GROC's CANDID GUIDE TO
ATHENS
&
TRAVELLING THE GREEK ISLANDS

For the package & villa holidaymaker,
backpacker & independent traveller
whether journeying by air, car, coach, ferry-boat or train.

by

Geoffrey O'Connell

Published by
Ashford
1 Church Road
Shedfield
Hampshire
SO3 2HW

Geoffrey O'Connell's highly personalised style of writing encompasses books on yacht building and maintenance, humour, travel as well as a magnum opus concerning the history of Southwick village, where he and fellow traveller and wife, Rosemary, live in a Georgian house on a centuries-old Hampshire estate.

They regard themselves as geriatric, if very knowledgeable backpackers whilst ferry-boating about the Greek islands gathering information for the next guidebook.

One of the CANDID GUIDE Series

CONTENTS

	Page No.
Introduction	1
PART ONE	
Chapter 1	3
Packing, insurance, medical matters, climatic conditions, conversion tables & a starter course in Greek	
Chapter 2	11
Getting to & from the Island Groups & Athens	
Chapter 3	33
Travel between Athens & the Islands	
Chapter 4	45
Island accommodation	
Chapter 5	51
Travelling around an island	
Chapter 6	57
Island Drink, Food & Medical Care	
Chapter 7	71
Shopping & Public Services	
Chapter 8	79
Greece: History, Mythology, Religion, Present-day Greece, Greeks, Animals & National Holidays	
PART TWO	
Chapter 9	85
Athens City	
Index	120

Artwork: Jonathan Duval & Geoffrey O'Connell
Plans & maps: Graham Bishop & Geoffrey O'Connell
Typeset: Disc preparation by Willowbridge Publishers
Output: Unwin Bros.
Tables & Headings
Typeset: County Productions

ILLUSTRATIONS

Illustration No. | **Illustration captions** | **Page No.**

No.	Caption	Page
	The Greek Islands	
1	Rail Routes	15
2	Brindisi	19
3	Car Routes & Ferry-boat Connections	23
4a	The Ionian	32
4b	The Cyclades	35
4c	The N E Aegean	37
4d	Mainland islands	39
4e	The Dodecanese	41
4f	Crete	42-43
5	Athens	84
6	Athens inset - The Plaka	89
7	Athens inset - The Railway Stations	113
8	Athens Environs, Suburbs, Bus & Metro Stations	119

Please do not forget that prices are given as a guide only and relate to the year in which the book is written. In recent years not only lodging and 'troughing' costs, but also transport charges, particularly ferry-boat fees, have escalated dramatically. The increased value of most other currencies to the Greek drachmae has compensated, to some extent, for apparently inexorably rising prices.

In an effort to keep readers as up-to-date as possible regarding these and other matters, I have introduced **GROC's GREEK ISLAND HOTLINE**. *See* elsewhere for details.

The series is entering its seventh year of publication and I would appreciate continuing to hear from readers who have any additions or corrections to bring to my attention. As in the past, all correspondence (except that addressed to 'Dear fifth' or similar endearments) will be answered.

I hope readers can excuse errors that creep (well gallop actually) into the welter of detailed information included in the body text. In order to keep the volumes as up-to-date as possible, the period from inception to publication is kept down to some six months which does result in the occasional slip up......

GROC's Candid Guides introduce to readers

Suretravel '89

A comprehensive holiday insurance plan that 'gives cover that many other policies do not reach', to travellers anywhere in the world. In addition to the more usual cover offered, the **SURETRAVEL HOLIDAY PLAN** includes (where medically necessary): 24 hour World Wide Medical Emergency Service including, where appropriate, repatriation by air ambulance.

Additionally, personal accident, medical and emergency expenses EVEN while hiring a bicycle, scooter or car.

An example premium, in 1989, for a 10-17 day holiday in Greece is £13.50 per person.

Note: All offers & terms are subject to the Insurance Certificate Cover

For an application form please complete the cut out below and send to:
Willowbridge Publishing, Bridge House, Southwick Village, Nr Fareham, Hants. PO17 6DZ

Mr/Mrs/Miss...Age..................

of...

....

request a **SURETRAVEL** application form.

Date of commencement of holiday........................Duration..................

Signature...Date..................

The Candid Guides unique
'GROC's Greek Island Hotline'

Available to readers of the guides, this service enables a respondent to receive a bang up-to-the-minute update, to supplement the extensive information contained in a particular Candid Guide.

To obtain this paraphrased computer print-out, covering the Introductory Chapters, Athens, Piraeus & the Mainland Ports as well as any named islands, up to twenty five in number, all that is necessary is to:-

Complete the form below, enclosing a payment of £1.50 (to include postage), and send to:-

Willowbridge Publishing, Bridge House, Southwick Village, Nr.Fareham, Hants. PO17 6DZ

Note: The information will be of no use to anyone who does not possess the relevant, most up to date GROC's Candid Greek Island Guide. We are unable to dispatch the Hotline without details of the guide AND which edition. This information is on the Inside Front Cover.

Planned departure dates ....
....
Mr/Mrs/Miss ....
of ....
....

I possess:		I require:
GROC's Greek Island Guides	Edition	**GROC's Greek Island Hotline**
to:		to: ....
....		....
....		....
....		....
....		....

and enclose a fee of £1.50. Signature...Date..................

I appreciate that the 'Hotline' may not be dispatched for up to 7-10 days from receipt of this application.

INTRODUCTION

This is the seventh in the series of GROC's Candid Guides to the Greek Islands. It details Athens, the epicentre of island travel, and the minutiae of travelling to and from the Greek island groups. The guide marks a fundamental change in the presentation of the publications and is based on Parts One and Two previously included in each and every one of the various island guides. Due to the ever increasing detail and contents it has, to date, been necessary to try and constrain the continuously expanding information contained in the introductory chapters. So 'The time has come'...

This guide continues the tradition of unbiased, factual comment, detailed and accurate information setting out in full the essentials of packing, insurance and medical matters, climate, as well as getting to and from Athens and the island groups. Also itemized are the aspects of accommodation, island travel, food and drink, shopping, the various public services, history, mythology, religion, the Greeks and their holidays.

Each **Candid Guide** is finally researched as close to the publication date as is possible.

The exchange rate has fluctuated quite violently in recent years and at the time of writing the final draft of this guide, the rate to the English pound (£) was hovering about 260drs. Unfortunately prices are subject to fluctuation, usually upward with annual increases varying between 10-20%. Happily the drachma tends to devalue by approximately the same amount.

Recommendations and personalities are almost always based on personal observation and experience, occasionally emphasised by the discerning comments of readers or colleagues. They may well change from year to year and be subject to different interpretation by others.

The series incorporates a number of innovative ideas and unique services which have evolved over the years and include:

The Decal: Since 1985 some of the accommodation and eating places recommended in the guides display a specially produced decal to help readers identify the particular establishment. The decals are dated so a reader can identify the relevancy of the recommendation. The current issue is the third (1989-91). Previous ones have been 1984-85 & 1986-88.

GROC's Greek Island Hotline: An absolutely unique service available to readers of the Candid Guides. Application results in a summary detailing all relevant comments and information that have become available since the publication of the particular guide – in effect, an up-to-date update. The Hotline is constantly being revised and incorporates bang up-to-the-moment intelligence. A payment of £1.50 (incl. postage) enables a respondent to receive the paraphrased computer print-out in respect of the various guides. An interested reader only has to complete the form requesting the Hotline, enclose the fee and post to Willowbridge Publishing, Bridge House, Southwick Village, Nr Fareham, Hants PO17 6DZ.

Travel Insurance: A comprehensive holiday insurance plan that 'gives cover that many other policies do not reach....' See elsewhere for details.

The author (and publisher) are very interested in considering ways and means of improving the guides and adding to the backup facilities, so are delighted to hear from readers with their suggestions.

Enjoy yourselves and 'Ya Sou' (welcome).
Geoffrey O'Connell 1989

ACKNOWLEDGMENTS

Every year the list of those to be formally thanked grows and this edition shows no diminution in their number which has forced the original brief entry from the inside front cover to an inside page.

Contributors who assisted in the presentation of this guide include Han Warr.

Apart from those numerous friends and confidants we meet on passage, there are the the many correspondents who are kind enough to contact me with useful information, all of whom, in the main, remain unnamed.

Rosemary who accompanies me, adding her often unwanted, uninformed comments and asides (and who I occasionally threaten not to take next time), requires especial thanks for unrelieved, unstinting (well almost unstinting) support, despite being dragged from this or that supposedly idyllic location.

Although receiving reward, other than in heaven, some of those who assisted me in the production of this edition require specific acknowledgement for effort far beyond the siren call of vulgar remuneration! These worthies include Graham Bishop, who drew the maps and plans, and Viv Hitié, who controls the word processor.

Lastly, and as always, I must admonish Richard Joseph for ever encouraging and cajoling me to take up the pen – surely the sword is more fun?

The cover picture of an Athens back street, is produced by kind permission of GREEK ISLAND PHOTOS, Willowbridge Enterprises, Bletchley, Milton Keynes, Bucks.

PART ONE

1 Packing, Insurance, Medical Matters, Climatic Conditions, Conversion Tables & a Starter Course in Greek

Leisure nourishes the body and the mind is also fed thereby; on the other hand, immoderate labour exhausts both. Ovid

Vacationing anywhere on an organised tour allows a certain amount of latitude regarding the amount of luggage packed, as this method of holiday does not preclude taking fairly substantial suitcases. On the other hand, ferry-boating and backpacking restricts the amount a traveller is able to carry and the means of conveyance. This latter group usually utilise backpacks and or roll-bags, both of which are more suitable than suitcases for this mode of travel. The choice between the two does not only depend on which is the more commodious. At the height of season it can be advantageous to be distinguishable from the hordes of other backpackers and the selection of roll-bags may help disassociation from the more hippy of 'genus rucksacker'. If roll-bags are chosen they should include shoulder straps. These alleviate the discomfort experienced whilst searching out accommodation on hot afternoons with arms just stretching and stretching and stretching.

In the highly populous, oversubscribed months of July and August, it is advisable for independent travellers to pack a thin foam bedroll and a lightweight sleeping bag, just in case a room cannot be located on the occasional night.

Unless camping, I do not think a sweater is necessary between the months of May and September. A desert jacket or lightweight anorak is a better proposition and a stout pair of sandals or training shoes are obligatory, especially if very much walking is contemplated. Leave out the evening suit and cocktail dresses, the Greeks are very informal. Instead take loose-fitting, casual clothes and do not forget sunglasses and a floppy hat. Those holiday-makers staying in one place and not too bothered about weight and encumbrances might consider packing a parasol or beach umbrella and an inflatable sun-bed. It will save a lot of money in daily rental charges paid over to the beach entrepreneurs.

Should there be any doubt about the electric supply (and you shave) include a pack of disposable razors. Ladies might consider acquiring one of the small, gas cylinder, portable hair-curlers prior to departure. Take along a couple of toilet rolls. They are useful for tasks other than that with which they are usually associated, including mopping up spilt liquid, wiping off plates, and blowing one's nose. It might be an idea to include a container of washing powder, a few clothes pegs, some string for a washing line and a number of wire hangers. We have found the best clothes washing medium is a liquid biological detergent, one including a brightener and safe stain removal agents. Recommended is *Ariel Rapide*.

Those visitors contemplating wide ranging travel should consider packing a few plastic, sealed-lid, liquid containers, a plate and a cup, as well as a knife and fork, condiments, an all-purpose cutting/slicing/carving knife as well as a combination bottle and tin opener. These all facilitate economical dining whilst on the move as food and drink, when available on ferry-boats and trains, can be comparatively expensive. Camping requires these elementary items to be augmented with simple cooking equipment.

Mosquito coils can be bought in Greece and a Japanese container is now available in England which holds the coil, stopping it from breaking and controlling the rate of burn. The best device to repel these noxious insects is a small, two prong, electric heater on which a wafer thin tablet is placed and almost every room has a suitable electric point.

They can be purchased locally for some 1000drs and come complete with a pack of the capsules. One trade name is *Doker Mat*. The odourless vapour given off certainly sorts out the mosquitoes and is (hopefully) harmless to humans. Mark you, we did hear of a tourist who purchased one and swore by its efficacy, not even aware it was necessary to place a tablet in the holder...

Whilst discussing items that plug in, why not pack an electric coil thus allowing the brew up of a morning 'cuppa'. Tea addicts can use a slice of lemon instead of milk. Those who like their drinks sweet can utilise those (often unwanted) packets of sugar that accompany most orders for a coffee or a spoonful of the honey that will be to hand for the morning yoghurt – won't it?

Consider packing a pair of tweezers, some plasters, calamine lotion, after-sun and insect cream, as well as a bottle of aspirin in addition to any pharmaceuticals usually required. It is worth noting that shampoo and toothpaste cost about the same but sun-tan oil, which was inexpensive, has now doubled in price and should be 'imported'. Including a small phial of disinfectant has merit, but it is best not to leave the liquid in the original glass bottle. Should it break, the disinfectant and glass, especially if mingled with clothing, can prove not only messy but will leave a distinctive and lingering odour. Kaolin and morphine is a very reliable 'tummy settler' but another excellent remedy, easily obtainable in Greece and that I have always found efficacious, is *Ercefurly forte 200*. Recent correspondence, from a knowledgable reader, suggests packing *Arret* or *Imodium* capsules, instead of kaolin and morphine. Soluable *Dioralyte* will help replace lost fluid and salts (as well as being helpful to the hung over!). Greek chemists dispense medicines and prescriptions that only a doctor would be able to mete out in many other Western European countries, so prior to summoning a medico, try the local pharmacy.

Insurance & medical matters While touching upon medical matters, a national of an EEC country should extend their state's National Health cover. United Kingdom residents can contact the local *Department of Health and Social Security* requesting form number *E111 UK*. When completed, and returned, this results in a *Certificate of Entitlement to Benefits in Kind during a stay in a Member State*. Well, that's super! In short, it entitles a person to medical treatment in other EEC countries. Even with this arranged, it is prudent to also seriously consider selecting a comprehensive holiday insurance policy. This should not only cover loss of baggage and money, but personal accident and medical expenses in addition to cancellation of the holiday and personal liability. Check the exclusion clauses carefully. It is no good an insured person imagining he or she is covered for 'this or that', only to discover the company has craftily excluded claims under a particular section. Should a reader intend to hire a scooter ensure this form of 'activity' is not debarred, as is often the case. Rather than rely on the minimal standard insurance cover offered by many tour companies, it is best to approach a specialist broker. For instance, bearing in mind the rather rudimentary treatment offered by the average Greek island hospital, it is almost obligatory to include the option of *Fly-Home Medicare* cover in any policy. A couple of homilies might graphically reinforce the argument. Firstly the Greek hospital system expects the patient's family to minister and feed the inmate 'out-of-hours'. This can result in holiday companions having to camp in the ward for the duration of any internment. Perhaps more thought-provoking is the homespun belief that a patient is best left the first night to survive, if it is God's will, and to pass on if not! After a number of years hearing of the unfortunate experiences of friends and readers, who failed to act on the advice given herein, as well as the inordinate difficulties I experienced in arranging cover for myself, I was prompted to offer readers an all embracing travel insurance scheme. Details are to be found elsewhere in the guide. **DON'T DELAY, ACT NOW**.

Most rooms do not have rubbish containers so why not include some plastic bin liners, which are also very useful for packing food as well as storing dirty washing. A universal sink plug is almost a necessity. Many Greek sinks do not have one but, as the water usually drains away very slowly, this could be considered an academic point.

Take along a pack of cards, and enough paperback reading to while away sunbathing sojourns and long journeys. Playing cards are subject to a government tax, which makes their price exorbitant, and imported books are very expensive. Happily, some shops, tour offices and lodgings operate a book-swap scheme.

Many flights, bus, ferry-boat or train journeys are scheduled for early morning departure, so a small, battery-operated alarm clock may well obviate sleepless, fretful nights prior to the dawn. A small, hand or wrist compass can be an enormous help orientating in towns and if room and weight allow, a torch is a useful addition to the inventory.

Readers must not forget their passport which is absolutely essential to (1) enter Greece, (2) book into most accommodation, as well as campsites, (3) change money and (4) hire a scooter or car.

In the larger, more popular, tourist orientated resorts *Diners* and *American Express (Amex)* credit cards are accepted, as increasingly are *Access Mastercards*. Personal cheques, up to 25000drs in value, may be changed when accompanied by a Eurocheque bank card. Americans can use an *Amex* credit card at their overseas offices to change personal cheques up to $1000. They may also, by prior arrangement, have cable transfers made to overseas banks, allowing 24hrs from the moment their home bank receives specific instructions.

It is wise to record and keep separate the numbers of credit cards, travellers's cheques and airline tickets in case they should be mislaid or stolen. Incidentally, this is a piece of advice I always give but rarely, if ever, carry out myself. Visitors are now allowed to import 100,000drs of Greek currency (in notes). Any further cash required must be in the form of traveller's cheques and or foreign currency. Originally the allowance was only 1500drs, then 3000drs followed by 6000drs (in 1988), a readjustment forced on the authorities by the continual decline in the value of the Greek drachma. Despite these more realistic figures, it may be necessary to change currency soon after arrival. This can prove to be a problem at weekends or if the banks are on strike, a not uncommon occurrence during the summer months. *See* **Banks, Chapter Seven** for further details in respect of banks and money.

Imported spirits are comparatively expensive (except on some of the duty free Dodecanese islands) but the official spirits allowance into Greece is up to one and a half litres of alcohol. So confirmed whisky or gin drinkers, who are partial to an evening sundowner, should acquire a bottle or two before arrival. Cigars are difficult to buy on the islands, so it may well be advantageous to take along the 75 allowed. On the other hand, cigarettes are so inexpensive that it hardly seems worthwhile 'importing' them. Note the above applies to fellow members of the EEC. Allowances for travellers from other countries are 1 litre of alcohol and 50 cigars. Camera buffs should take all the film required, as it is more costly in Greece than in most Western European countries.

Officially, the Greek islands enjoy some 3000 hours of sunshine per year, out of an approximate, possible 4250 hours. The prevailing summer wind is the northerly *Meltemi*, which can blow very strongly, day in and day out during July and August, added to which these months are usually painfully dry and very hot 24 hours a day. The sea in April is perhaps a little cool for swimming, but the last two weeks of May and June are marvellous months, as are September and October.

The best time of year to holiday The following indicates that probably the best months to vacation are May, June, September and October, July and August being too hot. Certainly, the most tourist crowded months, when accommodation is at a premium, are July, August and the first two weeks of September. Taking everything into account, it does not need an Einstein to work the matter out.

Conversion tables & equivalent

Units	Approximate conversion	Equivalent
Miles to kilometres	Divide by 5, multiply by 8	5 miles = 8km
Kilometres to miles	Divide by 8, multiply by 5	
Feet to metres	Divide by 10, multiply by 3	10 ft = 3m
Metres to feet	Divide by 3, multiply by 10	
Inches to centimetres	Divide by 2, multiply by 5	1 inch = 2.5 cm
Centimetres to inches	Divide by 5, multiply by 2	
Fahrenheit to centigrade	Deduct 32, divide by 9 and multiply by 5	77°F = 25°C
Centigrade to fahrenheit	Divide by 5, multiply by 9 and add 32	
Gallons to litres	Divide by 2, multiply by 9	2 gal = 9 litres
Litres to gallons	Divide by 9, multiply by 2	

Note: 1 pint = 0.6 of a litre and 1 litre = 1.8 pints

Pounds (weight) to kilos	Divide by 11, multiply by 5	5 k = 11 lb
Kilos to pounds	Divide by 5, multiply by 11	

Note: 16 oz = 1 lb; 1000g = 1 kg and 100g = 3.5 oz

Tyre pressures
Pounds per square inch to kilometres per square centimetre

lb/sq.in	kg/cm	lb/sq.in	kg/cm
10	0.7	26	1.8
15	1.1	28	2.0
20	1.4	30	2.1
24	1.7	40	2.8

The Greeks use the metric system but most 'unreasonably' sell liquid (i.e. wine, spirits and beer) by weight. Take my word for it, a 640g bottle of wine is approximately 0.7 of a litre or 1.1 pints. Proprietary wines such as *Demestica* are sold in bottles holding as much as 950g, which is 1000ml or $1\frac{3}{4}$ pints.

Electric points in the larger towns, smarter hotels and holiday resorts are 220 volts AC and power most American or British appliance. A few older buildings, in out-of-the-way places, might still have 110 DC supply. Remote pensions may not have any electricity, other than that supplied by a generator and even then the rooms might not be wired into the system. More correctly they may well be wired but not connected!

Greek time is 2 hours ahead of GMT and British Summer Time (and 7 hours ahead of United States Eastern Time). That is except for a short period when the Greek clocks are corrected for their winter at the end of September, some weeks ahead of the United Kingdom alteration.

Basics & essentials of the language These notes and subsequent **Useful Greek** at the relevant chapter endings are not, nor could be, intended to substitute for a formal phrase book or three. Accent marks have been omitted.

Whilst in the United Kingdom it is worth noting that the *British Broadcasting Co.* (Marylebone High St, London WIM 4AA) has produced an excellent book, *Greek Language and People*, accompanied by a cassette and record.

For the less committed, a very useful, pocket-sized phrase book that I always have to hand is *The Greek Travelmate* (Richard Drew Publishing, Glasgow) costing £1.99. Richard Drew, the publisher, recounts a most amusing, if at the time disastrous, sequence of events in respect of the launch of this booklet. It appears the public relations chaps had come up with the splendid idea of sending each and every travel writer a preview copy of the book, complete with an airline tray of the usual food and drink served mid-flight.

PACKING 7

This was duly delivered at breakfast time but, unlike Bob Newhart's record of the *HMS Codfish's* shelling of Miami Beach, this was not a 'slow newsday'. No, this was the day that Argentina chose to invade the Falklands, which dramatic event drove many stories off the pages for good, including the phrase book launch!

The Alphabet

Capitals	Lower case	Sounds like
A	α	Alpha
B	β	Veeta
Γ	γ	Ghama
Δ	δ	Dhelta
E	ε	Epsilon
Z	ζ	Zeeta
H	η	Eeta
Θ	θ	Theeta
I	ι	Yiota
K	κ	Kapa
Λ	λ	Lamtha
M	μ	Mee
N	ν	Nee
Ξ	ξ	Ksee
O	ο	Omikron
Π	π	Pee
P	ρ	Roh
Σ	σ	Sighma
T	τ	Taf
Y	υ	Eepsilon
Φ	φ	Fee
X	χ	Chi
Ψ	ψ	Psi
Ω	ω	Omegha

Groupings

αι	'e' as in let
αυ	'av/af' as in have/haff
ει/οι	'ee' as in seen
ευ	'ev/ef' as in ever/effort
ου	'oo' as in toot
γγ	'ng' as in ring
γκ	At the beginning of a word 'g' as in go
γχ	'nks' as in rinks
μπ	'b' as in beer
ντ	At the beginning of a word 'd' as in deer In the middle of a word 'nd' as in send
τζ	'ds' as in deeds

Useful Greek

English	Greek	Sounds like
Hello/goodbye	Γειά σου	Yia soo (informal singular said with a smile)
Good morning/day	Καλημέρα	Kalimera
Good afternoon/evening	Καλησπέρα	Kalispera (formal)
Good night	Καληνύχτα	Kalinikta
See you later	Θα σε δω αργοτερα	Tha se tho argotera

8 CANDID GUIDE TO ATHENS

English	Greek	Pronunciation
See you tomorrow	Θα σε δω αύριο	Tha se tho avrio
Yes	Ναι	Ne (accompanied by a downwards and sideways nod of the head)
No	Οχι	Ochi (accompanied by an upward movement of the head, heavenwards & with a closing of the eyes)
Please	Παρακαλώ	Parakalo
Thank you	(Σαζ) Ευχαριστώ	(sas) Efkaristo
No, thanks	Οχι ζυχαριστώ	Ochi, efkaristo
Thank you very much	Ευχαριστώ πολύ	Efkaristo poli
After which the reply may well be:-		
Thank you (& please)	Παρακαλώ	Parakalo
Do you speak English?	Μιλάτε Αγγλικά	Milahteh anglikah
How do you say....	Πως λενε...	Pos lene...
...in Greek?	...στα Ελληνικά	...sta Ellinika
What is this called?	Πως το λένε	Pos to lene
I do not understand	Δεν καταλαβαίνω	Then katahlavehno
Could you speak more slowly (slower?)	Μπορειτε να μιλάτε πιο αργά	Boreete na meelate peeo seegha (arga)
Could you write it down?	Μπορειτε να μου το γράψετε	Boreete na moo to grapsete

Numbers

English	Greek	Pronunciation
One	Ενα	enna
Two	Δύο	thio
Three	Τρία	triah
Four	Τέσσερα	tessehra
Five	Πέντε	pendhe
Six	Εξι	exhee
Seven	Επτά	eptah
Eight	Οκτώ	ockto
Nine	Εννέα	ennea
Ten	Δέκα	thecca
Eleven	Εντεκα	endekha
Twelve	Δώδεκα	thodhehka
Thirteen	Δεκατρία	thehka triah
Fourteen	Δεκατέσσερα	thehka tessehra
Fifteen	Δεκαπέντε	thehka pendhe
Sixteen	Δεκαέξι	thekaexhee
Seventeen	Δεκαεπτά	thehkaeptah
Eighteen	Δεκαοκτώ	thehkaockto
Nineteen	Δεκαεννέα	thehkaennea
Twenty	Εικοσι	eeckossee
Twenty-one	Εικοσι ένα	eeckcossee enna
Twenty-two	Εικοσι δύο	eeckcossee thio
Thirty	Τριάντα	treeandah
Forty	Σαράντα	sarandah
Fifty	Πενήντα	penindah
Sixty	Εξήντα	exhindah
Seventy	Εβδομήντα	evthomeendah
Eighty	Ογδόντα	ogthondah
Ninety	Ενενήτα	eneneendah
One hundred	Εκατό	eckato
One hundred and one	Εκατόν ένα	eckaton enna
Two hundred	Διακόσια	theeakossia
One thousand	Χίλια	kheelia
Two thousand	Δύο χιλιάδες	thio kheeliathes

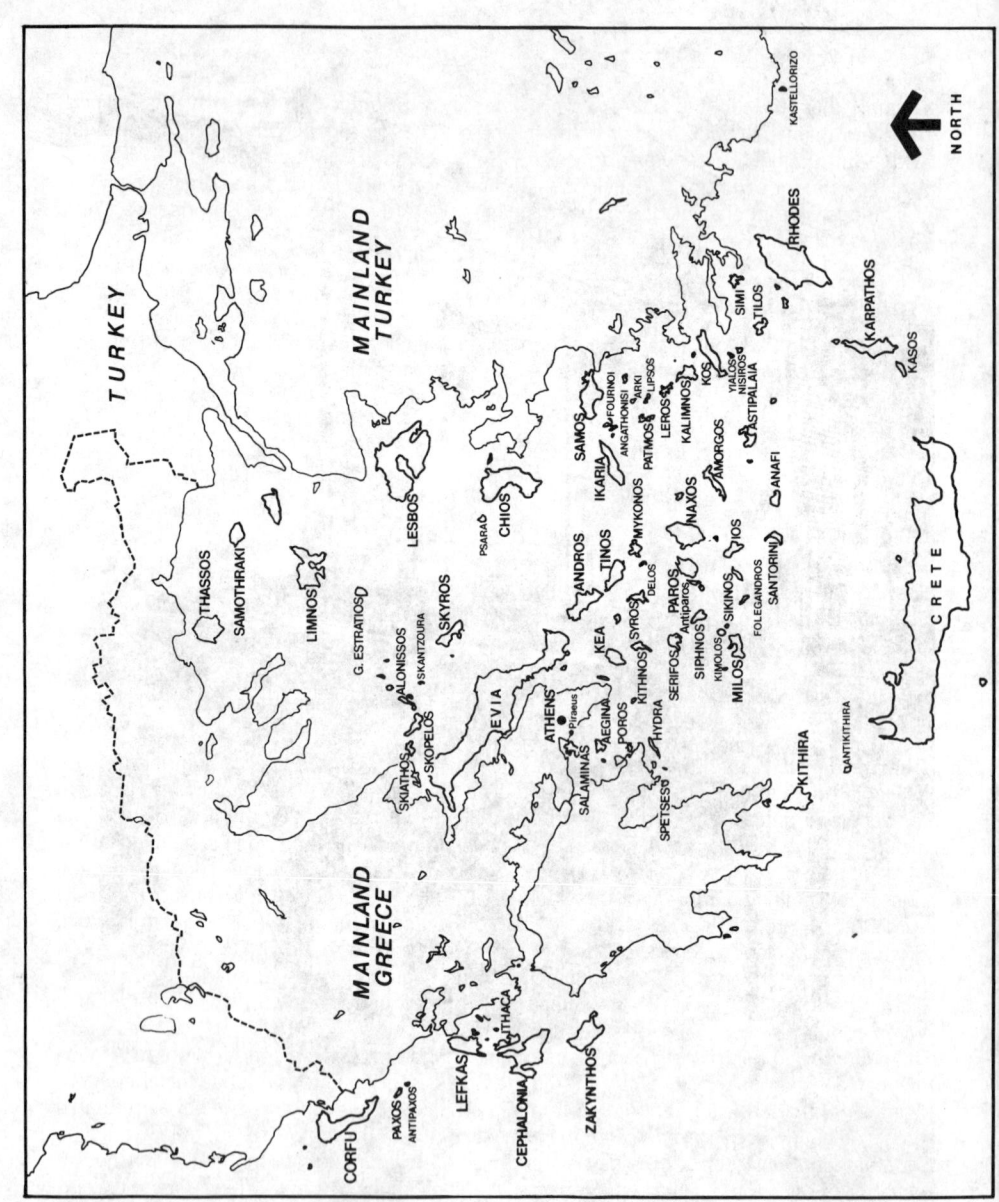

THE GREEK ISLANDS

2 Getting to & from the Island Groups & Athens

If all the year were playing holidays, to sport would be as tedious as work. William Shakespeare

To start this chapter off, first a word of warning. Whatever form of travel is utilised, travellers must not pack money or travellers cheques in luggage that is to be stowed away, out of sight. Some years ago, almost unbelievably, we met a young lady who, at the last moment and prior to checking-in at the airport, had stuffed some drachmae notes in a zipped side pocket of one of her suitcases. On arrival in Greece, surprise, surprise, she was minus the money.

BY AIR
From the United Kingdom

Scheduled flights Most proceed direct to Athens East (international) airport, from whence it is possible to transfer, by bus, to Athens West (domestic) airport in order to fly Olympic Airways to various of the islands. Both Olympic Airways international and domestic flights use the West Airport.

The various island groups allow other permutations in addition to the above, as follows:-
Crete It is possible to fly direct to Iraklion (via Athens?) courtesy of Olympic Airways.
Dodecanese There are flights direct to Rhodes (via Athens).
Ionian Direct flights are available to Corfu.

Heathrow to Athens (3¾hrs): daily, non-stop, via *British Airways, Olympic* and others.
East Midlands to Athens (8hrs): Mon-Sat, via Amsterdam with *Olympic*.
Edinburgh to Athens (7hrs): Tues, Thurs, Fri & Sat, via Amsterdam with *Olympic*.
Southampton to Athens (8hrs): Mon-Sat, via Amsterdam with *Olympic*.

Scheduled air fare options include: 1st class return, economy, excursion, APEX (Advanced Purchase Excursion Fare), PEX (instant purchase, and the cheapest scheduled fare) and Eurobudget.

Charter flights & package tours Some package tour operators keep a number of seats available on each flight for, what is in effect, a charter flight. A nominal charge is made for accommodation (which need not be taken up, but read on...), the cost of which is included in the return air fare. These seats are substantially cheaper than scheduled APEX fares and are known as 'Charter Cheapies'. Apart from the relatively low price, the normal two week holiday period can be extended by a further week or weeks for a small surcharge. There are a variety of United Kingdom departure airports including Birmingham, Bristol, East Midlands, Gatwick, Luton, Manchester and Newcastle. But, as one correspondent has pointed out, the frequency of charter flights tails off dramatically between October and March, as does the choice of airport departure points. Do not forget this when contemplating an out-of-season holiday.

An increasing tide of near penniless British youngsters taking a charter flight to Athens and causing various problems, prompted the Greek authorities to announce their intention, from 1988, to carefully monitor charter flight arrivals. Those who did not have irrefutable proof of authorised accommodation, as well as enough money to survive, would be repatriated immediately, at the carriers expense. In the consequent muddle of internecine squabbling between the charter companies and the Greeks, the authorities agreed to relax the originally stringent threat, but only for 1988. Certainly independent travellers should have sufficient money to convince the authorities that they are sufficiently well heeled as not to become a problem during any planned stay.

To ascertain what is on offer, scan the travel section of the Sunday papers as well as the weekly magazine *Time Out* and, possibly, *Private Eye*. There are many, varied packaged holidays available from the large tour operators whilst some of the smaller, more personal companies offer a bewildering array of multi-centre, fly-drive, budget-bed, self-catering and personally tailored holidays, in addition to the usual hotel accommodation.

Exceptionally reasonable charter flights, with the necessary accommodation vouchers, are available from *Owners Abroad Ltd*, Ilford, who also have offices in Birmingham, Glasgow and Manchester. Examples of their fares and destinations, in 1989, included:-

Two week return fares: Gatwick to Athens from £111.50 (Low Season) to £141.50 (High Season); to Corfu from £107.50/£137.50; to Iraklion(Crete) £119.50/£149.50; to Mykonos £144.50/£174.50; to Rhodes £121.50/£151.50; to Skiathos £135.50/£165.50.

The fares for three or four weeks are those above plus £25 whilst for five or six weeks an additional 50 per cent is charged. Note that the total number of weeks allowed in Greece for travellers who arrive and depart by charter flights is six, not twelve weeks.

Perhaps the least expensive flights available are obtainable from *Courier Flights*. These scheduled seats started off at about £75 return to Athens for the 1989 low season period. BUT passengers can only take a maximum of 10kg of hand luggage, one holdall measuring no more than 1ft x 2ft – no other baggage. Other restrictions result in only one passenger being able to travel at a time and for a minimum period of ten or fourteen days. The *cognoscenti* confirm that these seats are booked well ahead.

Companies offering interesting and slightly off-beat holidays in the various island groups are as follows:-

Crete *Aegina Club Ltd* and *Ramblers Holidays*. *Aegina* offer a wide range of tours, three different locations in up to three weeks and, additionally, will tailor a programme to fit in with client's requirements. *Ramblers*, as would be imagined, include walking holidays based on a number of locations with half-board accommodation. More conventional inclusions, many in smaller, more personal hotels, pensions and tavernas than those used by the larger tour companies, are available from *Small World* and *Martyn Holidays*. Both brochures have one or two more out of the way locations but equally the two firms allow a fair amount of 'glossing' to creep into individual descriptions. I suppose this is to be expected and, if taken into account, can be allowed for in any deliberations.

Cyclades *Aegina Club Ltd* and *Ramblers Holidays*. The more usual offerings are available from *Greek Sun*, *Laskarina Holidays* and *Simply Simon*, the latter company offering a selected number of interesting locations. The luxury end of the market is nobly catered for by *The Best of Greece*.

Dodecanese *Aegina Club Ltd* and *Ramblers Holidays*. The more down to earth, conventional requirements are coped for by *Timsway Holidays*. Their brochure includes many of the Dodecanese resorts including the less tourist ravaged islands of Karpathos and Pserimos. Other selective locations are offered by *Laskarina Holidays* whose islands neatly dovetail with *Timsway* as they include comparatively unexploited Chalki and Tilos. Mind you the firm with the most complete coverage of the Dodecanese must be *Twelve Islands*. They can offer package holidays at locations on islands that other firms simply 'haven't reached'. *Twelve Islands* also offer a range of interesting variations including 'Castaways', 'Painting', 'Botanical', 'Take-A-Chance', 'Two-and Multi-Centre' and 'Island Hopping' holidays. For those to whom money is no object *The Best of Greece* include a Rhodes hotel.

Ionian Amongst companies offering interesting and slightly off-beat holidays are the *Aegina Club Ltd* and *Greek Islands Club*. The latter also offer dinghy sailing, speed sailing and windsurfing holidays through an associated company, *Greek Islands Sailing Club*. Conventional inclusions, many in smaller, more personal hotels, pensions and tavernas than those used by the larger tour companies, are available from *Cricketers Holidays*,

Islands Unlimited, *Something Special* and *Timsway Holidays*. The luxury end of the market is nobly catered for by *The Best of Greece*.

Mainland including Argo-Saronic & Sporades *Aegina Club Ltd* and *Ramblers Holidays*. The brochure of *Laskarina Holidays* includes islands in both the Argo-Saronic and Sporades chains. Perhaps most importantly, the female representatives of this company are excellent, as I can vouchsafe, having met one in the course of research (not lechery – the 'Management Committee' was close by)..

NE Aegean *Aegina Club* and *Ramblers Holidays*. The brochure of *Greek Sun Holidays'* covers a number of the more popular NE Aegean islands and a few, individual, interesting locations but, in my opinion, their text is subject to a certain amount of hype. As long as this is allowed for in assessing the suitability of a location then no harm can be incurred by potential vacationeers.

Also *See* **Travel Agents, A To Z**, **Athens**, **Chapter Nine**.

Students Young people lucky enough to be under 26 years of age (oh to be 26 again) should consider contacting *STA Travel* who market a number of inexpensive charter flights (for adults as well). Students of any age or scholars under 22 years of age (whatever mode of travel is planned) should obtain an *International Student Identity Card (ISIC)*. This ensures discounts are available whenever they are applicable, not only in respect of travel but also for entry to museums, archaeological sites and some forms of entertainment.

If under 26 years of age, but not a student, it may be worthwhile applying for membership of *The Federation of International Youth Travel Organization (FIYTO)*, which guarantees discounts from some ferry and tour operators.

From the United States of America Scheduled Olympic flights include departures from:

Atlanta (via John F Kennedy (JFK) airport, New York (NY): daily
Baltimore (via JFK): daily
Boston (via JFK): daily
Chicago (Via JFK): daily
Dallas (via JFK): daily
Denver (via JFK): daily
Detroit (via JFK): daily
Houston (via JFK): daily
Los Angeles (via JFK): daily
Miami (via JFK): daily, 15 hours
Minneapolis (via JFK): daily
New York (JFK:) daily direct, approx. $10\frac{1}{2}$ hours
Norfolk (via JFK): daily
Philadelphia (via JFK:) daily, about 11 hours
San Diego (via JFK): daily
San Francisco (via JFK): daily, approx. $14\frac{1}{2}$ hours
Seattle (via London): daily
Tampa (via JFK): daily
Washington DC (via JFK): daily

Note that flights via New York's John F Kennedy airport involve a change of plane from, or to, a domestic American airline.

USA domestic airlines also run a number of flights to Greece and the choice of air fares is bewildering. These include economy, first class return, super APEX, APEX GIT, excursion, ABC, OTC, ITC, and others, wherein part package costs are incorporated.

Charter/stand-by flights & secondary airlines As in the United Kingdom, scanning the Sunday national papers' travel section, including the *New York Times*, discloses various companies offering package tours and charter flights. Another way to make the journey is to take a stand-by flight to London and then fly, train or bus on to Greece. Alternatively, there are a number of inexpensive, secondary airline companies offering flights to London, and the major Western European capitals.

Useful agencies, especially for students, include *Let's Go Travel Services*.

From Canada Scheduled Olympic flights include departures from:
Calgary (via JFK or La Guardia, NY): Mon, Tues, Thurs & Fri.
Edmonton (via Toronto, Amsterdam or London): daily
Montreal: twice weekly direct
  or (via Amsterdam, JFK or La Guardia, NY): daily
Toronto (via Montreal): twice weekly
  or (via Amsterdam, JFK or La Guardia, NY): daily
Vancouver (via Amsterdam): daily
Winnipeg (via Toronto & Montreal): Wed & Sat only.

As for the USA, not only do the above flights involve a change of airline but there is a choice of domestic and package flights as well as a wide range of differing fares.
   Student agencies include *Canadian Universities Travel Service*.

From Australia There are Australian airline scheduled flights to Athens from Adelaide (via Melbourne), Brisbane (via Sydney), Melbourne and Sydney. Flights via Melbourne and Sydney involve a change of plane from, or to, a domestic airline. Regular as well as excursion fares and affinity groups.

From New Zealand There are no scheduled flights.
   Various connections are available as well as regular and affinity fares.

From South Africa Scheduled Olympic flights include departures from:
Cape Town (via Johannesburg): Fri & Sun only.
Johannesburg: direct, Thurs, Fri & Sun.

Flights via Johannesburg involve a change of plane from, or to, a domestic airline. South African airline flights from Johannesburg to Athens are available as regular, excursion or affinity fares.

From Ireland Scheduled Olympic flights from:
Dublin (via London): daily, which involves a change of airline to *Aer Lingus*.

Note that when flying from Ireland, Australia, New Zealand, South Africa, Canada and the USA there are sometimes advantages in travelling to London, or other European capitals, on stopover and taking inexpensive connection flights to Greece.

From Scandinavia
include:
Denmark Scheduled Olympic flights from:
Copenhagen: daily
Sweden Scheduled Olympic flights from:
Stockholm (via Copenhagen or Vienna): Tues, Wed, Thurs, Fri & Sat.
Norway Scheduled Olympic flights from:
Oslo (via Frankfurt or Copenhagen): daily.

All the Scandinavian countries have a large choice of domestic and package flights with a selection of offerings. Contact *SAS Airlines* for *Olympic Airways* details.

AIRPORTS
United Kingdom Do not forget if intending to stay in Greece longer than two weeks, the long-stay car parking fees tend to mount up – and will the battery last for a 3 or 4 week layover. Incidentally, garage charges at Gatwick are about £32.00 for two weeks, £42.00 for three weeks and £52.00 for four weeks. The difficulty is that most charter flights leave and arrive at rather unsociable hours, so friends and family may not be too keen to act as a taxi service.

Athens Hellinikon airport is split into two parts, West (Olympic domestic and international flights) and East (foreign airlines). Coaches make the connection between the two airports. Olympic Airways buses travel to Athens centre as do city buses.
Western (or domestic) airport: City buses pull up alongside the terminal building. Across the road is a pleasant cafe/restaurant where the service becomes fairly chaotic when packed out. To the left of the cafe (*Facing*) is a newspaper kiosk and further on, across

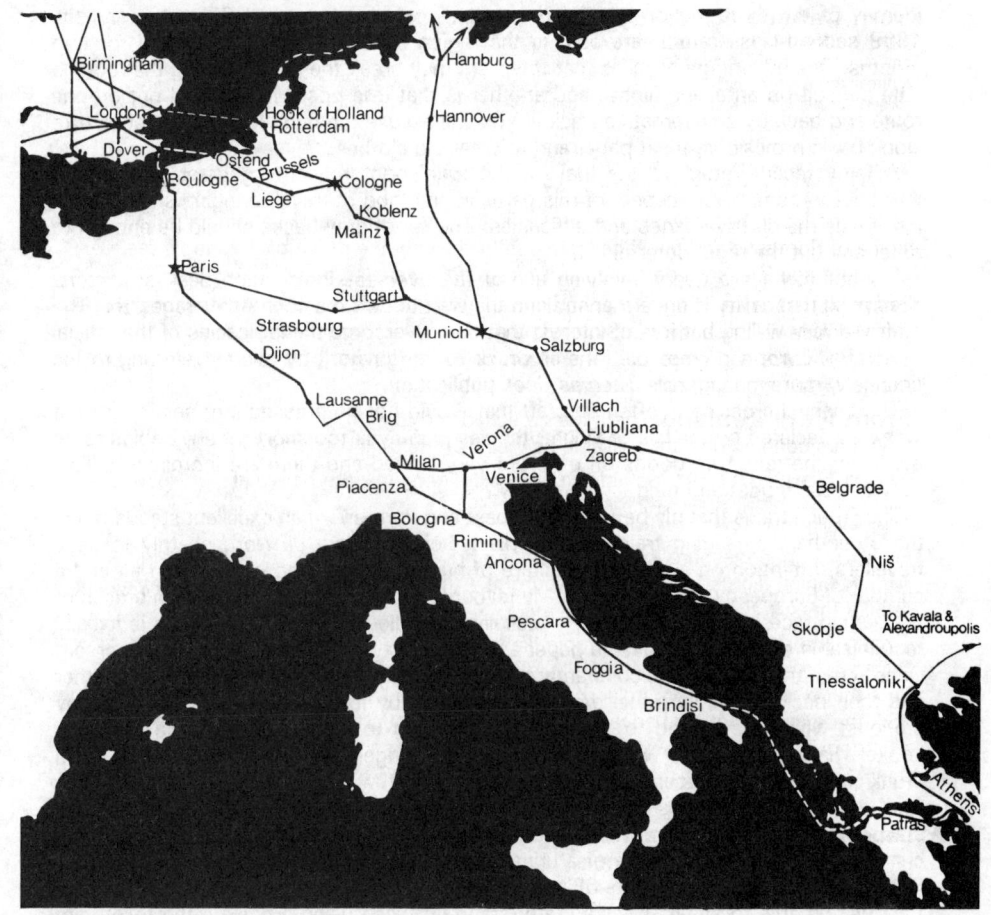

Illustration 1 Rail Routes

a side road, a Post Office is hidden in the depths of the first building.
Eastern airport Outwardly quite smart but can, in reality, become an expensive, very cramped and uncomfortable location if there are long delays. Let's not beat about the 'airport', the place becomes a hell-hole. Suspended flights occur when, for instance, air traffic controllers strike elsewhere in Europe. So remember to have enough money and some food left for an enforced stay. Flight departures are consistently overdue and food and drink in the airport are costly, with a plastic cup of coffee costing about 120drs. Furthermore, there are simply no facilities to accommodate a lengthy occupation by a plane load of passengers. The bench seats are very soon fully occupied – after which the floor of the concourse becomes covered with heaps of dejected travellers sleeping and slumped for as long as it takes the aircraft to depart. You have been warned.

BY TRAIN
From the United Kingdom & European countries (Illustration 1).
Recommended only for train buffs and masochists, but one of the alternative routes to be considered when a visitor intends to stay in Greece in excess of 6 weeks. The quickest

journey of the three, major scheduled overland routes takes about 60 hours, and the 1989 second-class return fare cost in the region of £230. Tickets are valid for two months. One advantage of rail is that travellers may break the journey along the route (a little difficult on an airline flight), and another is that it is possible to travel out on one route and back by an alternative track (if you will excuse the pun). It is important to take along basic provisions, toilet paper and to wear old clothes.

A fairly recent return to the 'day of the train' reinforced my general opinion and introductory remarks in respect of this particular method of travel, bringing sharply back into focus the disadvantages and difficulties. The list of drawbacks should be enough to deter any but the most determined.

Try not to have a query involving use of the overseas information desk at *Victoria Station* as the facility is undermanned and the wait to get to a counter averages ½hr. The staff are very willing but it is of interest that they overcome the intricacies of the official British Rail European timetable ('it's all Greek to me guvnor') by overtly referring to the (infinitely) more manageable *Thomas Cook* publication.

The channel crossing is often on craft that would not be pressed into service even if war was declared on the Isle of Wight; the sea journey is too short for any cabins to be available; the duty free goods on offer are very limited and there are inordinate delays between train, boat and train.

The French trains that ply between the coast and Paris are of an excellent standard. On the other hand changing trains at the 'black hole' of *Gare du Nord* sharply focuses travellers' attention on a whole subculture of human beings who exist in and around a number of European railway stations. My favourite example of this little known branch of the human race is the 'bag-shuffler' – usually a middle-aged lady. The genus is initially recognisable by the multitudinous paper and plastic bags festooned about their person. Once at rest the contents are constantly and interminably shuffled from one bag to another and then back again, the ritual being accompanied by low mutterings. French railway stations, which are heated to a temperature relating to gentle simmer on a domestic cooker, have perfected a waiting room seating arrangement that precludes any but a drunk contortionist stretching out for a nap. In common with most other railway stations, food and drink are expensive and credit cards impossible to use, even at the swanky station restaurants. The railway station's toilet facilities are minuscule and men are charged for other than the use of a urinal and washbasin. Ladies have to pay about 2 Francs (F), a private closet costs 6F and a shower 12F. Potential users must not imagine they will be able to sneak in for a crafty stand-up wash using a basin – the toilets are intently watched over by attendants who would only require knitting needles to irresistibly remind one of the women who sat at the foot of the guillotine.

The Metro connection between the railway stations of *Gare du Nord* and *Gare de Lyon* is not straightforward and involves a walk. The *Gare de Lyon* springs a minor trap for the unwary in that the inter-continental trains depart from platforms reached after a long walk along the far left platforms (*Facing the trains*). Don't some of the French trains now resemble children's rocket drawings?

Although it may appear to be an optional extra, it is obligatory to purchase a couchette ticket for the train journey. This is a Catch 22 situation brought about by the rule that only couchette ticket holders have the right to a seat! Yes, well, not so optional! It is also necessary to pack food and drink, at least for the French part of the journey, as usually there are no refreshment services. In Italy most trains are met, at the various station stops, by trolley pushing vendors of (rather expensive) sustenance.

Venice Station, signed *Stazione St Lucia*, is most conveniently sited bang-on the edge of the Grand Canal waterfront with shops and restaurants to the left. Some of the cake shops sell slabs of pizza pie for about 1000 lira (L), which furnishes good stand-by nourishment. The scheduled stopover here will have to be adjusted for any (inevitable)

TO ISLAND GROUPS

delay in arrival. Venice (on the outward journey) is the watershed where Greek, and the occasional Yugoslavian, carriages are coupled up, after which passengers can be guaranteed to encounter a number of nasties. The replacement compartments are seedier and dirtier than their French and Italian counterparts and the lavatories vary between bad to unspeakable. Faults include toilets that won't flush (sometimes appearing to mysteriously fill up), Greek style toilet paper (which apart from other deficiencies lacks body and – please excuse the indelicacy – through which fingers break), no toilet paper at all (which is worst?), no soap dispenser, a lack of coat hooks, water taps that 'don't' – and all very grimy.

From Venice the term 'Express' should be ignored as the train's progress becomes slower and slower and slower with long, unscheduled stops and quite inordinate delays at the Yugoslavian frontiers. During the Yugoslavian part of the journey it is necessary for passengers to lock themselves into their compartment as some of the locals have an annoying habit of entering and determinedly looting tourists' luggage. There have even been 'totally unsubstantiated rumours', in the last year or two, of callow fellows spraying an aerosol knockout gas through the keyholes, breaking in and at leisure relieving passengers of their belongings. I must stress I have not actually met victims and the story may be apocryphal. It is inadvisable to leave the train at *Belgrade* for a stopover as the accommodation available to tourists is extremely expensive, costing in the region of £80 plus for a double room, per night. Additionally, it is almost impossible to renegotiate a couchette for the remainder of the onward journey. There are trolley attendants at the major Yugoslavian railway stations but the innards of the rolls proffered are of an 'interesting' nature, resembling 'biltong' or 'hardtack' burgers. Certainly when poked by the enthusiastic vendors I'm sure their fingers buckle. Another item of 'nutriment' on offer are large, but rather old cheese curd pies. A railway employee wanders the length of the train, twice a day, with a very large aluminium teapot ostensibly containing coffee. Nobody is interested in payment with Yugoslavian dinars, but American dollars, English pounds sterling or German marks almost cause a purr of satisfaction. Travellers lucky enough to have the services of a Greek attendant may well find he keeps a cache of alcoholic drinks for sale. An aside is that Yugoslavians are obsessed by wheel-tapping and at all and every stop (almost at 'the drop of a sleeper') appear and perform. Much of the journey beyond Belgrade is on a single line track and should, for instance, a cow break into a trot the animal might well overtake the train. At the frontier, passengers may well be reminded of the drawbacks experienced behind the Iron Curtain as they will probably be subjected to rigorous, lengthy baggage and document checks by a 'swamp' of officials, whose numbers include stern faced, unsmiling, gun-toting police.

In stark contrast the friendly Greek frontier town of *Idomeni* is a tonic. Even late at night the station's bank is open, as is the taverna/snackbar with a scattering of tables on the platform and a buzz of brightly lit noise and activity.

To avoid the Yugoslavian experience a very pleasant alternative is to opt for the railway route that travels the length of Italy to:
BRINDISI PORT (Illustration 2). Here international ferry-boats can be caught to the mainland Greek ports of Igoumenitsa or Patras, from either of which buses make the connection with Athens, whilst Patras offers the possibility of another train journey on to Athens.

Despite the many thousands and thousands of tourists that pass through Brindisi every day, day in and day out, during the summer season, the town is in no way prepared for the influx. There is a total lack of public facilities to handle the disparate personal needs of the travellers. For instance, the station lavatory is locked 'out of hours', it being necessary to locate the other shower/toilet blocks available. Furthermore there is only a small public square on which the hordes have to flop out and while away the interminable hours whilst waiting for this or that ferry-boat or train.

Brindisi contains several traps for the unwary. For instance, the *Maritime Railway Station* (*Tmr* 1H6) and the quay (*Tmr* 2H7) for the Italy-Greek boats are some 200m apart, which on a hot day... The railway station has no formal ticket office or barrier. It is only necessary to dismount, turn left along the platform, left again, beside the concrete wall supporting the first floor concourse (which stretches over and above the platforms), across the railway lines and left again down the sterile dockland street, romantically named Via del Mare, to the ferry-boat complex. The road, hemmed in by a prefabricated wall on the right, curves parallel to the seawall on the left, from which it is separated by a high chain link fence, a number of railway lines and tarmacadam quay. But, before leaving the station, stop, for all the ticket offices and necessary officials are situated in the referred to upper storey buildings or in the 'Main Street', Corso Garibaldi. It is necessary to purchase a boarding pass from the Port office, on the first floor. Do not forget, as it is enough to try the patience of an angel (let alone a saint) to have to trudge all the way back to the Railway station in order to get the necessary bit of cardboard. I know from personal experience. Lastly, but not least, when booking rail tickets ask for *Brindisi Maritime*, as the town railway station is a kilometre or so inland. Another irritant is the advisability to 'clock in' at least 2 to 3 hours before a boat's departure, otherwise a traveller may be 'scratched from the fixture list' and have to rebook and pay again!

My favourite tour agency office, *Hellitalia* (*Tmr* 3G/H5/6 - tel 0831 222988), is across the road from the station, alongside a bank on the corner formed by the streets of Corso Garibaldi and Via del Mare. The staff, headed by Signor Fortunato Lorenzo, are very helpful and most informative. An attitude at odds with some of their business competitors in the High St who display Italian intransigence - rather different from Grecociliousness - the Italians are suaver! An example was the office where the man, when he deigned to serve us, advised without any apology "No the listed ferry-boat wouldn't be running later in the year, despite the printed timetable, so we couldn't take advantage of a return booking discount and no, he didn't accept American Express, despite the sticker advertising that he did".

Diagonally across the bottom of this end of the 'Main St' is the small, tree edged square, Piazza Vittorio Emanuele. As it is well endowed with park benches, it has become an unofficial waiting room with travellers and backpackers occupying all the available seating. as well as most of the flagstones. Fortunately, set in the trunk of a tree, on the quay side of the square, is a drinking water fountain. There is another beyond the *Trattoria Al Gabiano*, on Via Regina Margherita.

Lavatorial demands are satiated by one corporation and one private enterprise shower and lavatory facilities. The rather shabby, 'local authorities' unit is situated on Via del Mare (*Tmr* 4G/H6). The charges are L300 for the use of a toilet, L1500 for a chap to shower and, inexplicably, L2000 for a female to douche. The other, more wholesome but more expensive edifice (*Tmr* 5G4/5) is at No 11, beyond the imposing flight of steps along Via Regina Margherita. The owner is resident and a shower costs L2000. Unfortunately the only laundry/dry cleaners are of the 24 hour variety. There is one on Via Regina Margherita.

Most of the town's cafe-bars, restaurants, change and ticket offices are ranged along Via Corso Garibaldi, the High St. On the left (*Station behind one*) of this road, prior to the side-street of Via de Flagila, is a very useful supermarket, the *Eurospar* (*Tmr* 6G/H5/6). Apart from the full range of provisions, there is a bread counter on the left of the entrance hall, thus doing away with the necessity of going into the store proper.

There is an Information office (*Tmr* 7G5) on Via Regina Margherita, a Post Office (*Tmr* 8G/H5/6) set in the north end of the Maritime Railway Station, the main Post Office (*Tmr* 8F/G6) adjacent to Piazza Mercato and a Hospital (*Tmr* 9B/C7) alongside Piazza di Summa.

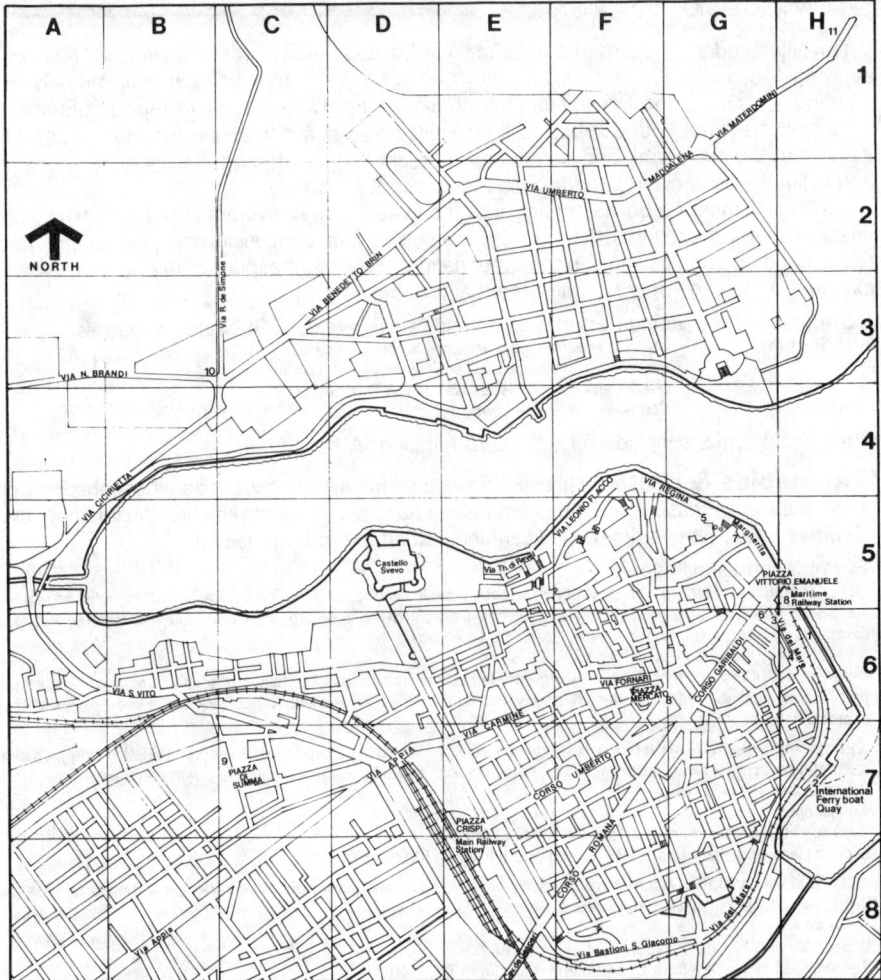

Illustration 2 Brindisi

Youth Hostel (*Tmr* 10B/C3) 2 Via Nicola Brandi Tel (0831) 413100
Directions: Unfortunately the Youth Hostel is some 5½km from the Maritime Railway Station, around the bay to the north. On the other hand, it is only 4km from the main Railway station, from whence Buses Nos 3, 4 & 5 pass the hostel.
 The cost of bed and breakfast is L8500.

The Campsite (*Tmr* 11HI) is even more of a trudge, being further to the east.

Those who haven't dozed off may well note that the matter of a boarding pass and port taxes has been mentioned elsewhere. These are not, repeat not, included in the ferry-boat ticket prices and, as they can cost as much as L7000 per person, must be allowed for in any monetary calculations, especially when funds are low. *See* **By Ferry-Boat** for the relevant details of the sea crossing.

Travellers under 26 years of age can take advantage of *British Rail's Inter-Rail Pass* by applying to *London Student Travel, Eurotrain* or by going to a London mainline railway station. Americans and Canadians may obtain a *Eurorail Pass* prior to reaching Europe. All these offers hold out a substantial discount on standard train and ferry fares, but are subject to various terms and conditions. Student outfits offering cut-price train, coach and airline flights include *London Student Travel (& Eurotrain)*.

Certainly it must be borne in mind that the Greek railway system is not extensive and unless travelling around other European countries, a concessionary pass might not represent much of a saving. On the other hand discounts in respect of the Greek railways extends to travel on some of the State Railway buses (OSE).

Examples of the various tickets, costs and conditions in 1989 were as follows:-

Inter-Rail ticket	Under 26 years of age, valid one month for use in 21 countries (and also allows half fare travel in the UK on *Sealink* and *B & I* ships, as well as *P & O* ferries, via Southampton and Le Havre).	£145

Other ticket options include B.I.G.E., Eurotrain and 'Athens Circle'.

Timetables & routes This section caused me as much work as whole chapters on other subjects. *British Rail*, whose timetable I have the greatest difficulty deciphering, and *Thomas Cook*, whose timetable I can understand, were both helpful.

Example routes include:
(1) London (Victoria Station), Dover (Western Docks), (jetfoil), Ostend, Brussels, Liege, Aachen, Cologne (change train, ½hr delay), Mainz, Mannheim, Ulm, Munich (change train ½hr delay) Salzburg, Jesenice, Ljubljana, Zagreb, Belgrade (Beograd), Skopje, Gevgelija, Idomeni, Thessaloniki to Athens.
An example of the journey is as follows:
Departure: 1300hrs, afternoon sea crossing, evening on the train, late night change of train at Cologne, night on the train, morning change of train at Munich, all day and night on the train arriving Athens very late, some 2¼ days later at approx 2315hrs.

(2) London (Charing Cross/Waterloo East stations), Dover Hoverport, (hovercraft), Boulogne, Paris (du Nord), change train (and station) to Paris (de Lyon), Strasbourg, Munich, Salzburg, Ljubljana, Zagreb, Belgrade (change train 1¾hrs delay), Thessaloniki to Athens.
An example:
Departure: 0955hrs and arrive 2¼ days later at 2315hrs.
Second class single fare from £135.20 and return from £230.90.

(3) London (Victoria), Folkestone Harbour, (ferry-boat), Calais, Paris (du Nord), change train (and station) to Paris (de Lyon), Venice, Ljubljana, Zagreb, Belgrade, Thessaloniki to Athens.
An example:
Departure: 1415hrs and arrive 2¼ days later at 0840hrs.
Second class single fare from £134.00 and return from £229.40.

(4) London (Liverpool St), Harwich (Parkeston Quay), (ferry-boat), Hook of Holland, Rotterdam, Eindhoven, Venlo, Cologne (change train), Mainz, Mannheim, Stuttgart, Ulm, Munich, Salzburg, Jesenice, Ljubljana, Zagreb, Belgrade, Nis, Skopje, Gevgelija, Idomeni, Thessaloniki to Athens.
An example:
Departure: 1940hrs, night ferry crossing, change train at Cologne between 1048 and 1330hrs, first and second nights on the train and arrive Athens, middle of the day, at 1440hrs.

An alternative is to take the more pleasurable train journey through Italy and make a ferry-boat connection to Greece as follows:
(5) London (Victoria), Folkestone Harbour, Calais, Boulogne, Amiens, Paris (du Nord), change train and station to Paris (de Lyon), Dijon, Vallorbe, Lausanne, Brig, Domodossala, Milan (Central), Bologna, Rimini, Ancona, Pescara, Bari to Brindisi.
(5a) Brindisi to Patras sea crossing.
(5b) Patras to Athens.
An example:
Departure: 0958hrs, day ferry crossing, change of train at Paris to the Parthenon Express, one night on the train and arrive at Brindisi at 1850hrs. Embark on the ferry-boat departing at 2000hrs, night on the ferry-boat and disembark at 1300hrs the next day. Take the coach to Athens, arriving at 1600hrs.

Note it is possible to disembark at Ancona and take a ferry-boat, but the sailing time is about double that of the Brindisi sailing. See **By Ferry-boat**.

TO ISLAND GROUPS 21

On all these services children benefit from reduced fares, depending on their age. Couchettes and sleepers are usually available at extra cost and Jetfoil sea crossings are subject to a surcharge.

Details of fares and timetables are available from *British Rail Europe* or *The Hellenic State Railways (OSE)*. One of the most cogent, helpful and informative firms through whom to book rail travel must be *London Student Travel/Eurotrain*. It is well worth contacting *Thomas Cook Ltd*, who have a very useful range of literature and timetables available from their Publications Department.

From the Continent & Scandinavia to Athens
Link up with one of the aforementioned main lines by using the appropriate connections sketched in Illustration 1.

Departure terminals from Scandinavia include Helsinki (Finland); Oslo (Norway); Gothenburg, Malmo and Stockholm (Sweden); Fredrikshavn and Copenhagen (Denmark).

The above are only a guide and up-to-date details must be checked with the relevant offices prior to actually booking.

BY COACH This means of travel is for the more hardy voyager and or young. If the description of the train journey has caused apprehension, the tales of passengers of the less luxurious coach companies should strike terror into the reader. Common 'faults' include lack of 'wash and brush up' stops, the presence of smugglers, prolonged border customs investigations (to unearth the smugglers), last minute changes of route and vehicle breakdowns. All this is on top of the forced intimacy with a number of widely disparate companions, some of whom may be wildly drunk, in cramped, uncomfortable surroundings.

For details of the scheduled *Euroway Supabus* apply c/o Victoria Coach Station or to the *National Express Company*. In 1989 a single fare cost from £79 and a return ticket from £140, via Germany. This through service takes 4 days plus, with no overnight layovers but short stops at Cologne, Frankfurt and Munich, where there is a change of coach. Fares include ferry costs but exclude refreshments. Arrival and departure in Athens is at either the Peloponissos Railway Station or 44 Karageorgis Servias St, Syntagma Sq.

The timetable is as follows:
Departure from Bay 20, Victoria Coach Station, London: Fri & Sat at 2030hrs, arriving at 1100hrs, 4¼ days later.
Return journey
Departure from Filellinon St, Syntagma Sq, Athens: Wed & Fri at 1300hrs, arriving London at 0800hrs, 4 days later.

Eurolines Intercars (Uniroute) operate a coach service that shuttles between Athens and Paris on a three day journey. The buses depart twice a week on Wednesday and Saturday, at 1030hrs, for a cost of about 13,000drs, but note that baggage costs an extra 200drs. The French end of the connection is close by the *Metro Station Porte Vincennes* and the Athens terminus is alongside the *Stathmos Larissis Railway Station*. These air conditioned buses are comfortable but do not possess a toilet. The 'leg-stretching' stops are absolutely vital, not only for passengers to relieve themselves but in order to purchase victuals. To help make the journey acceptable passengers should consider packing enough food and drink to tide them over the trip. It is a problem that the standard of the 'way-station' toilets and snackbars varies from absolutely awful to luxurious. And do not forget that the use of the lavatories is usually charged for in Greece, Italy and Yugoslavia.

There are sufficient stops in Greece at, for instance, Livadia, Larissa and Thessaloniki, as well as at the frontier. The border crossing can take up to some 2¼hrs. The Yugoslavian part of the route passes through Belgrade and at about two-thirds distance there is a lunchtime motorway halt. At this sumptuous establishment (surprise, surprise) Amex credit cards are accepted and the lavatories are free – a welcome contrast to the previous, 'mind boggling' Yugoslavian stop, where even the Greeks blanch at the sight of the toilets! The bus and driver change at Trieste, which is probably necessary after the rigours of the Yugoslavian roads.

Use of the lavatories in the Trieste bus station has to be paid for and they are very smelly and there is the possibility of encountering a lecherous attendant 'masterminding' the ladies toilet. One of the two Italian stops is at a luxurious motorway complex. It is worth noting that all purchases at Italian motorway cafe-bars and restaurants have to be paid for first. A ticket is issued which is then exchanged for the purchaser's requirements. This 'house rule' even applies to buying a cup of coffee.

The route between Italy and France, over the Alps, takes a tediously long time on winding, narrow mountain roads with an early morning change of driver in France. It may well be necessary to 'encourage' the driver on this section to make an unscheduled halt in order to save burst bladders. The bus makes three Paris drop-offs, at about midday, three days after leaving Athens.

The best disembarkation point depends on a traveller's plans. Devotees of the Le Havre channel crossing must make for the *Gare St Lazare Railway Station*. The Metro, with one change, costs about 5 francs (F) per person and the coach's time of arrival allows passengers to catch an afternoon Paris to Le Havre train. This departs on the three hour journey at 1630hrs and the tickets cost some 100 F each. No information in respect of cross-Channel ferries is available at the Paris railway station, despite the presence of a number of tourist information desks.

Incidentally, the walk from the *Le Havre Railway Terminus* to the cross-Channel embarkation point is a long haul but there are reasonably priced taxis between the two points. The superb restaurant *Le Southampton*, conveniently across the street from the Ferryboat Quay, may well compensate for the discomfort of the trudge round, especially as they accept payment by *Amex*.

'Express' coach companies include *Consolas Travel*. This well-established company runs daily buses during the summer months, except Sunday. *London Student Travel* quotes a single ticket at a cost of £72 and a return ticket £125. Other services are run by various 'pirate' bus companies. The journey time is about the same and prices, which may be slightly cheaper, also do not include meals. The cheaper the fare, the higher the chance of vehicle breakdowns and or the driver going 'walkabout'. On a number of islands, travel agents signs still refer to the *Magic Bus*, or as a fellow traveller so aptly put it – the 'Tragic Bus', but the company that ran this renowned and infamous service perished some years ago. Imitators appear to perpetuate the name.

In the United Kingdom it is advisable to obtain a copy of the weekly magazine *Time Out*, wherein the various coach companies advertise. For return trips from Athens, check shop windows in Omonia Sq, the American Express office in Syntagma Sq, or the Students Union in Filellinon St, just off Syntagma Sq. Also *See* **Travel Agents, A To Z, Athens, Chapter Nine**.

BY CAR (Illustration 3) Motoring to Greece is usually only a worthwhile alternative method of travel if there are at least two adults who are planning to stay for longer than three weeks, as the journey from England is about 1900 miles and takes approximately 50hrs non-stop driving.

Vehicle owners should ensure that spares are likely to be plentiful. An instance will illuminate. Recently I drove to Greece in a Mazda camping van and the propshaft went on the 'blink'. It transpired there was only one propshaft in the whole of Greece – well that was the story. Spare parts are incredibly expensive and our replacement finally cost, with carriage and bits and pieces, 36,000drs. The $\frac{1}{2}$hr labour required to fit the wretched thing was charged at about £18 an hour. At the time the total worked out at approximately £194 which seemed a bit steep, even when compared to English prices. This cautionary tale prompts me to remind owners to take out one of the vehicle travel insurance schemes. The *AA* offers an excellent *5 Star Service Travel Pack* and other motoring organisations have their own schemes. At the time of making the decision, the insurance premium

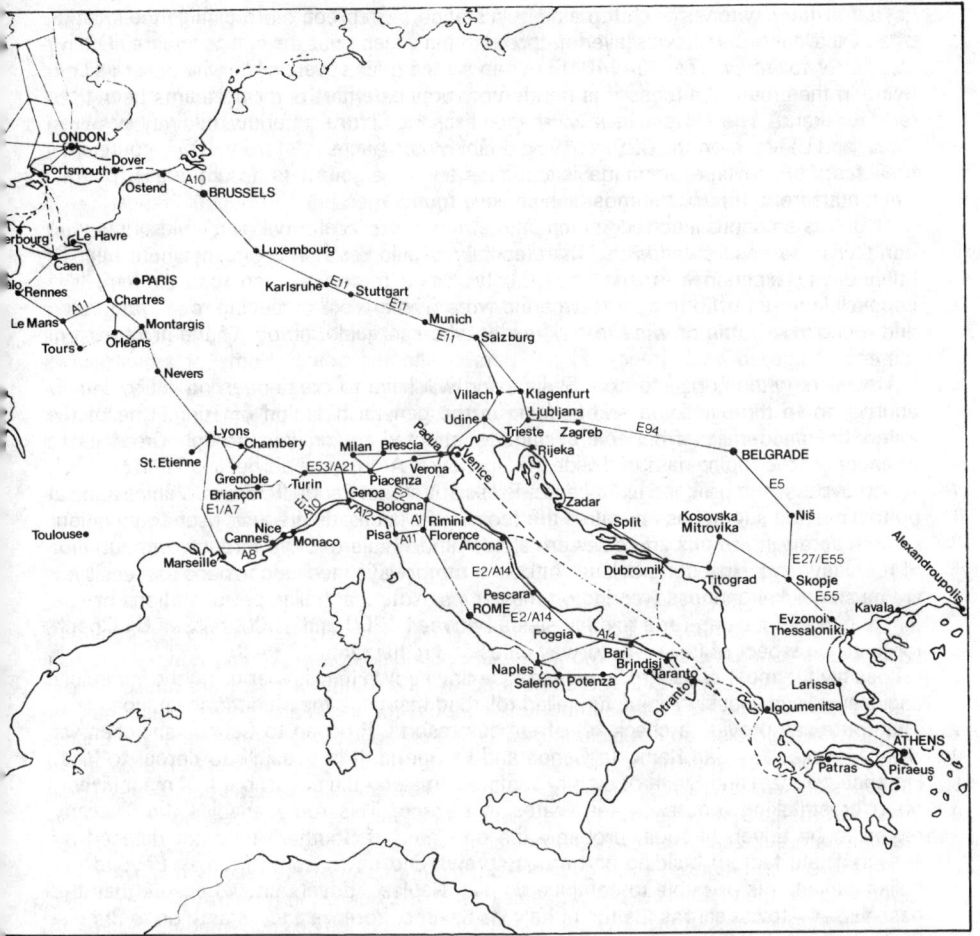

Illustration 3 Car Routes & Ferry-boat Connections

might seem a trifle expensive. Conversely, when faced with possibly massive inroads into available currency, the knowledge that a pack of credit vouchers is available, with which to effect payment for repairs, is very reassuring. The motoring organisations will prepare routes from their extensive resources. Certainly the *AA* offers this service but individual route plans now take 2-3 weeks to compile.

One of the shortest routes from the United Kingdom is via a car-ferry to Ostend (Belgium), on to Munich, Salzburg (Germany), Klagenfurt (Austria) and Ljubljana (Yugoslavia). There the Autoput E94 is taken to Zagreb, Belgrade (Beograd) and Nis on the E5, where the E27 and E55 are used, via Skopje, to the frontier town of Gevgelija/Evzonoi. Major rebuilding works can cause lengthy delays on the road between Zagreb and Nis.

For those who wish to drive across France, there are a number of ferry-boat ports from which to choose, including Le Havre, Cherbourg and St Malo, where the *Brittany* ferry terminal building contains some excellent shower and toilet facilities. Whichever port is used, for those who wish to stop a night in France, I am prepared to divulge the location of an excellent hotel I have stayed at three or four times over the last ten years. The ivy clad *Hotel de France*, (Tel 43444016) overlooks the main square of La Chatre sur Le Loir. Being in the area of Le Mans it is rightly very popular with the racing teams during the race weekend. The village, usually 'mapped' as La Chatre, is about midway between Tours and Le Mans on the D29. In 1988 double room prices cost from 100F, continental breakfast 18F, whilst evening meals in the restaurant, a gourmets delight, a gastronomic treat, start from 58F for the most inexpensive tourist menu.

That was an unqualified recommendation, now for a 'health warning'. Motorists who don't wish to pass away with frustrated fury should resist routing anywhere near St Etienne. My experience is that once on this city's motorway ring road system, it is impossible to get off. I'm sure there are drivers who are still careening round and round and round... A bottle of wine to any reader who can guide me out of the nightmare of the encircling road.

Travellers who choose to skirt Switzerland will have to cross over into Italy, usually angling down through Lyon and heading in the general direction of Turin. One of the loveliest Franco-Italian frontier crossings is effected by driving through Grenoble to Briancon for the Alpine pass of Col de Montgenevre. Across the border lies Turin (Torino), which bypass, and proceed to Piacenza, Brescia, Verona, Padua (Padova), Venice and cut up to Trieste. I say bypass because the ordinary Italian roads are just 'neat aggravation' and the sprawling towns and cities are almost impossible to drive through without a lot of problems and exhausting delays. Although motorways involve constant toll fees they are much quicker and less wearing on the nerves. Note that Italian petrol stations have a 'nasty habit' of closing for a midday siesta between 1200 and 1500hrs. See **By Coach** for hints in respect of Italian motorway cafes and restaurants.

Possibly the most consistently picturesque drive down Italy is that using the incredibly engineered, audaciously Alpine tunnelled toll road that hugs the Mediterranean coastline. This route can provide a check list of famous resorts. Proceed to Cannes and then via Nice, Monaco, and San Remo to Genoa and La Spezia. It is possible to detour to Pisa, Florence (Firenze) and Siena or simply continue on along the coast, but this magnificent, often breathtaking motorway terminates at Livorno. This route enables the Tuscany region to be driven through, probably the only area of Southern Italy not defaced by indiscriminate factory building and urban sprawl, and on to Rome (Roma). Beyond the Italian capital, it is possible to continue on past Naples – drivers should ensure that it is past Naples – to cut across the toe of Italy via Salerno, Potenza and Taranto on to Brindisi Port. Note the insistence 'on past Naples', as this city is infamous for its modern-day highwaymen. A dubious honour indeed, but reports include motorists being waved down for flat tyres or simulated road accidents and then being systematically robbed. You have been warned!

I do not wish to be seen knocking the country but, whilst on the subject, it behoves me to warn travellers to be extra careful in respect of personal belongings in the larger Italian towns. Despite the presence of an awesome number of police, most of whom are armed, pickpockets and robbers are very much at large. The police appear to be more interested in enforcing the traffic laws than catching thieves, but that may just be an impression.

An alternative route through Italy is via Turin, Milan, Bergamo, Brescia, Verona and on to Trieste which leads around the southern edge of a few of the lakes, in the area of Brescia. Excursions to Padua and Venice are obvious possibilities. From Trieste the most scenic (and winding) route is to travel the Yugoslavian Adriatic coast road via Rijeka, Zadar and Split to Dubrovnik. This latter, lovely medieval inner city is well worth a visit. At Petrovac the pain starts as the road swings up to Titograd, around to Kosovska Mitrovika, Pristina, Skopje and down to the Greek border at Gevgelija. The stretch from

Skopje to the frontier can be rather unnerving due to the vast plains crossed and countless Muslims, endlessly trekking backwards and forwards. Signposting in Yugoslavia is usually very bad; always obtain petrol when the opportunity occurs and lastly, but not least, city lights are often turned off during the hours of darkness (sounds a bit Irish to me!), making night driving in built-up areas extremely hazardous. To save the journey on from Petrovac, it is possible, at the height of the season, to catch a ferry from Dubrovnik to Igoumenitsa or Patras on the Greek mainland. (*See* **By Ferry-boat**)

Detailed road reports are available from the *Automobile Association*, but I would like to stress that in the Yugoslavian mountains, especially after heavy rain, landslips can (no will!) result in parts of the road disappearing, as well as the surface being littered with rocks. There you go! Also note that the very large intercontinental lorries may prove even more of a hazard, the drivers appearing to regard the middle of the sometimes narrow roads as their own territory.

The main road through Greece to Athens, via Pirgos, Larissa and Lamia, is wide and good but the speed of lorries and their trailer units can prove disquieting. Vehicles being overtaken are expected to move right over and tuck well into the wide, hard shoulders. From Evzonoi to Athens, via Thessaloniki, is 340 miles (550km) and some of the major autoroute is now a toll road. Drivers approaching Athens via the Corinth Canal should use the Toll road as the old route is murderously slow, especially in bad weather.

To sum up, my favourite choice of route used to be crossing the Channel to Le Havre to drive through France, which holds few perils for the traveller, via Evreux, Chartres, Pithiviers, Montargis, Clamecy, Nevers, Lyon and Chambery to the Italian border at Modane. Here the fainthearted can take the tunnel whilst the adventurous wind their way over the Col du Mont Cenis. That was until I 'discovered' the Briancon route.

In Italy, rather than face the rigours of the Yugoslavian experience, it is worth considering cutting down the not-all-that attractive Adriatic seaboard to one of the international ferry-boat ports of Ancona, Bari, or Brindisi. Boats connect to Corfu, as well as Igoumenitsa and Patras on the Greek mainland (*See* **By Ferry-boat & By Train**).

General Vehicle & Personal Requirements Documents required for travel in any European country used to include an *International Driving Licence*, and a *Carnet de Passages en Douanes* (both issued by the AA and valid for one year) but these are not now necessary in many countries including France, Italy, Switzerland, Germany, Greece and Yugoslavia. Drivers must have their United Kingdom driving licence and one document not to be forgotten is the *Green Insurance Card*. It is recommended to take the vehicle's registration documents, as proof of ownership, and the conveyance must bear a nationality sticker of the approved pattern and design. If a car owner carries out all the strictures each country demands, everything should be in order!

Particular countries' requirements include:

France Every year the French police carry out purges of motorists, and exceeding speed limits may well result in stiff, on the spot, fines. Headlights must be treated to allow for both right hand lane driving and the necessity to have yellow headlamp glass.

Italy All cars entering Italy must possess both right and left hand external driving mirrors. Drivers' licences have to be accompanied by an Italian translation, which is obtainable from one of the motoring organisations.

To help counter the disproportionately expensive price of petrol, tourists may apply to the relevant Italian Tourist Office for a package of concessionary petrol coupons and motorway vouchers. These go some way to offsetting the Hobson's choice in respect of the motorways, vis-a-vis the ordinary roads, and the resultant toll fees, which can mount up to about £50 for a north to south journey. Import allowances are as for Greece.

Switzerland Motorists should remember that the authorities require the vehicle and all the necessary documents to be absolutely correct (they would). The authorities have a nasty habit of stopping vehicles some distance beyond the frontier posts in order to make thorough checks.

Yugoslavia A valid passport is the only personal document required for citizens of, for example, Denmark, West Germany, Finland, Great Britain and Northern Ireland, Republic of Southern Ireland, Holland and Sweden. Americans and Canadians must have a visa and all formalities should be checked with the relevant Yugoslavian Tourist Office.

It is compulsory to carry a warning triangle, a first aid kit and a set of replacement vehicle light bulbs. The use of spotlights is prohibited and drivers planning to travel during the winter should check the special regulations governing the use of studded tyres.

Visiting motorists do not now have to buy petrol coupons in order to obtain fuel. But it is still advantageous to purchase them as they are the most cost effective method of buying petrol. The coupons are available at the frontier. Carefully calculate the number required for the journey and pay for them in foreign currency. Not only is the exchange rate allowed very advantageous, compared to that if the coupons are paid for in Yugoslavian dinars, but their acquisition allows for 10% more fuel. Petrol stations are often far apart, closed or have run out of fuel, so fill up when possible.

Photographers are only allowed to import five rolls of film; drinkers a bottle of wine and a quarter litre of spirits and smokers 200 cigarettes or 50 cigars. Each person may bring in unlimited foreign currency but only 15000 Yugoslavian dinars.

Fines are issued on the spot and the officer collecting one should issue an official receipt. To obtain help, in the case of accident or breakdown, dial 987 and the *SPI* will come to a driver's assistance.

Greece It is compulsory to carry a first aid kit, a fire extinguisher and a warning triangle in a vehicle. Failure to comply may result in a fine. It is forbidden to carry petrol in cans. In Athens the police are empowered to confiscate and detain the number plates of illegally parked vehicles. The use of undipped headlights in towns is strictly prohibited.

Speed Limits
See table below - all are standard legal limits which may be varied by signs.

	Built-up areas	Outside built-up areas	Dual Carriageways	Motorways
France	37mph (60kph)	56mph (90kph)	68mph (110kph)	81mph (130kph)
Greece	31mph (50kph)	49mph (80kph)	49mph (80kph)	62mph (100kph)
Italy	31mph (50kph)	56mph (90kph)	68mph (110kph)	81mph (130kph)
Switzerland	31mph (50kph)	49mph (80kph)	49mph (80kph)	74mph (120kph)
Yugoslavia	37mph (60kph)	49mph (80kph)	62mph (100kph)	74mph (120kph)

ALLOWANCES Customs allow the importation of 200 cigarettes or 50 cigars, 1 litre of spirits or 2 litres of wine. Visitors from the EEC may import 300 cigarettes or 75 cigars, 1½ litres of spirits or 5 litres of wine.

BY FERRY-BOAT (Illustration 3) . Some of the descriptive matter in this chapter, under the heading **By Train**, is relevant as it refers to both inter-country and ferry-boat travel, especially that relating to Brindisi Port and the international ferry-boats.

The ferry-boats on this run generally divide neatly into two. The expensive, but rather shambolic Greek ferries and the expensive, but luxurious and well-appointed Italian ferries. The Greek boats are really nothing more than an inter-island ferries of 'middling' quality, with the 'threat' of a cabaret and casino. They can be in appalling condition and the reception staff are often rude. The trappings of the Italian boats may well include a sea-water swimming pool, a ladies' hairdresser and beauty salon, a number of restaurants, a self-service cafeteria, a coffee bar and a disco. Food and drink on the craft of both countries is simply expensive. Examples include a coffee costing 165drs, a beer 150drs, *petit dejeuner* for two, of coffee and cake, 600drs and dinner 1500-2500drs a head. On the Greek craft the gourmet standards are average and the service poor whilst the Italian service and offerings are excellent, all at about the same price. Moral, try not to eat on board. Fares, in 1989, ranged from about 6000drs for deck class and 9200drs for a simple berth to 17000drs for a two berth cabin with en suite bathroom. Travellers should not rely on the purser to carry out normal currency exchange transactions and must remember that, apart from the cost of a ticket, there is the embarkation/boarding pass fee to pay. This latter costs about 800drs.

Due to the popularity of Brindisi (Illustration 2 – *See* **Brindisi Port**, **By Train**, this Chapter), height of the season travellers must be prepared for crowds, lengthy delays and the usual ferry-boat scrum (scrum not scum). That is why the knowledgeable head for the other departure ports, more especially Ancona. Motorists should note that the signposting from the Ancona autoroute mysteriously runs out, failing to indicate the turn off to the Ferry-boat Quay – it is the south exit. But once alongside, all the formalities for purchasing a ticket and currency exchange are conveniently to hand in the concourse of an adjacent, very large, square, Victorian, 'neo something' building.

Those making the return journey from Greece to Italy must take great care when purchasing the ferry-boat tickets, especially at Igoumenitsa (Greek mainland). The competition is hot and tickets may well be sold below the published price. If so, and a traveller is amongst the 'lucky ones', it is best not to 'count the drachmae' until on board. The port officials carefully check tickets and if they find any that have been sold at a discount they are confiscated and the purchaser is made to buy full price replacements. Ouch!

Passengers must steal themselves for the monumentally crass methods employed by the Italian officials to marshal the passengers prior to disembarking at the Italian ports. The resultant delays and queues that stretch throughout the length of the boat's corridors appear to be unnecessary and turn normally meek and mild people into raging psychos.

Sample Ferry-boat Services from Italy & Yugoslavia (1988)
From Italy:

Brindisi to Patras: (& vice versa)	(April-Oct) daily	Companies include:- Fragline,5a Rethymnou St,10682 Athens.Tel(010301)8214171/8221285. CF Eolos & Ouranos
		Seven Islands Lines,22 Perikleous St, Syntagma Sq,10562 Athens. Tel(010301)3232756 CF Ionis & Ionian Glory
		HML,28 Amalias Ave,Athens. Tel(010310)3236333. CF Egnatia,Poseidonia, Corinthia & Lydia.
		Agapitos Lines,99 Kolokotroni St,185 35 Piraeus.Tel(010301)4136246. CF Corfu Diamond & Sea.

			Low Season	High Season
Sample ferry-boat fees To Patras:- per person:	deck	from	4/5000drs	7000drs

28 CANDID GUIDE TO ATHENS

	aircraft seats		6000drs	8000drs
	2/4 berth cabin		7500drs	11000drs
	c/w washbasin			
	2 berth cabin		13/15000drs	19/2000drs
	c/w bathroom			
cars (over 4¼m)			5500drs	10500drs

Voyage duration: 20hrs.

Brindisi to Igoumenitsa: (April-Oct) daily
& Patras: (& vice versa)

Companies include:-
Fragline. (See above)

Nausimar, 9 Filellinon St, 185 36 Piraeus.
Tel(010301)4524290
CF Hellenic Spirit

Agapitos Lines, (See above)

HML. (See above)

Seven Islands Lines. (See above)

Sample ferry-boat fees To Igoumenitsa:-			Low Season	High Season
per person:	deck	from	4/5000drs	7000drs
	aircraft seats		5500drs	7500drs
	2/4 cabin		6/7000drs	10500drs
	c/w washbasin			
	2 berth cabin		12/14000drs	19000drs
	c/w bathroom			
cars (over 4¼m)			5000drs	9500drs

Voyage duration: 11½hrs.

Ancona to Patras: (April-Oct) Mon, Wed, Fri & Sat.
(& vice versa)

Karageorgis Lines, 26-28 Akti-Kondyli, Piraeus. Tel(010301)4110461/4173001.
CF Mediterranean Sea & Sky

Sample ferry-boat fees To Patras:-			Low season	High season
per person:	deck	from	5500drs	7000drs
	aircraft seats		–	–
	2/4 berth cabin		10500drs	13000drs
	c/w washbasin			
	2 berth cabin		16000drs	19000drs
	c/w bathroom			
cars (over 4¼m)			12000drs	15000drs

Voyage duration: 35hrs

Ancona to Igoumenitsa
& Patras (& vice versa)

(May-June)	Wed & Sat	
(June-Oct)	Wed, Thurs Sat & Sun	
(May-Sept)	Wed & Sat	
(July-Aug)	additionally Sun, Thurs & Fri.	
(April-May & Oct)	Mon, Tues & Thurs.	
(June-Sept)	Mon, Thurs & Sat.	
(July-Aug)	Mon, Tues, Thurs & Sat.	

Companies include:-
Minoan Lines, 2 Leoforos Vasileos, Konstantinou, Athens. Tel(010301) 7512356.
CF El Greco & Fedra

Marlines, 38 Akti Possidonos, 185 31 Piraeus. Tel(010301)4110777
CF Princess M, Countess M & Queen M

Strintzis Lines, 26 Akkti Possidonis, 185 31 Piraeus. Tel(010301)4129815.
CF Ionian Sun, Star & Galaxy

Sample ferry-boat fees To Igoumenitsa:-			Low season	High season
per person:	deck	from	5500drs	7000drs

TO ISLAND GROUPS

aircraft seats	6500drs	8500drs
2/4 cabin c/w washbasin	8500drs	10500drs
2 berth cabin c/w bathroom	16000drs	19500drs
cars (over 4¼m) Voyage duration: 24hrs.	12000drs	15000drs

Bari to Igoumenitsa & Patras: (& vice versa)	(mid-April) (May) (June & Oct) (July-Sept)	Wed & Fri Fri & Sun. Wed,Fri & Sun. daily	Ventouris Ferries,91 Pireos Kithiron Sts,18541 Piraeus.Tel(010301) 4181001 CF Grecia Express, Patra & Athens Express

Sample ferry-boat fees
To Igoumenitsa:-
per person:

		Low season	High season
deck	from	3500drs	4500drs
aircraft seats		4200drs	6000drs
2/4 cabin c/w washbasin		8500drs	13500drs
2 berth cabin c/w bathroom		11500drs	15500drs
cars (over 4¼m) Voyage duration: 13hrs.		4500drs	10000drs

Sample ferry-boat fees
To Patras:-
per person:

		Low season	High season
deck	from	4500drs	5500drs
aircraft seats		5000drs	6500drs
2/4 cabin c/w washbasin		9000drs	15300drs
2 berth cabin c/w bathroom		12200drs	17500drs
cars (over 4¼m) Voyage duration: 20½hrs.		4500drs	11500drs

From Yugoslavia

Dubrovnik to Igoumenitsa: (& vice versa)
(July-Aug)   Mon,Tues & Thurs.   Jadrolinija Line,c/o Hermes en Greece 3 Iassonos St,185 37 Piraeus Tel(010301)4520244.
Voyage duration: 20hrs.

Rijeka to Igoumenitsa:
(July-Aug)   Mon,Wed & Sun   Jadrolinija Line (*See* above)
Voyage duration: 43hrs.

Split to Igoumenitsa:
(July-Aug)   Tues,Thurs & Sat   Jadrolinija Line (*See* above)
Voyage duration: 29hrs

Zadar to Igoumenitsa:
(July-Aug)   Tues.   Jadrolinija Line (*See* above)
Voyage duration: 36hrs.

Ferries that dock at Igoumenitsa can connect with Athens by scheduled bus services and those that dock at Patras connect with Athens by both scheduled bus and train services.

Note the above services are severely curtailed outside the summer months, many ceasing altogether.

Travellers that dock at Igoumenitsa can connect with Athens by scheduled bus services, whilst those disembarking at Patras may journey to Athens by either scheduled bus or train services.

The Greek mainland ports of Igoumenitsa and Patras are detailed in **GROC's Candid Guide to Corfu, The Ionian Islands, West Coast Ports & Athens.**

Do not forget that the availability of ferry-boat sailings must be continually checked, as must airline, bus and train timetables. This is especially necessary during the months of October through to the beginning of May when the services are usually severely curtailed. So be warned.

USEFUL NAMES & ADDRESSES
The Automobile Association, Fanum House, Basingstoke, Hants. RG21 2EA.   Tel (0256) 20123
AA Routes   Tel (0256) 20123
The Greek National Tourist Organisation, 195-197 Regent St, London W1R 8DL.   Tel (01) 734 5997
The Italian State Tourist Office, 1 Princess St, London W1R 8AY.   Tel (01) 408 1254
The Yugoslavian National Tourist Office, 143 Regent St, London W1R 8AE.   Tel (01) 734 5243
British Rail International, PO Box 303, London SW1 1JY.   Tel (01) 834 2345 *(Author's note – keep ringing)*
The Hellenic State Railways (OSE), 1-3 Karolou St, Athens, Greece.   Tel (010301) 01 5222 491
Thomas Cook Ltd, Publications Dept, PO Box 36, Thorpewood, Peterborough PE3 6SB.   Tel (0733) 63200

Other useful names & addresses mentioned in the text include:
Time Out, Southampton St, London WC2E 7HD.   Tel (01) 836 4411
Courier Flights/Inflight Courier, 45 Church St, Weybridge, Surrey KT13 8DG.   Tel (0932) 857455/56
Owners Abroad Ltd, Valentines House, Ilford Hill, Ilford, Essex IG1 2DG.   Tel (01) 514 8844
Olympic Airways, 164 Piccadilly, London W1V 9DE.   Tel (01) 846 9080
Aegina Club Ltd, 25A Hills Rd, Cambridge CB2 1NW.   Tel (0223) 63256
The Best of Greece (Travel) Ltd, Rock House, Boughton Monchelsea, Maidstone, Kent ME17 4LY.
                                                                              Tel (0622) 46678
Ramblers Holidays, 13 Longcroft House, Fretherne Rd, Welwyn Garden City, Herts AL8 6PQ.   Tel (07073) 31133
Greek Sun Holidays, 1 Bank St, Sevenoaks, Kent TN13 1UW   Tel (0732) 740317
Laskarina Holidays, St Mary's Gate, Wirksworth, Derbyshire, DE4 4DQ.   Tel (062 982) 2203/4
Simply Simon Holidays, 1/45 Nevern Sq, London SW5 9PF   Tel (01) 373 1933
Greek Islands Club, 66 High St, Walton-on-Thames, Surrey KT12 1BU.   Tel (0932) 220416
Cricketers Holidays, 4 The White House, Beacon Rd, Crowborough, East Sussex TN6 1AB   Tel (08926) 64242
Islands Unlimited, Bignor, Nr Pulborough, West Sussex RH20 1QD   Tel (07987) 308
Something Special Travel Ltd, 13 Maidenhead St, Hertford, Herts SG14 1AN   Tel (0992) 552231
Timsway Holidays, Penn Place, Rickmansworth, Herts. WD3 IRE.   Tel (02404) 5541
Twelve Islands Angel way, Romford, Essex RM1 1AB   Tel (0708) 752653
Small World, Old Stone House, Judges Terrace, East Grinstead RH19 1AQ   Tel (0342) 27272
Martyn Holidays, West Leigh House, 390 London Rd, Isleworth, Middx.   Tel (01) 847 5855
STA Travel, 38 Store St, London WC1E 7BZ.   Tel (01) 580 7733
London Student Travel, (Tel (01) 730 3402/4473) & **Eurotrain**, Tel (01) 730 6525), both at 52 Grosvenor Gdns, London SW1N 0AG.
Euroways Supabus, c/o Victoria Coach Station, London, SW1.   Tel (01) 730 3466
or c/o National Express Co.
The Greek address is: 1 Karolou St, Athens.   Tel (010301) 5240 519/6
Eurolines Intercars (Uniroute), 102 Cours de Vincennes, 75012 Paris (Metro Porte Vincennes)
National Express Co, Westwood Garage, Margate Rd, Ramsgate CT12 6SL.   Tel (0843) 581333
or
Victoria Coach Station, 164 Buckingham Palace Road, London, SW1.   Tel (01) 730 0202
Consolas Travel, 29-31 Euston Rd, London NW1.   Tel (01) 833 4021/2026
The Greek address is: 100 Eolou St, Athens.   Tel (010301) 3219 228

Amongst others the agencies and offices listed above have, over the years and in varying degrees, been helpful in the preparation of the guides. I would like to extend my sincere thanks to all those concerned. Some have proved more helpful than others!

Olympic Airways overseas office addresses are as follows:
America: 647 Fifth Ave, New York, NY 10022.   Tel (0101 212)
                                                                              (Reservations) 838 3600
                                                                              (Ticket Office) 735 0290
Canada: 1200 McGill College Ave, Suite 1250, Montreal, Quebec H3B 4G7.   Tel (0101 418) 878 9691
        80 Bloor St West, Suite 502 Toronto ONT M5S 2VI.   Tel (0101 416) 920 2452
Australia: 44 Pitt St, 1st Floor, Sydney, NSW 2000.   Tel (01061 2) 251 2044
South Africa: Bank of Athens Buildings, 116 Marshall St, Johannesburg.   Tel (010127 11) 836 5951
Denmark: 4 Jernbanegade DK 1608, Copenhagen.   Tel (010451) 126-100
Sweden: 44 Birger Jarlsgatan, 11429 Stockholm.   Tel (010468) 113-800

TO ISLAND GROUPS 31

More useful overseas names & addresses include:
Let's Go Travel Services, Harvard Student Agencies, Thayer Hall B, Harvard University, Cambridge,
MA02138 USA   Tel 617 495 9649
Canadian Universities Travel Service, 187 College St, Toronto ONT M5T IP7 Canada.   Tel 417 979 2406
Automobile Association & Touring Club of Greece (ELPA), 2 Messogion Street, Athens. Tel (010301) 7791 615

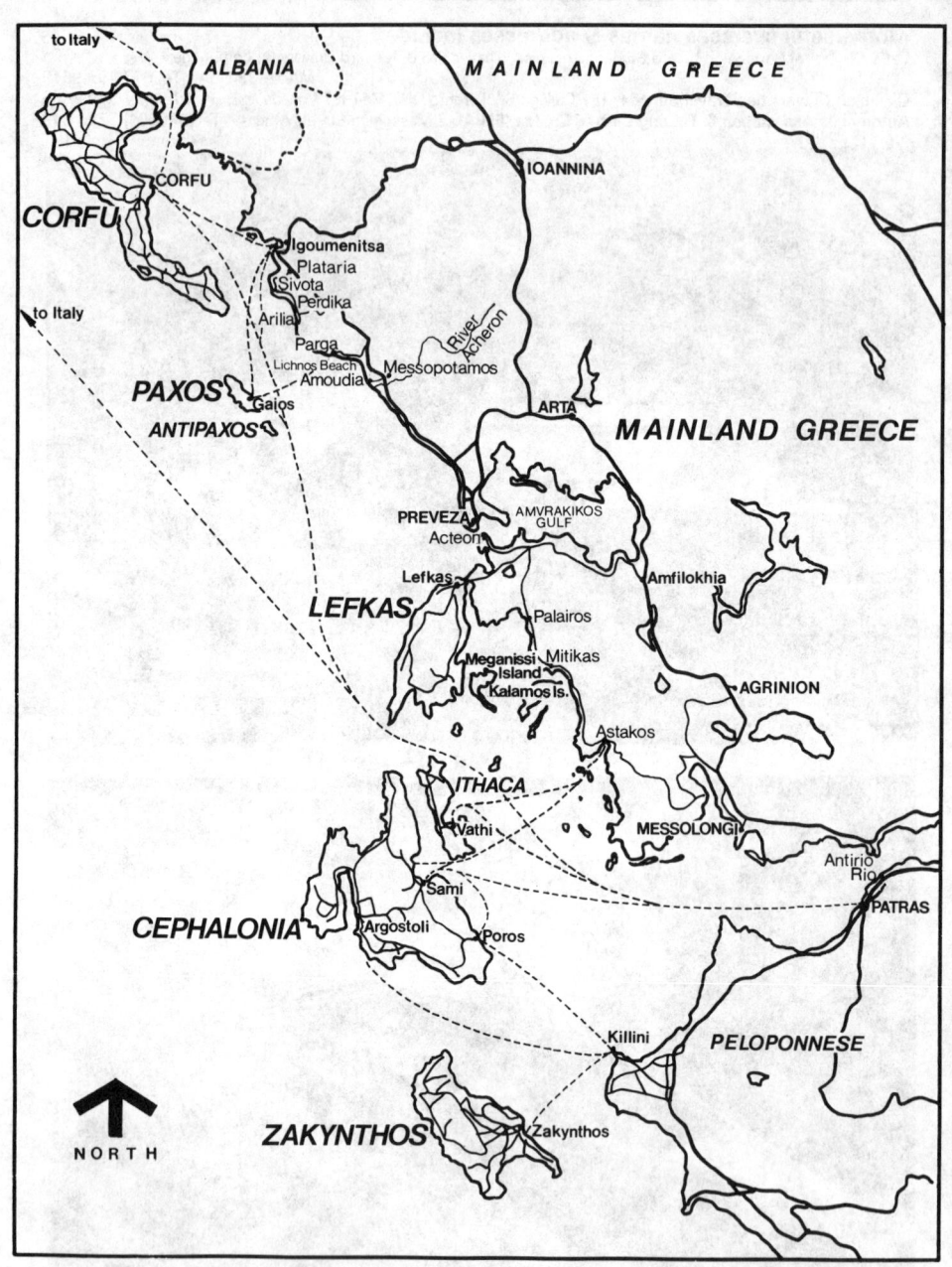

Illustration 4a The Ionian

3 Travel between Athens & the Islands

I see land. I see the end of my labour. Diogenes

The Greek islands are very thick on the water. They number between 1000 and 3000, depending upon which authority you wish to believe, of which approximately 100 are inhabited. Crete is the largest; some 24 are located in the Cyclades islands; 16 in the Dodecanese; 8 in the Ionian; 12 in the Mainland Group of the Argo-Saronic & Sporades islands and 11 in the NE Aegean.

In the past, the only way of setting foot on an island was to make for the relevant port and board a ferry-boat. Over the years a specialised and efficient system of water-borne travel developed.

The creation of a number of airfields on the smaller islands (which must be regarded as a mixed blessing) has made it possible to fly to Athens and take an onward flight to the chosen destination.

ARRIVAL BY AIR It can prove difficult to obtain a seat for domestic flights on the spot, especially at the height of the tourist season, as Greeks now utilise the services extensively. It may be preferable to forward book, through a local Olympic office, prior to arrival. Ferry-boat travel was always much cheaper than flying, but for a few years this differential all but disappeared. In fact, in some cases flying was even cheaper than a 3rd class ferry-boat ticket and certainly less expensive than a 2nd class fare. Savage price hikes in air fares, between 1986-88, restored the ferries economic advantage. The uplift is such as to restore the old differentials, ferry-boat travel now being at least 50% cheaper than flying.

Travellers arriving in Athens, other than by aircraft, and wanting a domestic flight from the West airport, can catch one of the city buses to the airport. (*See* **Arrival By Air, Athens, Chapter Nine**). Approximately an hour must be allowed between catching the airline bus and the relevant plane check-in time.

Many travellers do not wish to stop over in Athens. If this is the case, and arriving other than on an Olympic flight, it is possible to travel from the East to the domestic, West, airport using the connecting bus service.

The staff of Olympic, the Greek airline, are usually very helpful and their English good, although it is possible to fall foul of that sporadic Greek characteristic, intransigence.

It is worth considering utilising internal flights on one leg of a journey, especially if Athens is the point of arrival or departure. The possible extra cost of the flight, over and above the overland and ferry fares, must be balanced against the time element. For instance, Athens to Santorini island occupies some 40 mins by air, whilst the ferry takes about 12 hours. One other advantage of domestic air travel is that the fares can be paid for by the use of *American Express*, *Diners* or *Access Mastercard*, possibly saving precious drachmae, especially towards the end of a holiday. On the other hand, the cost of domestic flights has been steeply increased over the last couple of years (as have ferry-boat fares).

Cretan towns served by airports include Iraklion, Chania and Sitia.

Cycladean island airports include Mykonos, Paros and Santorini which are relatively sophisticated, with Santorini now able to accept the large jumbo jets. Unpolished Milos airport does not let the side down!

Dodecanese island airports take in the international facilities at Rhodes and Kos as well as smaller airfields on Karpathos, Kos and Leros. From Rhodes it is possible to fly on to Kastellorizo.

The **Ionian** island airports of Corfu, Cephalonia and Zakynthos are at the smarter end of the Greek island airports, bearing little resemblance to some of their 'country cousins' on the remoter islands. Preveza, the airport for Lefkas, was, until recently, a military airport but the shackles have been allowed to loosen.

Of the **Mainland** island group, Skiathos and Skyros of the Sporades islands and only Kithira of the Argo-Saronic islands possess airports.

NE Aegean island airports include those on Samos, Chios, Lesbos and Limnos. Mainland facilities relative to the group are Thessaloniki and Alexandroupoli.

ARRIVAL BY BUS *See* **Athens (Chapter Nine)** for details of daily scheduled bus services to the mainland ports that connect by ferry-boat to the various islands.

ARRIVAL BY FERRY In the following comments I am calling on many years experience of travelling third and tourist class on any number of ferry-boats.

In general, where sleeping arrangements are available, they will prove satisfactory if certain basic rules are followed. First claim a bunk by depositing luggage on the chosen berth, it will be quite safe as long as money and passports are removed. The position of a berth is important. Despite the labelling 'Men' and 'Women', a berth can usually be selected in either sleeping area. Try to choose one adjacent to stern deck doors to ensure some ventilation - due to the usual location of the third and tourist class accommodation beneath decks, it can get very hot and stuffy. A last tip is to lay a towel over plastic bunk covering to alleviate what otherwise would prove to be a sticky, uncomfortable night. Some ferries only have aircraft type, fold back seats in the 3rd/tourist class. Travellers should attempt, where possible, to find a lounge in which the television is muted and Gipsy children are noticeable, by their absence.

The third class lavatories are often in an unsightly condition even prior to a craft's departure. To help enjoy reasonable surroundings and have the use of a shower, quietly proceed into the next class and use their facilities (but don't tell everybody). Both the toilets and the showers suffer from the usual deficiencies listed under **Greek Bathrooms, Chapter Four**, so be prepared.

Important points to take into account when ferry-boating include the following:
1. The ferries are owned by individual steamship companies and an employee of one line will be unable, or unwilling, to give enquirers information in respect of another company's timetable. Incidentally, this individual ownership results in a wide disparity in quality of service and general comfort between different ferry-boats.
2. The distances and voyage times are quite often lengthy and tiring. Additionally the duration of the overall passage sometimes (no always) results in the timetable going awry, with delays in scheduled departure times at islands well into a ferry's voyage.
3. There are usually four basic fare classes: first, second, tourist and third/deck class. The published fares on scheduled ferries are government controlled and the third/deck class option represents good value. Purchasers must ensure that they state the fare class required as failure to do so may well result in a more expensive, tourist ticket being bought instead of the cheaper, deck class. Apart from the aforementioned four categories, there may well be a variety of first and second-class sleeping accommodation, including private and shared cabins.

There are a number of 'Express' ferries and tourist trip boats, usually plying a particular island-to-island journey, on which charges are considerably higher.

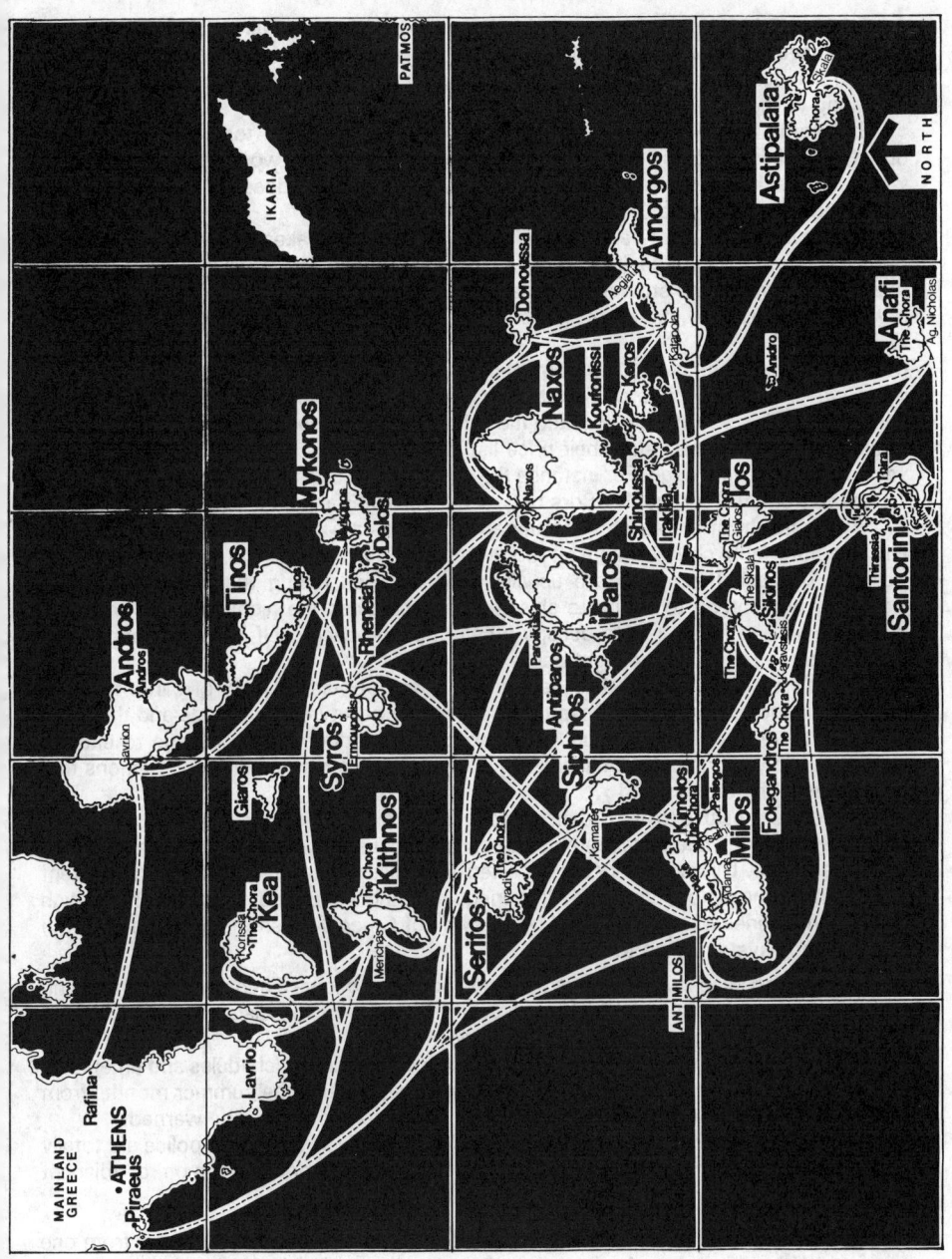

Illustration 4b The Cyclades

4. Food and drink on the ferries used to be comparatively expensive, but price rises on the land have not been mirrored at sea. On the other hand the service on the older boats is often discourteous and inefficient, so it still may be advantageous to pack provisions for a long voyage.

Wholesome and inexpensive ferry-boat picnic food includes: tomatoes, cucumber, bread, salami, ham, *Sunfix* orange juice and a bottle of wine (or two!). Take some bottled water. Greek chocolate (especially with nuts) is very good but does not keep well in the ambient daytime temperatures.

5. The state of the toilets and the lack of basic supplies makes it mandatory that one or two lavatory rolls are packed, easily to hand as it were. The usual lack of washroom facilities commends the stowage of a pack of 'wipes'. Quite frankly, on some occasions it will be necessary to stand on the rim of the toilet bowl as the only way of using the facility. Sorry!

6. Tickets should be purchased from a ticket agency prior to a voyage, as they can cost more when bought on board. Ticket agency offices vary from 'the plush' to boxed-in back stairs. Clients who have checked the scheduled prices should not go wrong. On the other hand they must be sure their price list is up-to-date as fare increases over recent years have been very large. For instance the cost of a 3rd class Piraeus to Santorini ticket increased from 1093drs to 1708drs between April 1985 and July 1988.

7. At the height of the season, the upper deck seats are extremely hot during the day and uncomfortably chilly at night. It is advisable to stake a claim to a seat as early as possible because the ferries are usually very crowded during the summer months. Voyagers who intend to lay out a sleeping bag and sleep the night away on the deck would do well to remember to occupy a seat, not the deck itself, which is more often than not sluiced down in the night hours.

8. Travellers should ensure they have a good fat book and a pack of cards to while away the longer sea voyages. Despite the awesome beauty of the islands and the azure blue sea, there are often long, unbroken periods of Mediterranean passage to endure, interrupted only by the occasional passing ship and the dramatic activity and ructions that take place during a port call.

9. Travellers sensitive to discordancy, and who find disagreeable a cacophony, a clamour of sound, may well find unacceptable the usual raucous mix experienced in the average 3rd class lounge. This is auditory assault often embodies two televisions (tuned to different programmes, the picture constantly flickering, suffering a snowstorm or horizontally high jumping in a series of stills) overlaid by the wail of Greco-Turkish music piped over the ship's tannoy system. Best to fly!

One delight is to keep a weather eye open and hope to observe a shoal of dolphins diving and leaping in the ship's wake. Their presence is often made discernible by the loud slapping noise they make when re-entering the water.

Ferry-boaters must take care when checking the connections, schedules and timetables as they can, no do, change during the year, especially outside the summer months from May through to September, as well as from one year to another. So be warned.

Do not forget, when the information is at it's most confusing, the Port police are totally reliable, but often a little short on English. Their offices are almost always on, or adjacent to the quayside.

ARRIVAL BY FLYING DOLPHINS (Hydrofoils – Ceres) Apart from one or two isolated services in the Cyclades, the main thrust of hydrofoil activity is amongst the island groups of the Argo-Saronic and the Sporades. Where these speedy craft operate they cut ferry-boat timetables in half but the fares are about double. For instance the Piraeus(Zea) to Spetses ferry costs 777drs and takes $5\frac{1}{2}$hrs whilst the hydrofoil costs 1745drs with a 'flying' time of 2hrs.

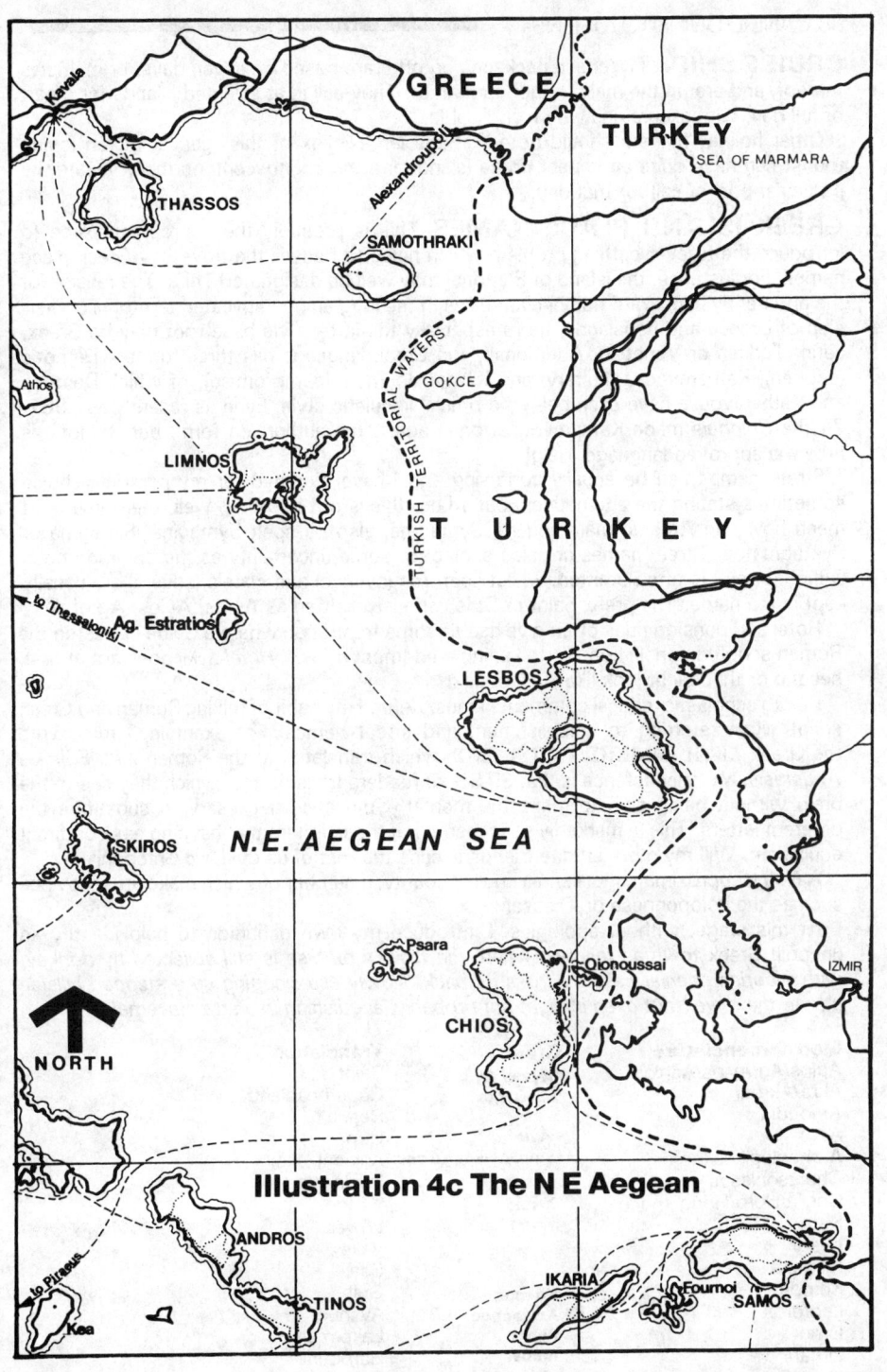

CRUISE SHIPS Fly/cruise packages on offer are based on seven days, or multiples thereof, and are, in the main, rather up-market. They call in at selected islands for a part or full day, with excursions where applicable.

Other holiday-makers should note that the large influx of this 'genus' of fun loving tourist can have quite an impact on an island, and the *cognoscenti* normally vacate the particular port of call for that day.

GREEK ISLAND PLACE NAMES This is probably the appropriate place to introduce the forever baffling problem which helps to bedevil the traveller – Greek place names. For instance, the island of Santorini may well be designated Thira. The reason for the apparently haphazard nomenclature lies in the long and complicated territorial ownership of Greece and its islands, more especially the latter. The base root may be Greek, Latin, Turkish or Venetian. Additionally the Greek language has three forms – Demotic (spoken), Katharevousa (literary) and Kathomiloumeni (compromise), of which Demotic and Katharevousa have each been the official linguistic style. Even as recently as 1967-74 the *Colonels* made Katharevousa, once again, the authorised form, but Demotic is now the approved language. Help!

Street names can be equally confusing and I have plumped for my personal choice sometimes stating the alternatives, but where this is not possible, well, there you go! I mean how can Athens' main square, Syntagma, also be spelt Syntagina, Sintagma or Syntagmatos? Street names are also subject to some uncertainty as the common noun Odhos (street) is often omitted, whilst Leoforos (avenue) and Plateia (square) are usually kept in the name. The prefix Saint or St is variously written as Agios, Ayios, Ag or Ai.

Hotel and pension titles often give rise to some frustration where a Guide has listed the Roman scripted appellation. To the uninitiated (most of us?), *Hotel* Αυλη does not at first, second or third sight look like *Avli*, does it?

Due to scholastic, critical comments I must defend my habit of mixing Roman and Greek script when referring to establishment and street names. For example, I may write the Greek ΑΚΤΗ ΕΘΝΙΚΗΣ ΑΝΤΙΣΤΑΣΗΣ, which translates to the Roman *Akti Ethnikis Antistasis*. My only defence is that 99.9% of readers transmit that which they see to the brain without being able to make the mental gymnastics necessary to substitute the different letters. This is markedly so in respect of those letters that have no easy or direct equivalent. Will my more erudite friends excuse the rest of us dyslexic Grecophiles!

A *Nome* approximates to a small English county, a number of which make up a province such as the Peloponnese or Thessaly.

At this stage, without apologies, I introduce my own definition to help identify an unspoilt Greek town as follows: *where the town's rubbish is still collected by donkey, with wooden panniers slung across its back, slowly clip-clopping up a stepped hillside street, the driver, not even in sight but probably languishing in a stray taverna!*

Map nomenclature	Greek	Translation
Agios/Ag/Ayios/Aghios	Άγιος/ Άγια	Saint
Akra/Akrotiri	Ακρωτήρι	Cape/headland
Amoudia		Beach
Ano	Άνω	Upper
Archeologikos (horos)	Αρχαιολογικός χώρος	Ancient (site)
Cherssonissos		Peninsula
Chora/Horo/Horio/khorio	Χωριό	Village
Kato	Κάτω	Lower
Kiladi		Valley
Klimaka		Scale
Kolpos	Κόλπος	Gulf
Leoforos	Λεωφόρος	Avenue
Limni	Λίμνη	Lake/marsh
Limani	Λιμάνι	Harbour

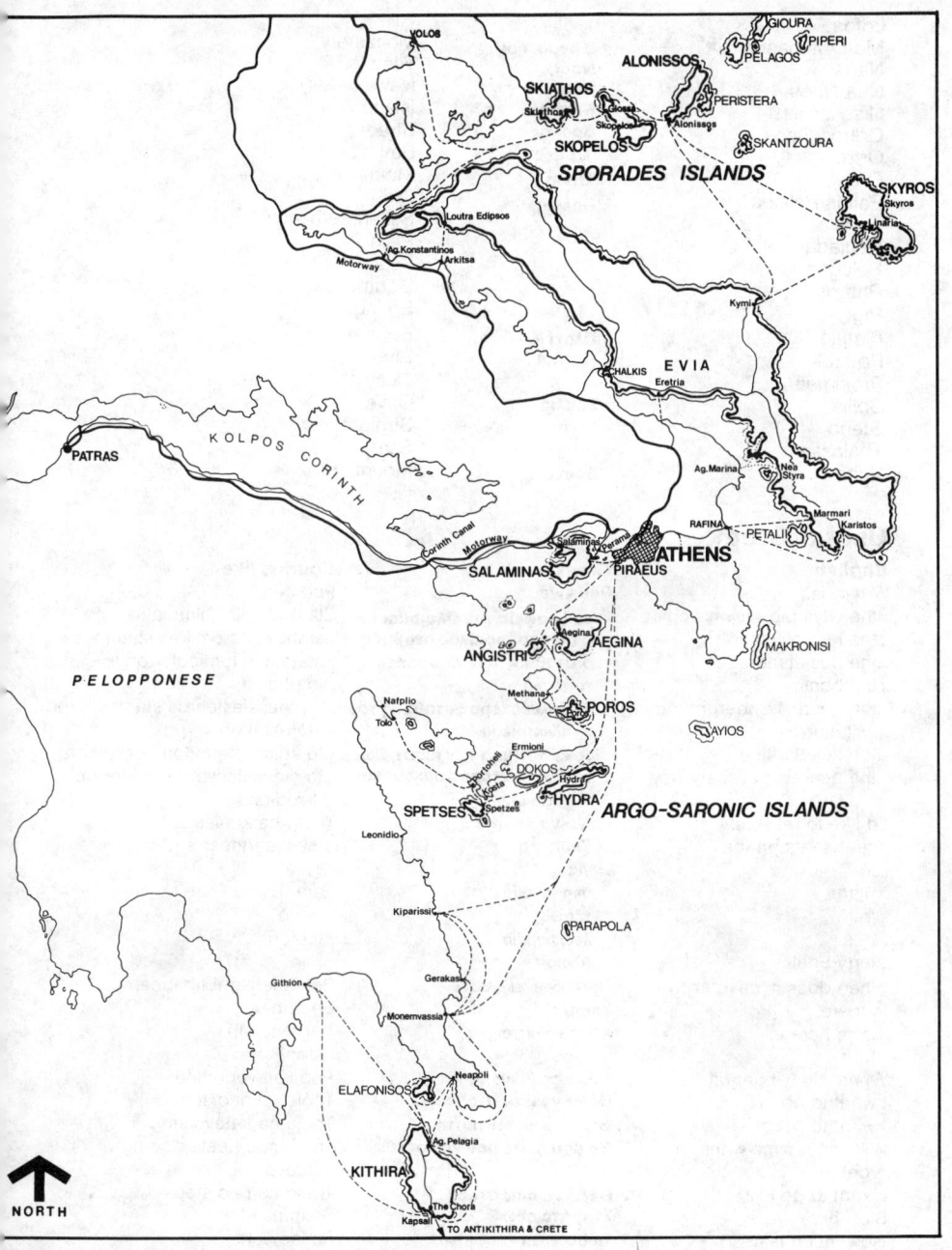

Illustration 4d Mainland islands

English		Greek	Sounds like
Lofos			Hill
Moni/Monastiri		Μοναστήρι	Monastery
Naos		Ναός	Temple
Nea/Neos		Νέο	New
Nissos/Nissi		Νήσος	Island
Odhos/Odos		Δρόμος	Street
Ormos		Όρμος	Bay
Oros		Όρος	Mountain
Palios/Palaios		Παλιός	Old
Paralia			Seashore/beach
Pediada			Plain
Pelagos			Sea
Pharos			Lighthouse
Pigi			Spring
Plateia		Πλατεία	Square
Potami		Ποτάμι	River
Prokimea			Quay
Spilia		Σπηλιά	Cave
Steno			Straight
Thalassa			Sea
Vuno		Βουνό	Mountain

Useful Greek

English	Greek	Sounds like
Where is...	Που ειναι	Poo eene...
...the Olympic Airways office	τα γραφεία της Ολυμπιακής	...ta grafia tis Olimbiakis
...the railway station	ο σιδηροδρομικός σταθμός	...sidheerothromikos stathmos
...the bus station	ο σταθμοζ των λεωφορειων	...stathmos ton leoforion
...the boat	το πλοιο	...to plio
...the nearest underground station	ο πλησιέστερος σταθμός του ηλεκτρικοο	...o pleessiestehros stathmos too eelektrikoo
...the ticket office	το εκδοτήριο των εισιτηρίων	...to eckdhoterio ton eessitirion
...the nearest travel agency	το πλησιέστερο πρακτορείο ταξιδιων	...to pleessiestehro praktorion taxidion
I'd like to reserve...	Θελω να κρατησω	Thelo na kratiso
...seat/seats on the	θέση για	...thessee/thessis ghia
...to	για	...ghia
...plane	αεροπλανο	...aeroplano
...train	τραινο	...treno
...bus	λεωφορειο	...leoforio
...ferry-boat	πλοιο	...plio
When does it leave/arrive	Ποτε φευγει/φθανει	Poteh fehvghi/fthanee
Is there...	Υπαρχει	Eeparhee...
...from here to	απ εδωστο	...Apetho sto
...to	στον	...ston
Where do we get off	Που κατεβαινομε	Poo katevenomhe
I want to go to	Θέλω να πάω στους ...	Thelo na pao stoos...
I want to get off at	Θελω να κατεβω στο	Thelo na katevo sto...
Will you tell me when to get off	Θα μου πείτε πού να κατέβω;	Thah moo peete poo nah kahtevo
I want to go to...	Θέλω να πάω στους ...	Thelo na pao stoos
Stop here	Σταμάτα εδώ.	Stamata etho
How much is it	Ποσο ειναι	Posso eene
How much does it cost	Πόσο κάνει η μεταφορά	Posso kani i metafora
...to	στο	...sto
Do we call at	Θα σταματήσουμε στην ...;	Tha stamatissome stin

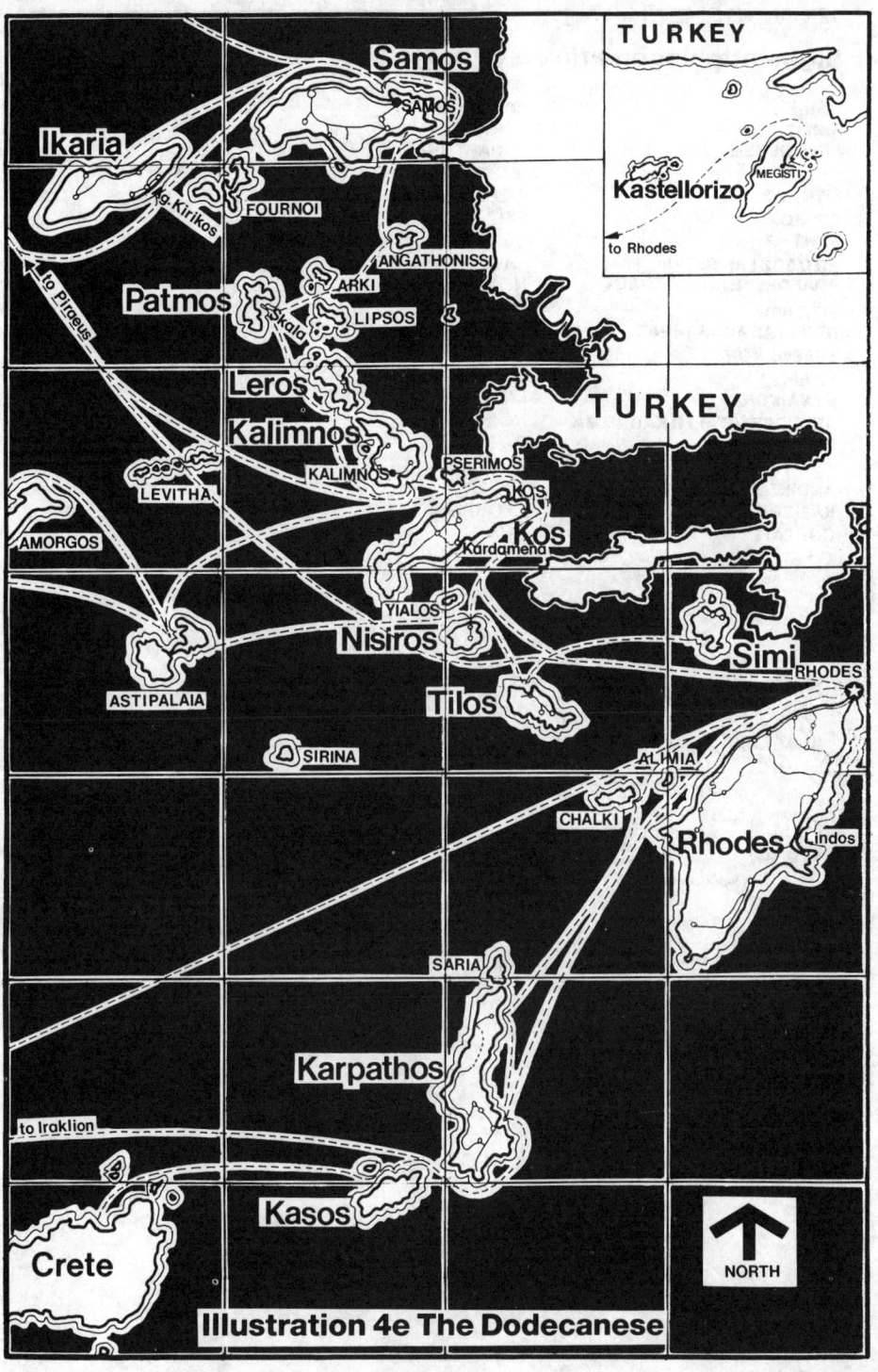

Signs often seen affixed to posts & doors

Greek	English
ΑΦΙΞΙΣ	ARRIVAL
ΑΝΑΧΩΡΗΣΙΣ	DEPARTURE
ΣΤΑΣΙΣ	BUS STOP
ΕΙΣΟΔΟΣ	ENTRANCE
ΕΞΟΔΟΣ	EXIT
ΚΕΝΤΡΟ	CENTRE (as in town centre)
ΕΙΣΟΔΟΣ ΕΛΕΥΘΕΡΑ	FREE ADMISSION
ΑΠΑΓΟΡΕΥΕΤΑΙ Η ΕΙΣΟΔΟΣ	NO ENTRANCE
ΕΙΣΙΤΗΡΙΑ	TICKET
ΠΡΟΣ ΤΑΣ ΑΠΟΒΑΘΡΑΣ	TO THE PLATFORMS
ΤΗΛΕΦΩΝΟΝ	TELEPHONE
ΑΝΔΡΩΝ	GENTLEMEN
ΓΥΝΑΙΚΩΝ	LADIES
ΑΠΑΓΟΡΕΥΕΤΑΙ ΤΟ ΚΑΠΝΙΣΜΑ	NO SMOKING
ΤΑΜΕΙΟΝ	CASH DESK
ΤΟΥΑΛΕΤΕΣ	TOILETS
ΑΝΟΙΚΤΟΝ	OPEN
ΚΛΕΙΣΤΟΝ	CLOSED
ΩΘΗΣΑΤΕ	PUSH
ΣΥΡΑΤΕ	PULL

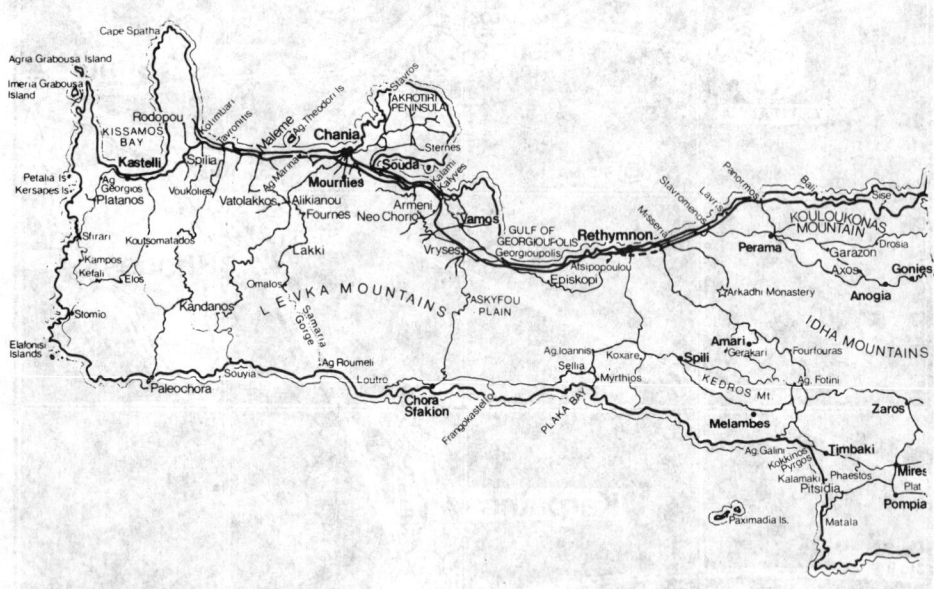

Illustration 4f Crete

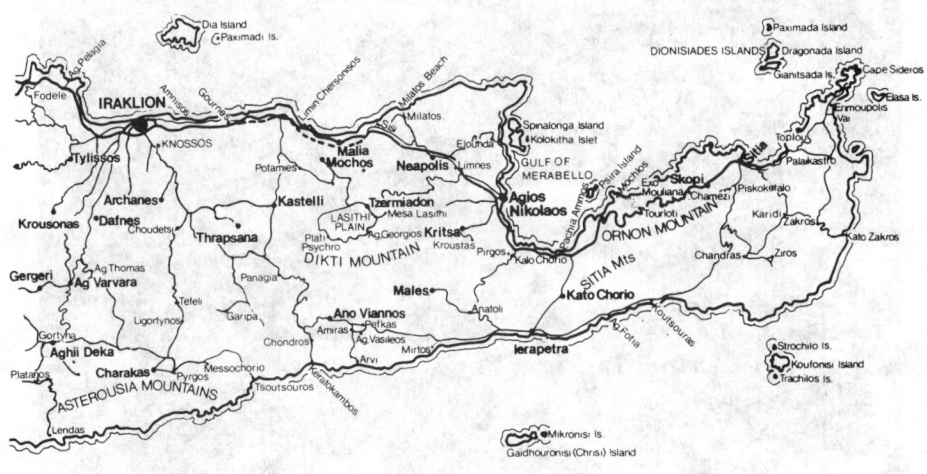

4 Island Accommodation

How doth man by care oppressed, find in an inn a place of rest. Combe

Package villa and tour organised holiday-makers will have accommodation arranged prior to arrival in Greece. In contrast, the most important matter to the independent traveller is undoubtedly the procurement of lodgings, especially the first overnight stay on a new island or at an untried location.

The choice and standard of accommodation is bewildering, ranging from extremely simple **Rooms**, in private houses (usually clean but with basic bathroom facilities), to luxury class, almost indecently plush hotels able to hold their own with the most modern counterpart, almost anywhere else in the world. The deciding factor must be the budget and a person's sensibilities. My comments in respect of standards reflect comparisons with Western European establishments. Those referring to prices are usually in relation to other Greek options, as the cost is averagely in excess of half that of the United Kingdom equivalents.

Travellers stepping off an island ferry-boat are usually a wisp in a swarming throng made up of Greeks, tourists and backpackers engulfed by a quayside mass of Greeks, tourists and backpackers struggling to get aboard the same craft. Visitors may well be approached by men, women and youngsters offering accommodation. It is a matter of taking pot-luck there and then, or searching around the town to make a more measured selection. The later in the day, the more advisable it is to take an offer, unseen. But it is obligatory to establish the price, if the rooms are with or without a shower, is the water hot and how far away they are located. It can prove unnerving to be 'picked up' and then commence on an ever-lengthening trudge through the back streets of a strange place, especially as Greek ideas of distance are rather optimistic.

Any accommodation usually requires a traveller's passport to be relinquished. As a passport is also required to change money and to hire a car, or a scooter, it is a good idea, if married or travelling with friends, to have separate documents. Then, if necessary, one passport can be left with the landlord and another kept for other purposes, as required.

Official sources and many guidebooks lay much emphasis on the role of the Tourist police in finding accommodation, but this cannot be relied upon as the offices may well be closed on arrival. Moreover changes in the structure of the various police forces, over the last few years, has resulted in the once separate and independent Tourist police being integrated with the Town police. I for one regard this as a very retrograde step. Such a pity that the Greeks, innovators of this excellent service, should now abandon the scheme, more especially in the light of the ever increasing number of tourists. Perhaps, having achieved their goal of ensuring Greece as a number one holiday spot, the authorities are going to allow the tour guides and couriers (that go 'hand in sand' with the ever increasing number of package tourists) to take over the Tourist police role in an *ex officio* capacity? Preposterous! I hope so.

A fruitful source of accommodation leads are tavernas, which more often than not result in an introduction to a **Room** or pension owner. Failing that, they usually send out for someone.

BEDROOMS Greek bedrooms tend to be airy, whitewashed and sparsely furnished. The beds are often hard, as are the small pillows, and unyielding mattresses may well be laid directly on to bed-boards, not springs.

It is advisable to inspect bedroom walls for the evidence of blood-red splats. These indicate flattened, but once gorged, mosquitoes and result from a previous occupant's night-time vigil. Well designed rooms usually have a top-opening window screened off with gauze so that they can be left ajar without fear of incursions by winged, creepy-crawlies. Where no gauze is in evidence, it is best to keep the windows tightly closed at night, however alien this may be. Those not in possession of a proprietary insect repellent may well have to reconcile themselves to a sleepless night. Tell-tale buzzing echoing in the ears indicates one has already been bitten. It is comparable to being attacked by Lilliputian Stuka night-fighters.

Hanging points are noticeable by their absence. Often there will be no wardrobe. If one is *in situ*, there is unlikely to be any hangers, not even the steel-wire type, and the cupboard doors may be missing. A rather idiosyncratic feature is that clothes hooks, when present, are often very inadequate, being more suitable for hanging coffee mugs by the handles.

Even more maligned and even more misunderstood than Greek food is:
THE GREEK BATHROOM I use the descriptive word bathroom, rather than refer simply to the toilets, because the total facility requires some elucidation. The following will not apply to Luxury, Class A or B hotels – well, it should not!

The plumbing is quite often totally inadequate. Instead of the separate wastes of the bath, shower and sink being plumbed into progressively larger soil pipes, thus achieving a 'venturi' effect, they are usually joined into a similar diameter tube to that of the individual pipes. This inevitably causes considerable back pressure with inescapable consequences. If this were not sufficient to cause a building inspector (who?) nightmares, where 'Mama' owns a washing machine it is invariably piped into the same network. That is why the drain grill, cunningly located at the highest point of the bathroom floor, often foams. The toilet waste is almost always insufficient in size and even normal, let alone excessive, use of toilet paper results in dreadful things happening, not only to the bathroom, but probably to a number of bathrooms in the building, street and possibly the village. If this were not enough... the header tank rarely delivers sufficient 'flush'. It has to be pointed out that Greeks have had, for many years, to be economic in the use of water and some islands ration it, turning off the supply for a number of hours per day, in the height of the summer. (*See* **Drinking Water, Chapter Six**).

Common faults are to find the lavatory without a seat; flooded to a depth of some inches; the bathroom light not working; no toilet roll; door locks not fitted as well as dirty WC pans and or any combination of the above. Furthermore, the wash basin may well be without a drain plug. Amongst other reasons, the lack of a plug is to stop flooding if a sink tap is accidently left turned on, when the mains water is switched off, and not turned off when the water supply is resumed!

The most common type of en suite bathroom is an all purpose lavatory and shower room. Beware! Years of research reveals that the shower head is usually positioned in such a way as to not only wash down the occupant but to drench the (amazingly) absorbent toilet roll as well as the bathers clothes, towel and footwear. Incidentally, the drain point is usually located so as to ensure that the bathroom is kept awash to a depth of between 1" and 3" ... and the resultant pool invariably lies where a toilet sitter's feet fall – if you read my meaning.

It is not unusual for there to be no hot water, even if a heating system is in evidence. Government energy conservation methods, the comparatively high cost of electricity and the use of moderately sized solar heating panels all contribute to this state of affairs. Where solar panels are the means of heating the water, remember to beat the rush and shower as early as possible, for the water soon loses its heat. Why not share with a friend? If hot water is available, but it is not heated by solar energy, then it will be necessary to locate the relevant electric switch. This is usually a 4 way position, ceramic knob hidden away behind a translucent panel door. On the other hand... To be fair to owners of accommodation, it is standard practice to charge for the use of hot water showers so it pays the landlord to have the switch out of sight and reach. Room charges may well be increased by as much as 100drs per day, per head, for the use of a shower, but this ought to be detailed on the Government controlled price list that should be displayed, and is usually suspended on the back of the bedroom door.

One stipulation on water-short islands that really offends the West European (and North American?) sense of delicacy, is the oft present, hardly legible sign requesting guests to put their 'paper' in the wastebin supplied, and not down the pan! I must own up to not always obeying this dictum and have had to make a hurried departure from a number of islands, let alone a pension or village, when the consequences of my profligate use of toilet paper have become apparent.

THE BEACH Some backpacking youngsters utilise the shore for their night's accommodation. In fact all island hoppers must be prepared to consider the beach as a stand-by, at the more crowded locations, during the months of July and August. I have only had to spend two or three nights on the beach in the nine or ten years of island excursions but admit to not venturing forth during the height of season months of late July, August and early September. On the other hand, the weather could not be more ideal for sleeping under the stars, the officials are generally not too fussed and may well direct travellers to a suitable spot. But beware of mosquitoes and tar.

CAMPING In direct contrast to *ad hoc* sleeping on the beach, camping, except at approved sites, is strictly forbidden. The law is not always rigorously applied. The restriction comes about from a wish to improve general hygiene, to prohibit and discourage abuse of private property and as a precaution against forest fires. The NTOG operate most of the licensed sites, some of which are spectacularly located, but there are some authorised, privately run camping grounds, which are also price controlled. A *Carnet-Camping International*, although not normally requested, affords campers worldwide, third-party liability cover, may result in a discount and is available to United Kingdom residents from the AA and other, similar organisations.

If moved on by an official for sleeping on the beach or illegally camping, it is advisable not to argue and go quietly. The Greek police have fairly wide, autonomous powers and it is preferable not to upset them unnecessarily.

As a guide, campsite fees, in 1989, were charged as follows: Adults per person 450-550drs; children ½ adult rate; tent hire 600-750drs and motor caravans 800-900drs.

YOUTH HOSTELS (ΞΕΝΩΝΑΣ ΝΕΩΝ) Establishments in Athens include the *YMCA (XAN)* and *YWCA (XEN)* as well as the *YHA*, which also has one or three outposts on the islands. This latter appellation more often than not is applied to ethnic, privately owned pensions catering for young travellers. They are habitually rather down-at-heel and tend to be operated in a somewhat Spartan, slovenly manner.

It is preferable to have YHA membership, taking the Association's card along. Approximate prices per night at the YMCA and YWCA are 1200drs and in a Youth Hostel 500drs.

ROOMS The story goes that as soon as a tourist steps off the ferry, he (or she) is surrounded by women crying *Rooms (Dhomatio)*, and whoops, within minutes the traveller is ensconced in some wonderful Greek family's private home.

History may well have been like that, and in truth the ferries are still met at almost every island, the inhabitants offering not only rooms but pensions and lower category hotels. *Rooms* are the cheapest accommodation and are generally very clean, sometimes including the option of breakfast which is ordinarily charged extra. Prices reflect an island's popularity and the season, but the average 1988 mid-season cost was 1500-2500drs for a double room, depending upon the classification. Government approved and categorised rooms are subject to an official tariff and are more expensive than freelance houses.

At the more tourist popular island resorts an unwelcome phenomena has reared 'his' ugly head. This is the long stay, enterprising layabout who rents a large double or triple bedroom, for the summer season, from a hapless, unsuspecting owner of accommodation. The 'entrepreneur', a species to be avoided, then daily sublets out the room, cramming in some five or six unfortunates a night.

Apart from a prospect being approached leaving the ferry, the Tourist police would, in the past, advise about available accommodation but this role is being drastically reduced in their amalgamation with the Town police. The Tourist police offices were signed, if at all, 'ΤΟΥΡΙΣΤΙΚΗ ΑΣΤΥΝΟΜΙΑ'. Householders display the sign 'ΕΝΟΙΚΙΑΖΟΝΤΑΙ ΔΩΜΑΤΙΑ' or simply 'ΔΩΜΑΤΙΑ', when they have a room to rent.

PENSIONS ('PANSION, ΠΑΝΣΙΟΝ') This category of lodging was a natural progression from *Rooms* and now represents the most often found and reasonably priced accommodation on offer.

The older type of pension is rather reminiscent of those large, Victorian English houses, that have been divided up into bed-sits. In the main though they have been purpose built, usually during the Colonels' regime (1967-74) when government grants were freely available for the construction of tourist quarters. The owner more often than not lives in the basement and acts as concierge. The rooms are functional and generally the guests on each level share a bathroom and shower and (a rather nice touch when provided) a communal refrigerator in which visitors can store their various provisions and drinks. Mid-season charges for 1988 varied between 2000 and 2500drs for a double room.

Sometimes a breakfast of coffee, bread and jam, perhaps butter and a boiled egg, is available at a cost of about 150drs and represents fair value compared with the cost of a cafe breakfast.

TAVERNAS (ΤΑΒΕΡΝΑ) Tavernas are, first and foremost, eating places. Some tavernas, especially those situated by, or near, beaches, also have accommodation available. The drawback is that the more popular the taverna, the less likely guests are to get a full night's sleep, but the more involved they will be with the taverna's social life, which often continues into the small hours. Charges are similar to those of a Pension.

HOTELS (ΞΕΝΟΔΟΧΕΙΟΝ) Shades of difference and interpretation can be given to the nomenclature by variations of the bland, descriptive noun hotel. For instance ΞΕΝΟΔΟΧΕΙΟΝ ΥΠΝΟΥ indicates a hotel that does not serve meals and ΠΑΝΔΟΧΕΙΟΝ a low grade hotel.

Many independent travellers would not consider hotels as a first choice. The high classification ones are more expensive than pensions and the lower grade hotels often cost the same, but may well be rather seedy and less desirable than the equivalent class pension. Greek hotels are classified L (Luxury), A, B, C, D and E and the prices charged within these categories (except L) are controlled by the authorities.

It is unfortunately almost impossible to neatly pigeon-hole and differentiate between hotels and their charges as each individual category is subject to fairly wide standards, and charges are dependent on a multitude of possible percentage supplements and reductions as detailed below:

Shower extra (C, D and E hotels); number of days stayed less than three, plus 10 per cent; air conditioning extra (A and B hotels); out of season deductions (enquire); high season extra (ie months of July, August and the first half of September, plus 20 per cent; single occupancy of a double room, about 80 per cent of the double room rate. The higher classification hotels may well insist on guests taking demi-pension terms, especially in high season.

ACCOMMODATION

The following table must be treated as a guide only and is based on 1989 prices:

Class	Comments	Guideline, mid-season double-bedroom price
L	All amenities, a very high standard and price. Probably at least one meal in addition to breakfast will have to be purchased. Very clean. En suite bathrooms with very hot water	--
A	High standard and price. Most rooms have en suite shower or bath. Guests may well have to accept demi-pension terms. Clean. Hot water.	6500-9000 drs
B	Good standard. Many rooms have en suite shower or bath. Clean. Hot water.	4300-6300 drs
C	May be an older hotel but many new, purpose built, package tourist hotels plump for this category. If of the ancient variety, will exhibit faded elegance, shared bathrooms. Cleanish. Possibly hot water	2300-4300 drs
D	Older, more faded. Shared bathroom, which may well be 'interesting'. A shower, if available will be an 'experience', and the water cold.	1500-2800 drs
E	Old, very faded and of dubious cleanliness. The whole stay will be an 'experience'. Only (very) cold water.	1500-1800 drs

The prices indicated include government taxes, service and room occupancy until noon.
Where in the text reference is made to 'official rates', these are the prices listed in the *Guide to the Greek Hotels*. Generally prices detailed throughout this guide are those applicable to 1989.

THE XENIAS Originally government owned and promoted to ensure the availability of high standard accommodation at important tourist centres, but now often managed by private enterprise.

FLATS & HOUSES During the summer months this type of accommodation, referred to by travel agents and package tour operators as villas, is best booked prior to arriving in Greece. Not only will pre-booking be easier but, surprisingly, works out cheaper than flying out and snooping around.

The winter is a different matter, but probably not within the scope of most of our readers.

Further useful names & addresses
The Youth Hostel Association, 14 Southampton St, London WC2E 7HY.   Tel. 01 836 8541

Useful Greek

English	Greek	Sounds like
I want...	Θελω	Thelo...
...a single room	ενα μονο δωματιο	...enna mono dhomatio
...a double room	ενα διπλο δωματιο	...enna thiplo dhomatio
...with a shower	με ντους.	...me doosh
We would like a room for...	Θα θελαμε ενα δωματιο για	Tha thelame ena dhomatio ghia...
two/three days/a week/ until	δυο/τρεις μέρες/μια εβδομαδα/μεχρι	thio/trees meres/meea evthomatha/mekhri
Can you advise of another...	Ξερετε κανενα αλλο...	Xerete kanena alo...
house with rooms	σπίτι με δωμάτιο	speeti meh dhomatio
pension	πανσιον	panseeon
inn	πανδοχειο	panthokheeo
hotel	ξενοδοχείο	ksenodhokheeo
youth hostel	ξενώνα νέων;	xenonas neon
How much is the room for a night?	Ποσο κανει το δωματιο για τη νυχτα	Poso kanee dho dhomatio ghia ti neektah

50 CANDID GUIDE TO ATHENS

That is too expensive	Ειναι πολυ ακριβα	Eene polee akriva
Have you anything cheaper?	Δεν εχετε αλλο πιο φθηνο	Dhen ekhete ahlo pio ftheeno
Is there...	Υπαρχει	Eeparkhee
a shower	ενα ντουζ	doosh
a refrigerator	ενα ψυγειο	psiyeeo
Where is the shower?	Που ειναι το ντουζ	Poo eene dho doosh
I have to leave...	Πρεπει να φυγω	Prepee na feegho...
today	σημερα	simera
tomorrow	αυριο	avrio
very early	**πολύ νωρίς.**	polee noris
Thank you for a	Ευχαριστω για την	Efkareesto ghia tin
nice time	**συμπαθητική ώρα** *	simpathitiki ora

*This is the exact translation, which would never be used, however, in Greek. An expression meaning rather: 'thanks for the fun' is:

	Ευχαριστω για την	Efkaristo ghia
	διασκεδαση	tin thiaskethasi

5 Travelling around an Island

A man is happier for life from having once made an agreeable tour. Anon

A few introductory remarks may well be apposite in respect of holiday-makers' possessions and women in Greece. The matter is discussed elsewhere but it is not out of place to reiterate one or two points (Rosemary calls it 'carrying on').

PERSONAL POSSESSIONS Do not leave airline tickets, money, travellers' cheques and or passports behind at the accommodation. A man can quite easily acquire a wrist-strap handbag in which to conveniently carry these items. The danger does not, even today, lie with the Greeks, but with fellow tourists, down-and-outs and professional thieves 'working a territory'.

WOMEN There has been, in recent years, a downward slide towards the 'percentage ploy'. Young Greek men, in the more popular tourist areas, have succumbed to the prospects offered by sexually liberated, overseas women holiday-makers, especially those openly courting sun, sand and sex. Greek girls are still subject to rigorous parental control, so it is not surprising that the local lads turn their attentions to other, possibly more fruitful, pastures. Greeks who indulge in this pastime are derogatorily referred to as *Kamaki* – 'spearers of game', after the traditional fishing trident. It's up to you girls, there is no menace, only opportunities!

Now back to the main theme of the chapter, but, prior to expanding on the subject, a few words will not go amiss in respect of:
BEACHES A surprisingly large number of island beaches are polluted, in varying degrees, mainly by seaborne plastic and some tar. Incidentally, olive oil is an excellent medium with which to remove this black menace which sticks to towels, clothes and shoes better than the proverbial .... to a blanket.

Lack of anything but a small rise and fall of tide removes the danger of swimmers being swept out to sea but, on windy days, the tug of the sea's undertow might prove dangerous to a weak swimmer.

Jellyfish and sea urchins can occasionally be a problem in a particular bay, jellyfish increasingly so. One of my Mediterranean correspondents advises me that cures for the jellyfish sting include ammonia, urine (ugh) and a paste of meat tenderiser (it takes all sorts I suppose).

The biggest headache (literally) to a tourist is the sun, or more accurately, the heat of the sun. To give an example of the extremely high temperatures sometimes experienced, in Athens a few years ago birds were actually falling out of the trees, and they were the feathered variety! Every year dozens of tourists are carted off, suffering from acute sunburn. A little often (sun that is) must be the watchword. Generally the islands benefit from the relief of the prevailing summer wind, the *Meltemi*.

Nudism was once severely punished by puritanical authorities. Nowadays, as long as tourists, who wish to sunbathe topless, bottomless or both, utilise those beaches allocated for the purpose, there will be no trouble. These may be official or simply a relatively remote area where the proverbial blind eye is turned. Over the years, as Greek families have increasingly appreciated the delights of the beach, the 'home-grown' young women have increasingly gone topless. In the same spirit of 'permissive' adventure, more and more middle-aged Greek ladies have taken to the sea, often in all enveloping black costumes and straw hats. Some, to preserve their modesty, swim in everyday clothes.

Despite the utterly reasonable condemnation of modern day advances in technology by us geriatrics, one amazing, welcome leap forward for all travelling and beach bound mankind is the *Walk-Master* personal stereo-casettes. No more the strident, tinny beat of the transistor (or more commonly the 'ghetto-blaster'), now simply the jigging silence of headphone enveloped, transfixed faces. Splendid!

It may well be that a reader is a devoted sun worshipper and spends every available minute on the beach, patio or terrace, if so there is no need to read any further. On the other hand when a holiday-maker's daytime interests range beyond conversion of the sun's rays into painful, peeling flesh, and there is a wish to travel around a particular island, then the question of *modus operandi* must be given some thought.

First, purchase an island map and one of the colourful and extremely informative tourist guides available on the larger islands. After which consider the alternative methods of travel and appraise their value.

ROADS The main roads of most islands are passable but asphalted country lanes often degenerate alarmingly, becoming nothing more than heavily rutted and cratered tracks. Generally much road building and reconstruction is under way. Beware, as not all roads, indicated as being in existence by imaginative map makers, are anything more than, at the best, donkey tracks or may simply be non-existent. Evidence of broken lines, marking a road, must be interpreted as meaning that any highway will certainly not be paved.

ON FOOT Owing to the hilly terrain of the islands and the daytime heat encountered, readers might have had enough walking without 'looking for trouble'. A quick burst down to the local beach, taverna. shop or restaurant, and the resultant one hundred or so steps back up again, may well go a long way to satiating any desire to go 'walkies'. If needs be, walking is often the only way to negotiate the more rugged donkey tracks and the minimum footwear is a solid pair of sandals or 'trainers'. Plan not to walk during the midday hours, to wear a hat, to take along sufficient clothes to at least cover up, should the sun prove too hot, and pack a bottle of drinking water.

HITCHING The comparative paucity of privately owned cars makes hitch-hiking an unsatisfactory mode of travel. On the other hand, if striking out to get to, or return from a particular village, most Greek drivers stop when thumbed down. It may well be a lift in the back of a Japanese pick-up truck, possibly sharing the space with some chickens, a goat or sheep or all three!

DONKEY Although once a universal 'transportation module', the donkey is only available for hire,nowadays,on a specific journey basis in particular locations. A personal prejudice is to consider donkey rides part of the unacceptable face of tourism, added to which it tends to be exorbitantly expensive.

BUSES Buses (and taxis) are the universal method of travel in Greece, so the services are widespread if, naturally enough, a little Greek in operation. Generally they run approximately on time and the fares are, on the whole, extremely reasonable. Passengers must expect to share the available space with fairly bulky loads and, occasionally, livestock.

The trick is to first find the square on which the buses 'terminus'. Then locate the bus office where the tickets are pre-purchased and on the walls or windows of which might be displayed timetables and the fares structure. The real fun starts if the bus is not only 'sardine packed', but fares are collected by a conductor who has to somehow make his way through, round and over the passengers. Be available well prior to scheduled departure times as buses have a 'nasty habit' of departing early. Try to ensure any luggage is placed in the correct storage compartment for the particular destination, otherwise it may go missing.

Buses are often crowded, especially when a journey coincides with a ferry-boat

ISLAND TRAVEL 53

disgorging its passengers. The timetables are more often than not scheduled so that a bus or buses await a ferry-boat's arrival, except perhaps very early or late arriving craft. A bus rarely leaves a potential client standing, they just encourage everyone aboard.

Do not fail to observe the decorations festooned around and enveloping the driver. Often these displays resemble a shrine which, taking account of the way some of the drivers propel their bus, is perhaps not so out of place. Finally, do have change available as coins are always in short supply. It is helpful to know that local buses may be labelled TOPIKO (TOΠIXO).

A critic took me to task for not stressing that the summer bus schedules listed throughout the text of the Guides are subject to severe curtailment, if not total termination, during the winter months from October through to May. So, smacked hand Geoffrey, and readers please note.

TAXIS As indicated, taxis are the 'other' mode of island travel, are usually readily available and can be remarkably modern and plush. On the other hand...

Ports and towns nearly always have a main square on which the taxis rank, but, come the time of a ferry-boat's arrival, they also queue on the quayside. Fares are governed by the local authorities and, at the main rank, are often displayed giving examples of the cost to various destinations. Charges are reasonable by European standards, but it is essential to establish the cost, prior to hiring.

It may come as a shock for a 'fare' to have his or her halting, pidgin Greek answered in 'pure' Australian or American. But this is not surprising when one considers that many island Greeks have spent their youth on merchant ships or emigrated to the New World for ten to fifteen years. On their return home, with the future relatively financially secure, many take to taxi driving to supplement their income (and possibly to keep out of the little woman's way?).

BICYCLE, SCOOTER & CAR HIRE On a general note, it is very sad to notice the increasing incidence of *No Parking* and *Free Parking* signs at the very popular resorts.

On the whole, bicycles are very hard work and poor value in relation to, say, the cost of hiring a scooter – an option endorsed when the mountainous nature of most islands, and the midday heat, is taken into consideration. The once popular Italian machines are progressively being replaced by the ubiquitous, semi-automatic Japanese motorcycles. Although the latter do away with the necessity to fight the gears and clutch, they are not entirely suited to transporting two heavyweights. I once had the frightening experience, when climbing a steep mountainside track, of the bike jumping out of gear, depositing my passenger and I on the ground, leaving the scooter whirling found like a crazed mechanical Catherine wheel.

It is amazing how easy it is to get a good tan while scootering. The moderate wind draws the sun's heat, the air is laden with the smell of wild sage and oleanders and with the sun on one's back... marvellous!

Very rarely is a deposit requested when hiring a bike or motorbike but a passport is required. Always shop around to check out various companies' charges. Generally the nearer to a port, town or city centre a hirer is, the more expensive the machines will be. Take a close look over the chosen mode of transport prior to parting with any money, as the maintenance of any mechanical unit in Greece is usually poor to non-existent. Bicycles and scooters, a few years old, will be 'pretty clapped out'. A client must check the brakes, they will be needed, and should not be fobbed off without making sure there is a spare wheel.

Increasingly, the owners of two wheeled vehicles are also hiring crash helmets of dubious appearance. Flash young Greek motorbike riders usually wear their 'Space Age' headgear on the handlebars, where no doubt it will protect them (that is the handlebars) from damage. A useful tip when hiring a scooter is to take along a towel. It not only provides additional padding for the pillion passenger's bottom, whilst driving on rocky roads, but saves having to sit on painfully hot, plastic seating should a rider forget to raise the squab when parked. Sunglasses are necessary to protect the eyes from airborne insets. Out of the height-of-season and early evening it tends to become very chilly, so a sweater or jumper is a good idea and females may well require a headscarf, whatever the time of day or night.

Fuel is served in litres and five litres of two-stroke costs about the same as in the United Kingdom. Fill up as soon as possible as fuel stations are still in fairly 'short supply' outside the main towns. Increasingly the gap between the scooter and the car is being catered for by the provision of more sophisticated machinery, including moon-tyred and powerfully engined Japanese trials motorbikes, as well as beach-buggies.

Typical daily hire rates are: for a bicycle 250-500drs; a scooter 1500-2000drs; a car from 5000-8500drs, including full insurances and taxes but mileage may cost extra, calculated at so much per kilometre. Out of season and period hire for all forms of conveyance can benefit from 'negotiation'. Car hire companies require a daily deposit, which varies between 10,000-20,000drs per day, as well as a hirer's passport and driving licence details. Due to this large outlay it is almost mandatory to pay by credit card, which most car hire companies 'gratefully grab'.

Be very careful to establish what (if any) insurance cover is included in the rental fees, and that the quoted hire charges include any compulsory taxes. One contentious area that causes unpleasant disputes is the increasing habit of the hire companies to charge comparatively expensively for any damage incurred, and I mean any damage, however slight. A hirer's detailed reasons for the causes of an accident, the damage and why it should not cost anything falls on deaf ears. Furthermore it is no use threatening to involve the police as they will not be at all interested in the squabble. It is noticeable that I and many readers regard car hire as a legalised rip-off.

Several other words of warning might not go amiss. Taking into account the uncertain state of the roads, do not hire a two-wheeled conveyance if not thoroughly used to handling one. There are a number of very nasty accidents every year, involving tourists and hired scooters. Additionally the combination of poor road surfaces and usually inadequate to non-existent vehicle lights should preclude any night-time scootering. Anyone intending to hire two wheeled transport must ensure they are fully covered for medical insurance, including an unscheduled, *Medicare* flight home, prior to departing for the holiday. And do ensure that a general holiday policy does not exclude accidents incurred on hired transport, especially scooters.

The glass-fronted metal framed shrines mounted by the roadside are graphic reminders of a fatal accident at this or that spot. Incidentally, on a less macabre note, if the shrine is a memorial to a man, the picture and bottle often present (more often than not of Sophia Loren and whisky) reputedly represent that person's favourite, earthbound desires.

But back to finger-wagging. The importance of the correct holiday insurance cover cannot be over-stressed. The tribulations I have encountered in obtaining inclusive insurance, combined with some readers' disastrous experiences, has resulted in an all-embracing scheme being featured in the Guides. This reminder should be coupled with the strictures in **Chapter One** also drawing attention to the policy devised for readers of the Candid Guides. Enough said!

Useful Greek

English	Greek	Sounds like
Where can I hire a...	Που μπορώ να νοικιάσω ένα	Poo boro na neekeeaso enna...
...bicycle	ποδήλατο	...pothilato
...scooter	σκούτερ	...sckooter
...car	αυτοκίνητο	...aftokinito
I'd like a...	Θα ήθελα ένα	Tha eethela enna...
I'd like it for...	Θα το ήθελα για	Tha dho eethela ghia...
...a day	μία μέρα (or: μιά)	...mia mera
...days	μέρες	...meres
...a week	μία εβδομάδα	...mia evthomadha
How much is it by the...	Πόσο κάνει την	Poso kanee tin...
...day	μέρα	...mera
...week	εβδομάδα	...evthomadha
Does that include...	Συμπεριλαμβάνονται σ' αυτό	Simberilamvanonte safto
...mileage	τα χιλιόμετρα	...tah hiliometra
...full insurance	μικτή ασφάλεια	...meektee asfaleah
I want some	Θέλω	Thelo
...petrol (gas)	βενζίνης	...vehnzini
...oil	λάδι	...lathi
...water	νερό	...nero
Fill it up	Γεμίστε το	Yemiste to
...litres of petrol (gas)	... λίτρα βενζίνης.	...litra vehnzinis
How far is it to...	Πόσο απέχει	Poso apechee
Which is the road for...	Ποιος είναι ο δρόμος για ...;	Pios eene o thromos ghia
Where are we now	Που είμαστε τώρα	Poo eemaste tora
What is the name of this place	Πώς ονομάζεται αυτό το μέρος;	Pos onomazete afto dho meros
Where is...	Που είναι	Poo eene...

Road Signs

ΑΛΤ	STOP
ΑΠΑΓΟΡΕΥΕΤΑΙ Η ΕΙΣΟΔΟΣ	NO ENTRY
ΑΔΙΕΞΟΔΟΣ	NO THROUGH ROAD
ΠΑΡΑΚΑΜΠΤΗΡΙΟΣ	DETOUR
ΕΛΑΤΤΩΣΑΤΕ ΤΑΧΥΤΗΤΑΝ	REDUCE SPEED
ΑΠΑΓΟΡΕΥΕΤΑΙ Η ΑΝΑΜΟΝΗ	NO WAITING
ΕΡΓΑ ΕΠΙ ΤΗΣ ΟΔΟΥ	ROAD REPAIRS
ΚΙΝΔΥΝΟΣ	BEWARE (Caution)
ΑΠΑΓΟΡΕΥΕΤΑΙ ΤΟ ΠΡΟΣΠΕΡΑΣΜΑ	NO OVERTAKING
ΑΠΑΓΟΡΕΥΕΤΑΙ Η ΣΤΑΘΜΕΥΣΙΣ	NO PARKING

6   Island Drink, Food & Medical Care

Let us eat and drink, for tomorrow we die. Corinthians

It is a pity that many tourists, prior to visiting Greece, have, in sundry 'replica' tavernas throughout Europe and North America, 'experienced' the offerings masquerading as Greek food. Unfortunately, neither food or drink cross the borders very well, in fact I don't think it is possible to recreate the unique quality of Greek cooking in foreign lands. Perhaps this is because they owe much of their taste to, and are in sympathy with, the very air, laden with the scent of the flowers and herbs, the very water, clear and chill, the very soil of the plains and scrub clad mountains, the ethereal and uncapturable quality that is Greece. Incidentally, many critics would postulate that it was impossible to recreate Greek food, full stop, but be that as it may...

Salad does not normally send me into ecstasy but, after a few days in Greece, the very thought of a peasant salad of endive leaves, sliced tomatoes and cucumber, black olives, olive oil and vinegar dressing, all topped off with feta cheese and sprinkled with oregano, parsley or fennel, sends me salivating to the nearest taverna.

Admittedly, unless you are lucky enough to chance across an outstanding taverna, the majority are surprisingly unadventurous and the choice of menu limited. Mind you there are one or two restaurants serving exciting and unusual meals, if the spelling mistakes are anything to go by. For instance I have observed, over the years, the following no doubt appetising dishes: *omeled, spachetti botonnaise, shrings salad, bowels entrails, lump cutlets, limp liver* (I know what they mean), *mushed pot, shrimps, crambs, kid chops, grilled meatbolls, spar rips, wine vives, fiant oven, swardfish, pork shops, staffed vine leaves, wild greens, string queens, wildi cherry, bater honi, gregg goti* (!), *mate with olive oil, bruised meat, forced meat balls, Creek salad, lamp kebab ....with rise, personal shrimps, mutton bowels served with pice, beef shoup, lame liver, intest liver, cububer, scorpines, chickey, greef beans, fried pataroes, bems giauts, veal roast in kettle, loveubrawn, walout kake, honey boiles, scruffed tomatoes*, (a fish called) *drowns, various complex* (in the coffee section) and *et cetera* – don't they sound interesting!

On a more positive note, whilst the usual dishes will be known to readers, a recommendation, a mention of a dish I haven't seen before and a couple of 'musing's' may not go amiss. As to the recommendation, where an eating house serves a good, creamy tzatziki and a Greek salad it makes a very refreshing dish to combine the two. Latterly I came across an offering I have not encountered previously, *pikileea*. This is a very tasty dish, originally a distinctive mezes, a meatless selection of appetisers. Diners lucky enough to locate a restaurant that serves *pikileea*, usually now as an hors d'oeuvres, will be served a plate including, for example, tomatoes, various dips, beetroot, aubergines, sweet peppers and kalamares. With regard to the musings, the ruminations, the brown studies, they relate to the humble potato and veal. Why, oh why, taking into account the copious plates of *patatas* available (thus proving the existence, in quantity, of the aforesaid tuber), are there no variations on the theme? Where are, oh where are mashed, roast or creamed potatoes to usurp the omnipresent, universal chip, just once in a while? Perhaps of course, the veal available in Greece is not the same veal as obtainable in the United Kingdom. I more than occasionally have an inkling that the meat labelled 'veal' may, only may be old beef or goat. One thing is for definite, there certainly aren't enough cows grazing 'in all of Greece' to 'grow' the amount of veal offered in the restaurants.

A FEW HINTS & TIPS Do not insist upon butter, the Greek variant is not very tasty to the European palate, is expensive and, tends to dissolve into greasy pools.

Sample the retsina wine and after a bottle or two a day, for a few days, there is every chance you will enjoy it. Moreover, retsina is beneficial (well that's what I tell myself), acting as a splendid anti-agent to the comparative oiliness of some of the food.

Bread is automatically served with a meal – and charged for – unless a diner indicates otherwise. It is very useful for mopping up excess olive oil and thus requires no butter to make it more greasy. It has become a noticeable and regrettable feature, in recent years, that the charge for bread has increased to between 10 and 30drs per head, and I have seen it as high as 50drs. Naughty! Many eateries have developed the nasty habit of lumping an extra tax calculation in with the bread charge, that is extra to the usual tax inclusive prices listed on the menu. This reminds me to point out that all establishments selling drink and food are Government controlled, the prices supposedly being listed and displayed for all clients to inspect. It is to be regretted that it is becoming increasingly evident that more and more establishments are 'failing' to carry out this simple task. Moreover, an increasing number of restaurants and tavernas are even omitting to supply clients with any menu, let alone a priced one. This 'naughty little' habit may not be unconnected with the diminished role of the Tourist police. Price lists should state the establishment's category and the price of every item served. When they do, two prices are shown. The first, being net, is not really relevant, whilst the second, detailing the price actually charged, includes all service charges and taxes.

Greek food tends to be served on the 'cool' side. Even if the meal started out hot, and by some mischance is speedily served, it will arrive on a thoroughly chilled plate. The selection of both food and drink available is usually rather limited and unenterprising, unless diners elect to frequent the more international restaurants (but why go to Greece?). On the other hand the choice of establishments in which to eat and drink is almost limitless, in fact the profusion is such that it can prove very confusing. If in doubt about which particular restaurant or taverna to patronise, use the well tried principle of picking one frequented by the locals. It is generally a waste of time to ask a Greek for guidance in selecting a good taverna or restaurant as he will be reluctant to give specific advice, in case the recommendation proves unsatisfactory.

Diners must not be shy and should assert their traditional right to look over the kitchen to see 'what's cooking'. If denied this traditional right, especially in the more rural areas, it would be best for clients to be on their guard. The food may well be pre-cooked, tasteless and plastic, particularly if the various meals available are displayed in a neon-lit showcase. Do not order the various courses all at once, as would be usual at home. If you do, they will probably be served simultaneously and or, worst, in the wrong sequence. Try to order course by course and take your time, everyone else does.

It is best for diners to appreciate that they are not being ignored or continually disregarded if the waiter does not approach the table for anything up to 20 minutes. He is probably overworked and taking his time. It certainly makes a visitor's stay in Greece very much more enjoyable, as well as helping to maintain a normal blood pressure, if all preconceived ideas of service can be forgotten. Lay back and settle into the glorious and indolent timelessness of the locals' way of life. When in a hurry, settle up as the order arrives for, if under the impression that it took a disproportionate time to be served, just wait until it comes to paying! It will probably take twice as long to extract the bill (*logariasmo*) as it did to receive the food.

Many meat dishes, and certainly chicken, are, more often than not, served with some chips. This should be borne in mind when making an order, if only to save having plate upon plate of the wretched things come forth. Fish appears expensive, in comparison with European prices, so readers can imagine the disparity with the cost of other Greek food. When ordering fish it is normal to select the choice from 'the ice' and, being priced by weight, it will be put on the scales prior to cooking. This is the reason that fish is listed at so many drachmae per kilo, which does reduce the apparently outrageous price, just a little. If seeking 'cost conscious' meals, and wishing for a change from the ubiquitous moussaka, beef steak, or for that matter, chicken and chips, why not plump (!) for squid (*kalamares*). They usually provide a filling, tasty, low budget cost meal at 300-400drs. It has to be admitted that demand has resulted in the more popular locations and areas serving imported Mozambique squid. These can often be recognised by their regular shape and sweet taste – probably suiting many palettes very well. From the late summer months, locally caught *kalamares* tend to be large and knobbly.

Food is natural and very rarely are canned or frozen items used, even if available. When frozen foods are included in the meal, the fact must be indicated on the menu by addition of the initials *KAT*. The olive oil used for cooking is excellent, as are the herbs and lemons, but it can take time to become accustomed to the different flavours these impart to the food. Before leaving the subject of hints and tips, remember that olive oil can be pressed into service for removing unwanted beach tar from clothes.

A most enjoyable road, quayside or ferry-boat breakfast is to buy a large yoghurt (*yiaorti*) and a small pot of honey (*meli*), mix the honey into the yoghurt and then relish the bitter-sweet delight. If locally produced, natural yoghurt (usually stored in cool tubs and spooned into a container) cannot be purchased, the brand name *Total* is a very adequate substitute, being made from cow's or sheep's milk. I prefer the sheep derived product and, when words fail, break into a charade of 'baa-ing'. It keeps the other shoppers amused, if nothing else. The succulent water melon, a common and inexpensive fruit, provides a juicy, lunchtime refreshment.

Apart from waving the tablecloth in the air, or for that matter the table, it is usual to call *parakalo* (please). It is also permissible to say *gharkon* or simply 'waiter'.

A disturbing habit, which is becoming increasingly prevalent in recent years, is the use of the word *Special/Spezial*. This is simply a ruse enabling establishments to charge extra for a dish, or offering, that would have, in the past, been the 'norm'. A good example is *Special souvlaki pita*, which is nothing more than that which was previously a conventional giro meat souvlaki. The now *Standard souvlaki* may well be an inferior substitute, nothing more than a slab of meat. That's improvement for you!

THE DRINKS
Non-alcoholic beverages Being a cafe (and taverna) society, coffee is drunk at all times of the day and night. Greek coffee (*kafe*) is in fact a leftover from the centuries long Turkish influence. The thick, grouty infusion is served without milk in small cups and always with a glass of deliciously cool water. Unless specified otherwise Greek coffee will be served sickly sweet or *varigliko*. There are many variations but the three most usual are *sketto* (no sugar), *metrio* (medium) or *glyko* (sweet). Be careful not to completely drain the cup, the bitter grains will choke an imbiber.

Except in the most traditional establishments (*kafeneions*), a client can ask for *Nes-kafe* or simply *Nes* which, as would be expected, is an instant coffee. This home-grown version often has a comparatively muddy taste. Those who require milk with their coffee must request *(Nes) meh ghala*. A most refreshing version is to order Nes chilled or *frappé*, which is served in a tall glass with ice cubes. French coffee (*ghaliko kafe*), served in a coffee pot with a separate jug of hot milk, espresso and cappuccino coffees are found in the larger, provincial towns, ports and international establishments. However, having made a detailed request, you may well receive any permutation of all the possibilities listed above, however carefully you may think you have ordered.

Tea, (*tsai*), perhaps surprisingly, is quite freely available, made of course with the ubiquitous teabag, which is not so outrageous since they have become universally commonplace. In more out of the way places herbal tea may be served.

Drinking Water It is sad to have to report that the once unquestionably superb, island drinking water supplies have, on many islands, become very suspect (with some notable exceptions). So much so that, in my opinion, at a few locations the situation is at a crisis level, when the demand is greatest. The cause is quite simply because the traditional shortages have been exacerbated by the overwhelming demands of tourism and the consequent, seemingly continuous construction of hotels, apartments and villas necessary to cope with the influx. Rumour has it that, at some resorts and in desperation, the resources have been topped up with questionable supplies during the height of summer months.

In many locations, the original water installations, never a byword of other than mediocrity, have suffered from less than exacting civil engineering standards, on being extended and expanded. Imperfections have even resulted in the unfortunate, unintentional 'marriage' of water and effluent. I can only advise holidaymakers, planning to visit the places in question, to pack some *Milton* as well as water purification tablets. Where the drinking water is at all suspect, it is absolutely essential to only drink bottled water, the cost of which is anything between 50-85drs for a $1\frac{1}{2}$ litre bottle. Brand names include *Loutraki, Nigita,* and *Sariza.*

Bottled mineral waters include *Sprite*, which is fizzy, and *lemonade/lemonatha*, a stillish lemonade. Orangeade (*portokaladha*), *visinatha*, a cherry flavoured soft drink, and various fruit juices are all palatable and sold, as often as not, under brand names, as is the universal *Koka-Kola*. A word of warning comes from a reader who reported that, in the very hot summer months, some youngsters drink nothing but sweet, fizzy beverages. This can result in mouth ulcers caused by fermenting sugar, so drink water every day.

Alcoholic beverages They are generally sold by weight. Beer comes in 330g tins and bottles, or, more usually, the larger 500g bottle. Purchase the 500g bottle, it is a good value measure and note that when purchasing to take-away, there is a deposit on the bottle of between 8-15drs. Wine is sold in 340/430g (a half sized bottle), 680/730g (1.1 pints) and 950g ($1\frac{3}{4}$ pints) sized bottles.

Beer Greek brewed or bottled beer represents good value except when served in cans. The latter are the export version and, in my opinion, a 'swindle'. This western European style of packaging should be resisted, if for no other reason than it means the cost, quantity for quantity, is almost double. The most widely available bottled beers are *Amstel, Henninger* and *Kaiser*. Draught lager is insidiously creeping into various resorts and should be avoided, not only for purist reasons, but because it is comparatively expensive, as are the imported, high alcohol content, bottled lagers. No names, no pack drill but *Carlsberg* is one that springs to mind. A small bottle of beer is referred to as a *mikri bira* and a large bottle as a *meghali bira*.

Wine Unresinated (*aretsinoto*) wine is European in style and palatable. Popular brands include red (*kokino*) and white (*aspro*) *Demestica, Cambas* or *Rotonda*. More refined palates may approve of the dry red and white wines of selected islands. On the other hand, Greek wines are not exactly famed for their quality, but if quantity of brands can make up for this, then the country will not let anyone down. When possible, red wine (*krasi kokino*), dark wine (*krasi mavro*) and white wine (*krasi aspro*) are best ordered draught (*huna*) or from the barrel (*apo vareli*), if for no other reason than they are much less expensive than the increasingly overpriced bottles.

Retsina, or resinated wine is achieved, if that can be considered the expression, by the barrels, in which the wine is fermented, being internally coated with pine tree resin. Most retsina is white, with a rosé (*kokkineli*) version sometimes available. Some consider the overall taste to be similar to chewing wet, lead pencils, but this is patently obviously a heresy. Retsina is usually bottled, and asking for *kortaki* ensures being served the traditional, economically priced, small bottle, rather than the comparatively expensive, full sized bottle. Rumour has it that the younger retsinas are more easily palatable, but that is very much a matter of taste. A particularly palatable brand of kortaki retsina is *Levkos Xnpos*, the white label of which is decorated with a maple leaf. Some tavernas serve 'open' (*apo vareli*) retsina (in metal jugs), which adjective is used to describe retsina available on draught, or more correctly, from the barrel. When purchasing for personal consumption, retsina can be found dispensed (into any container a client might like to press into service) from large vats, usually buried in side-street cellars. Whatever and wherever, a good 'starter' kit is to drink a bottle or two, twice a day, for three or four days and if the pain goes...

Spirits & others As elsewhere in the world, sticking to the national drinks represents good value. *Ouzo*, much maligned and blamed for other excesses, is, in reality, a derivative of the aniseed family of drinks (which include *Ricard* and *Pernod*). Taken with water, ouzo is a splendid 'medicine', traditionally served with *mezes* (or *mezethes*) – the Greek equivalent of Spanish tapas. These are small plates of, for instance, a slice of cheese, tomato, cucumber, possibly smoked eel, octopus and an olive. When served, mezes are charged for, costing some 20 to 50drs, but the tradition of offering them is disappearing in many tourist locations. Customers not wishing to be served mezes should request *khores mezes*. *Raki* is a stronger alternative to ouzo, more often than not 'created' in Crete. *Metaxa* brandy, available in three, five and seven star quality, is very palatable, but with a certain amount of 'body', whilst the *Otys* brand is smoother. Greek aperitifs include *Vermouth*, *Mastika* and *Citro*.

DRINKING PLACES Prior to launching into the various branches of this subject, I am at a loss to understand why so many cafe-bar and taverna owners select chairs that are designed to cause the maximum discomfort, even suffering. They are usually too small, for any but a very small bottom, too low and with a seat of wickerwork or raffia that painfully impresses its pattern on the sitter's bare (sun-burnt?) thighs.
Kafeneion (ΚΑΦΕΝΕΙΟΝ) A cafe, serving only Turkish, whoops, Greek coffee. Very Greek, very masculine and in which women are rarely seen. They are similar to a British working man's club, but with backgammon, worry beads and large open windows allowing a dim view of the smoke-laden interior.
Ouzeries (ΟΥΖΕΡΙ) As above, but the house speciality is (well, well) ouzo.
Cafe-bar (ΚΑΦΕΜΠΑΡ) As above, but serving alcoholic beverages as well as coffee, and women are to be seen.
Pavement cafes Rather French in style, with outside tables and chairs sprawling over the pavement, as well as the road. Open from mid-morning, throughout the day, to one or two o'clock the next morning. Snacks and sweet cakes are usually available.

Inside any of the above, the locals chat to each other in that peculiar Greek fashion which gives the impression that a full-blooded fight is about to break out, at any moment. In reality, they are probably just good friends, chatting to each other. Admittedly voices have to be raised to be heard over the blaring noise of the omnipresent television set, which is probably broadcasting a football match, a (sickly) American soap or a (ghastly) English 'comic' programme, the latter two with Greek subtitles.

Drinks can always be obtained at a taverna or restaurant, but a customer may be expected to eat, so read on. It is of course, possible to 'sip' at hotel cocktail bars, but why leave home!

EATING PLACES At the cheapest end of the market, and more especially found in Athens, are pavement-mounted stands serving doughnut-shaped bread (*koulouri*), which make for an inexpensive nibble, costing between 10-20drs
Pistachio nut & ice-cream carts The vendors push their wheeled trolleys around the streets, either selling a wide variety of nuts in paper bags, for 100-150drs, or ice-creams in a variety of flavours and prices.
Corn on the cob BBQ's Increasingly appearing on the pavements of resorts. The proprietors crouch over their simple tray of charcoal toasting' cobs of corn.
Galaktopoleio (ΓΑΛΑΚΤΟΠΩΛΕΙΟ) Shops selling dairy products, including milk, butter, yoghurt, bread and honey. Sometimes they serve omelettes and fritters with honey (*loukoumades*) for consumption on the premises or 'take-away'. A traditional, but more expensive, alternative to a restaurant/bar at which to purchase breakfast.
Zacharoplasteion (ΖΑΧΑΡΟΠΛΑΣΤΕΙΟΝ) Shops specialising in pastries, cakes (*glyko*), chocolates and soft drinks as well as, sometimes, a small selection of alcoholic drinks.
Galaktozacharoplasteion A combination of the two previously described establishments.
Snackbars, Souvlatzidika & Tyropitadika Snackbars are not so numerous in the less touristy areas, often being restricted to one or two in the main town. They represent good value for a stand-up snack. The most popular offering is *souvlaki pita*. This is pita bread (or a roll) filled with grilled meat or kebab (*doner kebab* – slices off a rotating, vertical spit of an upturned cone of meat, also called *giro*), and garnished with a slice of tomato, chopped onion and a dressing, all wrapped in an ice-cream shaped twist of greaseproof paper. Be careful, as *souvlaki* is not to be muddled with *souvlakia* which, when served at a snackbar, consists of wooden skewered pieces of lamb, pork or veal meat grilled over a charcoal fire. Confusingly, these are almost indistinguishable from *shish-kebab*, or *souvlakia*, served at restaurants or tavernas, where a plateful of metal-skewered meat pieces are interspersed with vegetables. Note increasingly, in tourist locations, the adjective *Special*, when applied to souvlaki pita, usually indicates an average, correctly made offering for which a comparatively extortionate price is charged. The cheaper alternative will simply be a slab of meat in place of the slices of giro meat.

Other 'goodies' include *tiropites* – hot flaky pastry pies filled with cream cheese; *boogatsa* – a custard filled pastry; *spanakopita* – spinach filled pastry squares or pies; a wide variety of rolls and sandwiches (*sanduits*) with cheese, tomato, salami and other spiced meat fillings, as well as toasted sandwiches (*tost*). This reminds me to point out to readers that if 'toast' is ordered, it is odds on that a toasted sandwich will be served.
Milk-shake bars Glitzy, neo-American milk-shake, soda pop and ice-cream emporiums – all stainless steel and chromium plate with bar stools and neon-lit pictures of the offerings available (Ugh!). Another symptom of Greek youths unbridled honeymoon with the American dream, as represented by Hollywood films of the 1960s.
Creperies These are intruding in the most concentrated package tourist resorts. Compared to the more traditional establishments, they serve very expensive sandwiches, pies and other 'exotica' including thin pancakes or crepes – thus the name.

They are a rather chic, smooth, smart version of their chromium, brightly neon lit 'cousins', the:-
Fast food joint A surely unwelcome import, selling ice-creams, hot-dogs and hamburgers. They also display garish, neon lit illustrations of the delights available.
Pavement cafes Snacks and sweets.
Pizzerias Seem to be on the increase and are, as one would expect, restaurants specialising in the Italian dish. They usually represent very good value and a large serving often feeds two.
Tavernas (ΤΑΒΕΡΝΑ), **Restaurants** (ΕΣΤΙΑΤΟΡΙΟΝ), **Rotisserie** (ΨΗΣΤΑΡΙΑ) **& Rural Centres** (ΕΞΟΧΙΚΟΝ ΚΕΝΤΡΟΝ) Four variations on a theme. The traditional Greek taverna

is a family concern, frequently only open in the evening. More often than not, the major part of the eating area is outside, sheltered by a vine trellis covered patio, spreading along the pavement and or on a roof garden.

Restaurants tend to be more sophisticated than tavernas, are often open all day, as well as evenings, but the definition between the two is rather blurred. The price lists may include a 'chancy' English translation, the waiter might be smarter and the tablecloth and napkins could well be linen, in place of the taverna's paper table covering and serviettes.

As tavernas often have a spit-roasting device 'tacked' on the side, there is little discernible difference between a rotisserie and a taverna. A grilled meat restaurant may also be styled ΨΗΣΤΑΡΙΑ.

The Rural Centre is a cafe-bar/taverna in, you've guessed it, a rural or seaside setting.

Fish tavernas (ΨΑΡΟΤΑΒΕΡΝΑ) Establishments specialising in fish dishes.

Hotels (ΞΕΝΟΔΟΧΕΙΟΝ). ΞΕΝΟΔΟΧΕΙΟΝ ΥΠΝΟΥ is a hotel that does not serve food, ΠΑΝΔΟΧΕΙΟΝ is a lower category hotel and ΧΕΝΙΑ, a Government-owned hotel. Xenias are usually well run, the food and drink international, the menu written in French with the prices reflecting all these 'attributes'.

In the more popular holiday resorts, an extremely unpleasant manifestation (to old fogies like me) is the prolification of menus, Greek bills of fare set out Chinese restaurant style. You know, 'Set Meal A' for two, 'Meal B' for three and Meal 'C' for four.

THE FOOD A summary of traditional dishes extolled in the past include:-
ΜΠΟΥΡΕΚΑΚΙΑ or *bourekakia*, which are long, thin tubes of battered ham filled with feta cheese and *saganaki*, a very tasty dish of scrambled eggs/omelette, in which are mixed sliced bacon and or sausage, prepared in an olive oil greased 6" pan.

MEDICAL CARE As has been pointed out in Chapter One, 'matters medical' require some preplanning. Travellers unfortunate enough to require the services of a doctor, must look out for the sign ΙΑΤΡΕΙΟΝ. This indicates a doctor's clinic or surgery. On larger islands, dialling 100 will, or should, whistle up an ambulance. The sign for a hospital, probably self-evident by its size alone, is ΝΟΣΟΚΟΜΕΙΟ.

The following represents a selection of the wide variety of menu dishes available.

Sample menu

Ψωμί (Psomi)	Bread
ΠΡΩΙΝΟ	BREAKFAST
Αυγά τηγανιτά με μπέικον και τομάτα	Fried egg. bacon & tomato
Τοστ βούτυρο μαρμελάδα	Buttered toast & marmalade
Το πρόγευμα (to pro-ye-vma)	English (or American on some islands) breakfast
ΑΥΓΑ	EGGS
Μελάτα	soft boiled
Σφικτά	hard boiled
Τηγανιτά	fried
Ποσσέ	poached
ΤΟΣΤ ΣΑΝΤΟΥΙΤΣ	TOASTED SANDWICHES
Τοστ με τυρί	toasted cheese
Τοστ (με) ζαμπόν και τυρί	toasted ham & cheese
Μπούρκερ	burger
Χαμπουρκερ	hamburger
Τσίσμπουρκερ	cheeseburger
Σάντουιτς λουκάνικο	hot dog

ΟΡΕΚΤΙΚΑ	APPETIZERS/HORS D'OEUVRES
Αντσούγιες	anchovies
Ελιές	olives
Σαρδέλλες	sardines
Σκορδαλιά	garlic dip
Τζατζικι	tzatziki (diced cucumber & garlic in yoghurt)
Ταραμοσαλάτα	taramosalata (a fish roe pate)
ΣΟΥΠΕΣ	SOUPS
Σούπα φασόλια	bean
Αυγολέμονο	egg & lemon
Ψαρόσουπα	fish
Κοτόσουπα	chicken
Ντοματόσουπα	tomato
Σούπα λαχανικών	vegetable
ΟΜΕΛΕΤΕΣ	OMELETTES
Ομελέτα μπέικον	bacon
Ομελέτα μπέικον τυρί τομάτα	bacon, cheese & tomato
Ομελέτα τυρί	cheese
Ομελέτα ζαμπόν	ham
Ομελέτα συκωτάκια πουλιών	chicken liver
ΣΑΛΑΤΕΣ	SALADS
Ντομάτα Σαλάτα	tomato
Αγγούρι Σαλάτα	cucumber
Αγγουροτομάτα Σαλάτα	tomato & cucumber
Χωριάτικη	Greek peasant/village salad
ΛΑΧΑΝΙΚΑ (ΛΑΔΕΡΑ*)	VEGETABLES
Πατάτες	potatoes **
Πατάτες Τηγανιτές	chips (french fries)
φρέσκα φασολάκια	green beans
Γίγαντες	(large) white beans
Σπαράγκια	asparagus
Κολοκυθάκια	courgettes or zucchini
Σπανάκι	spinach

*indicates cooked in oil.
**usually served up as chips

Note various methods of cooking include:
Baked – στο φούρνο; boiled – βραστά; creamed – με ασπρη σαλτσα; fried – τηγανιτα; grilled – στη σχαρα; roasted – ψητά; spit roasted – σούβλας.

ΚΥΜΑΔΕΣ	MINCED MEATS
Μουσακάς	moussaka
Ντομάτες Γεμιστές	stuffed tomatoes (with rice or minced meat)
Κεφτέδες	meat balls
Ντολμαδάκια	stuffed vine leaves (with rice or minced meat)
Παπουτσάκια	stuffed vegetable marrow (rice or meat)
Κανελόνια	canelloni
Μακαπόνια με κυμά	spaghetti bolognese (more correctly with mince)
Παστίτσιο	macaroni, mince and sauce
Σουβλάκι	shish-kebab
ΡΥΖΙ	RICE
Πιλάφι	pilaff
Πιλάφι (με) γιαούρτι	with yoghurt
Πιλάφι συκωτάκια	with liver
Σπανακόριζο	with spinach
Πιλάφι κυμά	with minced meat
ΠΟΥΛΕΡΙΚΑ	POULTRY
Κοτόπουλο	chicken, roasted

FOOD AND DRINK

Πόδι κότας	leg of chicken
Στήθος κότας	chicken breast
Κοτόπουλο βραστό	boiled chicken
Ψητό κοτοπουλο στη σούβλα	spit-roasted chicken

ΚΡΕΑΣ — MEAT

Νεφρά	kidneys
Αρνί	lamb†
Αρνίσιες Μπριζόλες	lamb chops
Παιδάκια	lamb cutlets
Συκώτι	liver
Χοιρινδ	pork†
Χοιρινές Μπριζόλες	pork chops
Λουκάνικα	sausages
Μπιφτέκι	steak (beef)
Μοσχαρίσιο	veal
Μοσχαρίσιες Μπριζολες	veal chops
Μοσχάρι	grilled veal
Ψητό Μοσχαράκι	roast veal

† often with the prefix suffix to indicate if roasted or grilled as above.

ΨΑΡΙΑ — FISH

Σκουμπρί	mackerel
Συναγριδα	red snapper
Μαρίδες	whitebait
Οκταπόδι	octopus
Καλαμάρια	squid
Μπαρμπούνι	red mullet
Κέφαλος	mullet
Αυθρίνι	grey mullet

ΤΥΡΙΑ — CHEESE

Φετα	feta (goat's-milk based)
Γραβιέρα	gruyere-type cheese
Κασέρι	cheddar-type (sheep's-milk based)

ΦΡΟΥΤΑ — FRUITS

Καρπούζι	water melon
Πεπόνι	melon
Μήλα	apple
Πορτοκάλι	oranges
Σταφύλια	grapes
Κομπόστα φρούτων	fruit compote

ΠΑΓΩΤΑ — ICE-CREAM

Σπέσιαλ	special
Παγωτό βανίλλια	vanilla
Παγωτό σοκολάτα	chocolate
Παγωτό λεμονι	lemon
Γρανίτα	water ice

ΓΛΥΚΙΣΜΑΤΑ — DESSERTS

Κέικ	cake
φρουτοσαλάτα	fruit salad
Κρέμα	milk pudding
Κρεμ καραμελέ	cream caramel
Μπακλαβας	crisp pastry with nuts & syrup or honey
Καταίφι	fine shredded pastry with nuts & syrup or honey
Γαλακτομπούρεκο	fine crispy pastry with custard & syrup

Γιαούρτι	yoghurt
Μέλι	honey

ΑΝΑΨΥΚΤΙΚΑ — COLD DRINKS/SOFT DRINKS

Πορτοκάλι	orange
Πορτοκαλάδα	orangeade
Λεμονάδα	lemonade made with lemon juice
Γκαζόζα (Gazoza)	fizzy lemonade
Μεταλλικό νερό	mineral water
Κόκα κολα	Coca-cola
Πέψι κολα	Pepsi-cola
Σέβεν-απ	Seven-Up
Σόδα	soda
Τονικ	tonic
Νερό (Nero)	water

ΚΑΦΕΔΕΣ — COFFEES

Ελληνικός (Καφές)	Greek coffee (sometimes called Turkish coffee ie. Τουπκικος Καφε)
σκέτο (skehto)	no sugar
μετριο (metrio)	medium sweet
γλυκό (ghliko)	sweet (very)

(Unless stipulated it will turn up 'ghliko'. Do not drink Turkish coffee before the grouts have settled.)

Νες καφέ	Nescafe
Νες (με γαλα) (Nes me ghala)	Nescafe with milk
Εσπρέσσο	espresso
Καπουτσινο	cappuccino
φραπέ	chilled coffee is known as 'frappe'
Τσάι	tea
Σοκαλάτα γάλα	chocolate milk

ΜΠΥΡΕΣ — BEERS

ΦΙΞ (ΕΛΛΑΣ) Μπύρα	Fix (Hellas) beer
φιάλη	bottle
κουτί	can
ΑΜΣΤΕΛ (Αμστελ)	Amstel
ΧΕΝΝΙΝΓΕΡ (Χέννινγκερ)	Henninger

(300g usually a can, 500g usually a bottle)

ΠΟΤΑ — DRINKS

Ούζο	Ouzo
Κονιάκ	Cognac
Μπράντυ	Brandy
Μεταξά	Metaxa
3 ΑΣΤ	3 star
5 ΑΣΤ	5 star
Ουίσκυ	Whisky
Τζιν	Gin
Βότκα	Vodka
Καμπάρι	Campari
Βερμούτ	Vermouth
Μαρτίνι	Martini

ΚΡΑΣΙΑ — WINES

Κόκκινο	red
Ασπρο	white
Ροζε Κοκκινέλι	rose
Ξηρό	dry
Γλυκό	sweet

Ρετσίνα e.g. Θεόκριτος Αρετσίνωτο e.g. Δεμέστιχα		resinated wine Theokritos unresinated wine Demestica

340g is a ½ bottle, 680g is a bottle, 950g is a large bottle

Useful Greek

English	Greek	Sounds like
Have you a table for...	Εχετε ένα τραπέζι για	Echete enna trapezee ghia...
I'd like...	Θέλω	Thelo...
We would like...	Θέλουμε	Thelome...
a beer	μιά μπύρα	meah beerah
a glass	ένα ποτήρι	ena poteeree
a carafe	μιά καράφα	meea karafa
a small bottle	ένα μικρό μπουκάλι	ena mikro bookalee
a large bottle	ένα μεγάλο	ena meghalo bookalee
bread	ψωμί	psomee
tea with milk	τσάι με γάλα	tsai me ghala
with lemon	τσάι με λεμόνι	me lemoni
Turkish coffee (Greek)	Τούρκικος καφές	Tourkikos kafes
sweet	γλυκός	ghleekos
medium	νέτριος	metreeo
bitter (no sugar)	πικρό	pikro
Black coffee	Nescafe xwpis γάλα	Nescafe horis ghala
Coffee with milk	Nescafe με γάλα	Nescafe me ghala
a glass of water	ενα ποτήρι νερό	enna poteeree nero
a napkin	μιά πετσέτα	mia petseta
an ashtray	ένα σταχτοδοχείο	enna stachdothocheeo
toothpick	μιά οδοντογλυφίδα	mea odontoglifidha
the olive oil	το ελαιόλαδο	dho eleolatho
Where is the toilet?	Που είναι η τουαλέττα	Poo eene i(ee) tooaleta?
What is this?	Τι είναι αυτό	Ti ine afto
This is...	Αυτό είναι	Afto eene
cold	κρύο	kreeo
bad	χαλασμένο	chalasmeno
stale	μπαγιάτικο	bayhiatiko
undercooked	άψητο	apseeto
overcooked	παραβρασμένο	paravrasmeno
The bill please	Το λογαριασμό παρακαλώ	To loghariasmo parakalo
How much is that?	Πόσο κάνει αυτό	Poso kanee afto?
That was an excellent meal	Περίφημο γεύμα	Pereefimo yevma
We shall come again	Θα ξανάρθουμε	Tha xanarthoume

7 Shopping & Public Services

Let your purse be your master. Proverb

Purchasing items in Greece is still quite an art form or subject for an *Open University* degree course. The difficulties have been compounded by the rest of the western world becoming nations of supermarket shoppers, whilst the Greeks have tended to favour the old-fashioned, traditional shops selling a fixed number of items and sometimes only one type of a product. On the other hand Greece is adopting many of the (retrograde?) consumer habits of its Western European neighbours. Nowadays, in the more cosmopolitan towns, cities and tourist exposed islands, credit cards, including *Visa, Access Mastercharge, Diners* and *American Express*, may well be accepted at tavernas and restaurants as well as by gift/souvenir shops.

The question of good and bad buys is a rather personal matter but the items listed below are highlighted on the basis of value for money and quality. Clothing and accessories that are attractive, and represent good value, include embroidered peasant dresses, leather sandals, woven bags, tapestries and furs. Day-to-day items that are inexpensive take in Greek cigarettes, drinks including *ouzo*, brandy and selected island wines. Suitable gifts for family and friends include ceramic plates, sponges, Turkish delight and worry beads (*komboloe*). Disproportionately expensive items embrace camera film, toiletries, sun oils, books and playing cards. Do not forget to compare prices and preferably shop in the streets and markets, not in airport and hotel concessionary outlets, which are often more expensive.

Try not to run short of small change, everybody else does, including bus conductors, taxi drivers and shops.

Opening hours Strict or old-fashioned summer shop hours are:
Mon, Wed & Sat: 0830-1400hrs; Tues, Thurs & Fri: 0830-1330hrs & 1730-2030hrs. These are changing to bring Greece in line with the other EEC countries and have become:-

Trade Stores
Mon & Wed   0900-1700hrs
Tues, Thurs & Fri 1000-1900hrs
Saturday   0830-1530hrs

Chemists
Mon & Wed   0800-1430hrs
Tues, & Thurs   0900-1400hrs
Friday   0800-1400 & 1700-2000hrs
Sat & Sun   A rota.

Food Stores
Mon & Wed   0900-1630hrs
Tues & Thurs   0930-1830hrs
Fri   0930-1900hrs
Sat   0830-1600hrs

Generally, during the summer months, shops in tourist areas are open Mon to Sat, from 0800-1300hrs. They then close for the siesta until 1700hrs, after which they open again until at least 2030hrs, if not 2200hrs. Sundays and Saints' days are more indeterminate, but there is usually a general shop open, somewhere. In very popular tourist resorts and busy ports, many shops open seven days a week.

Drink Available in the markets, at delicatessen meat/dairy counters, from 'off licence' type shops or from zacharoplasteions.

Smokers Imported French, English and American cigarettes are inexpensive, compared with European prices, at between 150 and 200drs for a packet of twenty. Greek cigarettes, which have a distinctive and different taste, are excellent. Try *Karellia*, which cost 100drs for twenty, and note that the price is printed around the edge of the packet. Even Greek cigars are almost unheard of on the islands, while in Athens they cost 15-25drs each. Dutch cigars work out at 35-50drs each, so, if a cigar smoker, take along your holiday requirements.

Newspapers & magazines The *Athens News* is published daily, except Mondays, in English and costs 60drs. Foreign language newspapers are available up to 24 hours after the day of publication and quality English papers cost 200drs.

Note that all printed matter is comparatively expensive.

Photography (Fotografion – ΦΩΤΟΓΡΑΦΕΙΟΝ) Photographers should carry all the film possible as, being imported, it is comparatively expensive. For instance, a roll of 35mm, 36 exposure colour film will cost a minimum of 1000drs, but more probably 1200drs. Despite the allure of the instant print shops that have sprung up on the more popular islands, it is probably best to wait until returning home. The quality of reproduction and focus of the development is 'variable'. That is not to say that the back-at-home, 'bucket-print' outfits, whose envelopes fall out of almost every magazine one cares to purchase, are infallible. I had a long drawn-out experience with a Shropshire company who managed to 'foul up' the development of five rolls of film. The problem is that a holiday-maker, who only has two or three films to develop and receives back the complete batch rather blurred, might consider it to be an 'own goal'. It is equally possible that the print company have botched the job.

When using colour film, blue filters should be fitted to the lens to counter the very bright sunlight in the height of summer months.

Radio To receive English language, overseas broadcasts, tune to 49m band on the *Short Wave*. In the evening, try the *Medium Wave*. English language news is broadcast by the Greek broadcasting system at 0740hrs on the *Medium Wave* (AM), somewhere between 700-800 Khz.

Tourist Guides & Maps Shop around before purchasing either, as the difference in price of the island guides can be as much as 150drs, that is between 350-500drs. Island maps cost from 100-150drs. Some major ports and towns have one authentic, well stocked bookshop, usually positioned a little off the town centre. The proprietor often speaks adequate English and courteously answers most enquiries.

SHOPS
Bakers & bread shops (ΑΡΤΟΠΟΙΕΙΟΝ, ΑΡΤΟΠΩΛΕΙΟΝ or ΠΡΑΤΗΡΙΟΝ ΑΡΤΟΥ) Bread shops, as distinct from bakers, tend to be few and far between. For some obscure reason bakers are nearly always difficult to locate, often being hidden away in or behind other shops. A pointer to their presence may well be a pile of blackened, twisted olive wood, stacked to one side of the entrance, and used to fuel the oven fires. They are almost always closed on Sundays and Saints days, despite which the ovens are often used by the local community to cook their Sunday dinners. Both bakers and bread shops may also sell cheese and meat pies. The method of purchasing bread can prove disconcerting, especially when sold by weight. Sometimes the purchaser selects the loaf and then pays but the most bewildering system is where it is necessary to pay first then collect the goods. Difficult if the shopper's level of Greek is limited to grunts, 'thank you' and 'please'! Greek bread has another parameter of measure other than weight, that is a graduation in hours – 1 hour bread, 4 hour bread and so on. After the period is up, the loaf is usually completely inedible, having transmogrified into a rock-like substance.

Butcher (ΚΡΕΟΠΩΛΕΙΟΝ) Similar to those at home, but the cuts are quite different (surely the Common Market can legislate against this deviation!).

Galaktopoleio *et al.* Cake shops (*Zacharoplasteion*) may sell bottled mineral water (ask for a cold bottle). See **Chapter Six**.

Markets The smaller ports and towns may have a market street and the larger municipalities often possess a market building. These are thronged with locals and all the basic necessities can be procured relatively inexpensively. Fruit and vegetable stalls are interspersed by butchers and dairy/delicatessen shops. During business hours, the proprietors are brought coffee and a glass of water by waiters from nearby cafes. The cups and glasses are carried, not on open trays but in round, aluminium salvers with a deep lid, held under a large ring handle, connected to the tray by three flat arms.

Mini-Market The nomenclature indicates a well stocked store in a small building.

Supermarkets (ΥΠΕΡΑΓΟΡΑ/ΣΟΥΠΕΡΜΑΡΚΕΤ) Very much on the increase and based on small town, self-service stores but not to worry, they inherit all those delightful, inherent Greek qualities, including quiet chaos. It has to be admitted, every so often, one does come across a 'real supermarket', recognisable by the check-out counters. Fortunately they no more than imitate their Western European equivalents, remaining 'organised' shambles.

Speciality shops Chanced upon in some big towns and Athens, whilst pavement browsing. Usually little basement shops which can be espied down steep flights of steps and specialising, for instance, in dried fruit, beans, nuts and grains.

Street Kiosks (Periptero/ΠΕΡΙΠΤΕΡΟ) These unique, pagoda-like huts stay open remarkably long hours, often from early morning to well after midnight. They sell a wide range of goods including newspapers, magazines (sometimes, surprisingly, in the larger cities, pornographic literature), postcards, tourist maps, postage stamps, sweets, chocolates, cigarettes and matches. Ownership is often a family affair – vested as a form of Government patronage and handed out to deserving citizens. Additionally they form the outlet for the pay phone system and, at the cost of 5drs, a local call may be made. It is rather incongruous, to observe a Greek making a possible important business call, in amongst a rack of papers and magazines, with a foreground of jostling pedestrians and a constant stream of noisy traffic in the background.

Alternate ways of shopping Then there are the other ways of shopping: from handcarts, their street-vendor owners selling, respectively, nuts, ice-cream, milk and yoghurt; from the 'back' of a donkey loaded down with vegetable-laden panniers or from two wheeled trailers drawn by fearsome sounding, agricultural rotovator power units. Often the donkey or trailer has an enormous set of scales mounted on the back end, swinging like a hangman's scaffold. If the vegetable/fruit is being sold by 'gypsy-types', then it is advisable to only purchase from those who have their prices on display, usually on a piece of cardboard. Even locals admit to being 'ripped off' by roadside merchants and these free market entrepreneurs are often prosecuted for breaking the law.

Frequently used shops include:
ΒΙΒΛΙΟΠΩΛΕΙΟΝ – bookshop; ΚΡΕΟΠΩΛΕΙΟΝ – butcher; ΙΧΘΤΟΠΩΛΕΙΟΝ – fishmonger; ΟΠΩΡΟΠΩΛΕΙΟΝ – greengrocer; ΠΑΝΤΟΠΩΛΕΙΟΝ – grocer; ΚΟΥΡΕΙΟΝ – hairdresser; ΚΑΠΝΟΠΩΛΕΙΟΝ – tobacconist. Readers may observe the above all have a similar ending and it is worth noting that shop titles which terminate in 'ΠΩΛΕΙΟΝ/πωλειον' are selling something, if that's any help!

SERVICES

The Banks (ΤΡΑΠΕΖΑ) & money The minimum opening hours are 0800-1330hrs Mon-Thurs and 0800-1300hrs on Friday. Some banks, in the most tourist ravaged spots, open for exchange transactions in the evenings and or even on Saturdays. Some smaller towns, villages or, for that matter, islands do not have a bank. Where this is the case there may be a local money changer acting as agent for this or that country-wide bank but, if not, the Post Office has increasingly become an option (*See* **Post Offices**). Do not forget that a passport is almost always required to change travellers' cheques. In the larger cities, personal cheques may be changed at selected banks when backed by a *Eurocheque* (or similar) bank guarantee card. A commission of between $\frac{1}{4}-1\frac{1}{2}\%$ is charged on all transactions, depending upon I know not what! Whereas Eurocheques used to be changed in sums of no more than £50 (English sterling), the arrangement now is that a cheque is cashed in drachmae, up to a total of 25,000drs. As the charges for changing cheques are based on a sliding scale, weighted against smaller amounts, this new arrangement helps save on fees.

Generally the service varies from absent minded inattention, curt discourtesy to downright rudeness. Averagely only one employee, if at all, reluctantly speaks English. Ensure the correct bank is selected to carry out a particular transaction (such as changing a personal cheque), a task made easier by their displaying a window sticker indicating which tourist services are transacted. There is nothing worse, after queuing for half an hour or so, than to be rudely told to go away. I once selected the wrong bank to carry out some banking function, only to receive a loud blast of abuse, that followed me through the swing doors, about a long-departed foreigner's bouncing cheque. Most embarrassing.

Change offices cash travellers cheques, as do the larger hotels, but at a disadvantageous rate compared to the banks. For instance, the commission charged may be 2%, or up to double that charged by the banks. Ouch! *See* **Post Office** for another interesting and less expensive alternative.

The basis of Greek currency is the drachma. This is nominally divided into 100 lepta and occasionally menus still show a price of, say, 62.60drs. As prices are rounded up (or down) and devaluation has considerably reduced the value of one drachma, in practice, the lepta is never encountered. Notes are in denominations of 50, 100, 500 and 1000drs and coins in denominations of 1 and 2drs (bronze), 5, 10, 20drs (nickel), and 50drs (goldy bronze). Do not run out of change, it is always in demand. Repetitious I know, but well worth remembering.

Museums The following is a mean average of the information available, but each museum is likely to have its own peculiarities. In the summer season (1st April-31st Oct) they usually open daily 0845-1500/1900hrs, Sun & holidays 0930-1430/1530hrs and are closed Mon or Tues. They do not open for business on 1st Jan, 25th March, Good Friday, Easter holiday and 25th Dec. Admission costs range from nothing to 100/500drs, whilst Sundays and holidays are sometimes free.

Post Offices (ΤΑΧΥΔΡΟΜΕΙΟΝ/ΕΛΤΑ**)** Stamps can be bought from kiosks (plus a small commission) and shops selling postcards as well as from Post Offices. In 1989 postage rates for cards to the United Kingdom were 60drs for a postcard. Post boxes are scattered around, are usually painted yellow, are rather small in size and often difficult to find, being fixed, high up, on side-street walls. When confronted by two letter-box openings, the inland service is marked ΕΣΩΤΕΡΙΚΟΥ/Εσωτερικου and the overseas ΕΞΩΤΕΡΙΚΟΥ/Εξωτερικου.

Most major town Post Offices are modern and the counter staff's attitude is only slightly less rude than that 'handed out' by bank employees. They are usually open Mon-Fri between 0730-2030hrs for stamps, money orders and registered mail; 0730-2000hrs for poste restante and 0730-1430hrs for parcels, which have to be collected. Letters sent poste restante will require sight of a passport for them to be handed over.

In recent years the range of Post Office services has been expanded to include cashing Eurocheques and Travellers Cheques, in addition to currency exchange. All but the most out-of-the-way island offices now offer these facilities. This can prove very useful knowledge, especially on busy tourist islands where the foreign currency desks of the banks are usually subject to long queues. More importantly the commission charged can be up to half that of the banks. Another interesting source of taking currency abroad, for

SHOPPING

United Kingdom residents, is to use *National Giro Post Office* cheques, which can be cashed at any Post Office in Greece. Detailed arrangements have to be made with the international branch of Giro.

Telephone Office (OTE) A separate organisation from the Post Office. One way to make an overseas or long-distance telephone call is to proceed to the OTE office. Here are a number of booths and the counter clerk indicates which compartment is to be used. Alongside him are mounted the instruments to meter the cost. Ensure that the meter is zeroed prior to making a connection. Long queues often form at offices in busy locations. Payment is made after completion of the call, at a current rate of 7drs per unit. Opening days and hours vary enormously. Smaller offices may only open weekdays for say 7 hours between 0830-1530hrs, whilst some of the larger city offices are open 24 hours a day, seven days a week.

As the Greek telephone system improves there is an increase in the number of kafeneions and tavernas, which possess a metered telephone, from which overseas calls can be made.

Overseas dialling codes
Australia	0061
Canada & USA	001
New Zealand	0064
South Africa	0027
United Kingdom & Ireland	0044
Other overseas countries	161

Inland services
Directory enquiries	131
Provincial enquiries	132
General information	134
Time	141
Medical care	166
City police	100
Gendarmerie	109
Fire	199
Tourist police	171
Roadside assistance	104
Telegrams/cables	165

To dial England, drop the '0' from all four figure codes. Thus to make a call to, say, Portsmouth, for which the code is 0705, dial 00 44 705 ...

The internal service is both very good and reasonably priced. Local telephone calls can be made from some bars and the pavement kiosks (periptero) and cost 5drs, which is the 'standard' coin. Some phones take 10 and 20drs coins. The presence of a telephone is often indicated by the sign ΕΔΩΤΗΛΕΦΩΝΕΙΤΕ, a blue background denoting a local phone, and an orange one an inter-city phone. Another sign, Εδω Τηλεφωνειτε (the lower case equivalent), signifies 'telephone from here'. The method of operation is to insert the coin and dial. If a connection cannot be made, on placing the receiver back on the cradle, the money is returned.

Telegrams may be sent from either the OTE or Post Office.

Useful Greek

English	Greek
Stamps	ΓΡΑΜΜΑΤΟΣΗΜΑ
Parcels	ΔΕΜΑΤΑ

English	Greek	Sounds like
Where is...	Που είναι	Poo eenne...
Where is the nearest...	Που είναι η πλησιέστερη	Poo eenne i pleesiesteri

English	Greek	Pronunciation
baker	ο φούρναρης/ψωμάς	foornaris/psomas
bakery	Αρτοποιείον	artopieeon
bank	η τράπεζα	i(ee) trapeza
bookshop	το βιβλιοπωλείο	to vivleeopolieo
butchers shop	το χασάπικο	dho hasapiko
chemist shop	το φαρμακείο	to farmakio
dairy shop	το γαλακτοπωλείο	galaktopolieon
doctor	ο γιατρός	o yiahtros
grocer	το μπακάλης	o bakalis
hospital	το νοσοκομείο	to nosokomio
laundry	το πλυντήριο	to plintirio, (plintireeo, since i = ee
liquor store	το ποτοπωλείο	to potopolio (potopoleeo)
photographic shop	το φωτογραφείο	to fotoghrafeeo
post office	το ταχυδρομείο	to tahkithromio
shoe repairer	το τσαγκαράδικο	to tsangkaradiko
tailor	ο ραπτης	o raptis
Have you any...	Εχετε	Ekheteh...
Do you sell...	Πουλάτε	Poulate...
How much is this...	Πόσο κάνει αυτό	Posso kanee afto...
I want...	Θέλω	Thelo...
half kilo/a kilo	μισό κιλό/ένα κιλό	miso kilo/ena kilo
aspirin	η ασπιρίνη	aspirini
apple(s)	το μήλο/μήλα	meelo/meela
banana(s)	η μπανάνα/μπανάνες	banana/bananes
bread	το ψωμί	psomee
butter	το βούτυρο	vutiro
cheese	το τυρί	tiree
cigarettes (filter tip)	το τσιγάρο (με φίλτρο)	to tsigharo (me filtro)
coffee	καφές	cafes
cotton wool	το βαμβάκι	to vambaki
crackers	τα κρακεράκια	krackerakia
crisps	τσιπς	tsseeps
cucumbers	το αγγούρι	anguree
disinfectant	το απολυμαντικό	to apolimantiko
guide book	ο τουριστικός οδηγός	o touristikos odhigos
ham	το ζαμπόν	zambon
ice-cream	το παγωτό	paghoto
lemons	το λεμόνια	lemonia
lettuce	το μαρούλι	to marooli
map	το χάρτης	o khartis
a box of matches	ενα κουτί σπίρτα	ena kuti spirta
milk	το γάλα	to ghala
pate	πατέ	pate
(ball point) pen	το μπικ	to bik
pencil	το μολύβι	to molivi
pepper	το πιπέρι	to piperi
(safety) pins	μια παραμάνα	mia (meea) paramana
potatoes	οι πατάτες	patates
salad	η σαλάτα	i salatah
salami	το σαλάμι	salahmi
sausages	το λουκάνικα	lukahniko
soap	το σαπούνι	to sapooni
spaghetti	σπαγγέτο	spayehto
string	ο σπαγκος	o spangos
sugar	η ζάχαρη	i zakahree
tea	το τσάι	to tsai
tomatoes	η ντομάτες	domahdes
toothbrush	η οδοντόβουρτσα	odhondovourtsa
toothpaste	η οδοντόκρεμα	odhondokrema
writing paper	το χαρτί γραψίματος	to kharti grapsimatos

8 Greece: History, Mythology, Religion, Present-day Greece, Greeks, Animals & National Holidays

All ancient histories, as one of our fine wits said, are but fables that have been accepted. Voltaire

HISTORY Excavations have shown the presence of Palaeolithic man up to 100,000 years ago. Greece's history and mythology are, like the Greek language, formidable to say the least, with legend, myth, folk tales, fables and religious lore often inextricably mixed. Interestingly archaeologists have increasingly established that at least some mythology is based on ancient facts.

Historically Greeks fought Greeks, Phoenicians and Persians. With Alexander the Great at the helm they conquered Egypt and vast tracts of Asia Minor. Then they were in turn conquered by the Romans. After the splitting of the Roman Kingdom into Western and Eastern Empires, the Greeks, with Constantinople as their capital, were ruled by the Eastern offshoot. They then fell into the hands of the Franks, about AD 1200, who were followed by the Turks. During this latter period the Venetians, Genoese and, finally, the Turks ruled most of the islands.

In 1821 the War of Independence commenced, which eventually led to the setting up of a Parliamentary Republic in 1829. Incidentally, Thessaly, Epirus, Macedonia, Thrace, the North East Aegean islands, Crete and the Dodecanese islands remained under Turkish rule. By the time the Dodecanese islanders had thrown out the Turks, the Italians had taken over. If you are now confused, give up, because it gets even more difficult to follow.

The Greek monarchy, which had come into being in 1833 and was related to the German Royal family, opted, in 1913, to side with the Axis powers. The chief politician Eleftherios Venizelos, disagreed, was dismissed and set up a rival government, after which the King, under Allied pressure, retired to Switzerland. In the years following the end of the First World War the Turks and Greeks agreed, after some fairly bloody fighting, to exchange a total of one and a half million people.

In 1936 a General Metaxas became dictator and achieved immortal fame by booting out Mussolini's representative. This came about when, in 1940, Mussolini demanded permission for Italy's troops to traverse Greece and received the famous *Ochi* (No). This day became a national festival known as *Ochi Day*, celebrated on 28th October. The Italians demurred and marched on Greece, the soldiers of whom, to the surprise of everybody, including themselves, reinforced the refusal by routing the invaders. The Italians were only saved from total humiliation by the intervention of the Germans, who then occupied Greece for the duration of the Second World War. At the end of hostilities, all the Italian held Greek islands were reunited with mainland Greece. As the wartime German ascendancy declined, the Greek freedom fighters split into royalist and communist factions and proceeded, in the first civil war, to knock even more stuffing out of each other than they had out of the Germans. Until British intervention, followed by large injections of American money and weapons, it looked as if Greece would go behind the Iron Curtain. A second civil war broke out between 1947 and 1949 and these two internal conflicts were reputed to have cost more Greek lives than were lost during the whole of the Second World War.

In 1951, both Greece and Turkey became full members of NATO, but the issue of the ex-British colony of Cyprus was to rear its ugly head, with the resultant, renewed estrangement between Greece and Turkey. The various political manoeuvrings, the involvement of the Greek monarchy in domestic affairs and the worsening situation in Cyprus, led to the *coup d'etat* by the *Colonel's Junta*, in 1967, soon after which King Constantine II and his entourage fled to Italy. The extremely repressive dictatorship of the Junta was apparently actively supported by the Americans and condoned by Britain. Popular country-wide feeling and, in particular, student uprisings between 1973-1974, which were initially put down in Athens by brutal tank attacks, led to the eventual collapse of the regime in 1974. In the death-throes of their rule, the Colonels, using the Cyprus dream to distract the ordinary people's feeling of injustice, meddled and attempted to overthrow the vexatious priest, President Makarios. The net result was that the Turks invaded Cyprus and made an enforced division of that unhappy, troubled island.

In 1974, Greece returned to republican democracy and in 1981 joined the EEC (God help them). Greek elections are an eye-opener to citizens of other European countries, being accompanied by a certain amount of violence and dynamite throwing.

RELIGION The Orthodox Church prevails everywhere but there are small pockets of Roman Catholicism, as well as very minor enclaves of Muslims on the Dodecanese islands and mainland, western Thrace. The schism within the Holy Roman Empire, in 1054, caused the Catholic Church to be centred on Rome and the Orthodox Church on Constantinople. The Turkish overlords encouraged the continuation of the indigenous church, probably to keep their bondsmen quiet, but it had the invaluable side effect of keeping alive Greek customs and traditions during the centuries of occupation. This nationalism was fostered by the inmates of the various religious orders operating *Krifo Scholio*. These were illegal, undercover schools at which the local children were introduced to the intricacies of the Greek religion and way of life.

The bewildering profusion of small churches, scattered 'indiscriminately' throughout the countryside, is not proof of the church's wealth, although the Greek people are not entirely convinced of that fact! It is, in fact, evidence of the piety of the families or individuals who paid to have them erected, in the name of their selected patron saint, as thanksgiving for God's protection. The style of religious architecture changes between the island groups. Many churches only have one service a year, on the name day of the particular patron saint, and this ceremony is named *Viorti* or *Panayieri*. It is well worth attending one of these self-indulgent extravaganzas to observe and take part in celebratory village religious life and music. One and all are welcome to the carnival festivities, which include eating and dancing in, or adjacent to, the particular churchyard.

The words *Byzantine* and *Byzantium* crop up frequently, with especial reference to churches and appertain to the period between the fourth and fourteenth centuries AD. During this epoch Greece was, at least nominally, under the control of Constantinople (Istanbul), built by the Emperor Constantine on the site of the old city of Byzantium. Religious paintings executed on small wooden panels during this period are called *Icons*. Very, very few original icons remain available for purchase, so beware if offered an apparent 'bargain'. Icons usually depict a holy person or personages. If legends and folklore are to be believed, during the Middle Ages the Mediterranean would appear to have been almost awash with unmanned rowing boats and caiques, mysteriously ferrying icons hither and thither.

Inside the churches, the altar area is separated from the worshippers by a 'screen' of timber or stonework, usually honeycombed by a number of doors, varying from the very simple to the most ornately carved and fretworked constructions. Especially noticeable are the pieces of shining, thin metal placed haphazardly around or pinned to wooden carvings. These *tamata* or *exvotos* represent limbs or portions of the human body and are purchased by worshippers as an offering, in the hope of an illness being cured and or limbs healed.

Male and female visitors to all and every religious building must be properly clothed. Men should wear trousers and a shirt. Ladies clothing ought to include a skirt, or if unavoidable trousers, a blouse and, if possible, a headscarf. Many monasteries simply will not allow entrance to scantily or 'undressed' people. With that marvellous duality of standards the Greeks evince, there is quite often a brisk 'clothes hire' business transacted on the very entrance steps, but it is not wise to rely on this arrangement being in force.

GREEKS In making an assessment of the Greek people and their character, it must be remembered that, perhaps even more so than the Spaniards or the Portuguese, Greece has only recently emerged into the twentieth century. Unlike other countries 'discovered' in the 1960s by the holiday industry, they have not, except in the most tourist swamped islands, degraded or debased their principles or character, despite the onrush of tourist wealth. For a people to have had so little and to face so much demand for European 'necessities', would have subverted the character of a less right-minded and sober people.

The country's recent emergence into the western world is evidenced by the still patriarchal nature of their society, a view supported, for instance, by the oft-seen spectacle of men lazing in the kafeneion whilst their womenfolk work in the fields (and why not?).

More often than not, even the smallest village, on the remotest island, manifests an English-speaking islander who has lived abroad at some time in his life, earning a living through seafaring, as a hotel waiter or as a taxi driver. Thus, while making an escape from the comparative poverty at home, for a period of good earnings in the more lucrative world, a working knowledge of English, American or Australian will have been gained. 'Greek strine' (used to describe the sounds of a Greek with the overtones of an Australian accent) or, as usually contracted, 'grine', simply has to be heard to be believed.

The greatest hurdle to comprehending the national character is undoubtedly the language barrier, a difficulty compounded by Greek often seeming unable to communicate with fellow Greek! Certainly, on occasions, they appear not to understand each other and the subject matter has to be repeated a number of times. Perhaps that is the reason for all that shouting!

There can be no doubt that the traditional Greek welcome to the *Xenos* or *Singrafeus*, now increasingly becoming known as *Touristas*, has become rather lukewarm in the more 'besieged' areas. It is often difficult to reconcile the shrugged shoulders of a seemingly disinterested airline official or bus driver, with being stopped in the street by a gold-toothed, smiling Greek proffering some fruit. But remember, the bus driver has probably weighed the difficulty of overcoming the language barrier, may be very hot, has been working long hours earning a living and is not on holiday. Sometimes a drink appears, mysteriously, at one's taverna table, the donor being indicated by a nod of the waiter's head, but a word of warning here. Simply smile and accept the gift graciously. Any attempt to return the kindness, by 'putting one in the stable' for your new-found friend, only results in a 'who buys last' competition, which will surely be lost. I know, I am speaking from 'battle-weary' experience. Whilst Greeks are very welcoming, and may invite a tourist to their table, do not expect more. They are reserved and have probably had previous, unhappy experiences of ungrateful, rude, overseas visitors.

Women tourists can travel quite freely in Greece without fear except, perhaps, from other tourists. On the other hand, females should not wear provocative attire or fail to wear sufficient clothing. This is especially so when in close social contact with Greek men, who might well be inflamed into 'action', or Greek women, whom it will offend, probably because of the effect on their men! Certainly all the above was the case, until very recently, but the constant stream of 'available', young tourist ladies on the more popular islands has resulted in the local lads taking both a 'view' and a chance. It almost reminds one of the *Costa Brava* in the early 1960s. The disparate moral qualities of the native and tourist females has resulted in a conundrum for young Greek women. To compete for their men's affections they have to loosen their principles (and more!) with a previously unheard of and steadily increasing number of speedily arranged marriages, if you know what I mean.

Do not miss the summer's evening *Volta* (Βολγα), the still traditional, family 'walkabout' on the square of any large settlement. Dressed for the event, an important part of the ritual is to show off the marriageable daughters. Good fun and great watching, but the Greeks are rather protective of their family and all things Greek... It is acceptable to comment favourably, but adverse criticism and familiarity should be kept to oneself.

It is interesting to speculate on the influence of the Greek immigrants on American culture. To justify this hypothesis consider the American habit of serving water with every meal, the ubiquitous hamburger (which is surely a poorly reproduced and inferior souvlaki pita – now being re-imported) and some of the official uniforms, more particularly the flat, peaked hats of American postmen and policemen.

ANIMALS After a letter from the worthy *Greek Animal Welfare Fund* requesting me to mention their cause, I decided not only to so do, but to air the subject from a personal viewpoint. First things first. The Fund represents all that is best in the English. (I can write this with little self-congratulatory feelings, as it is the viewpoint of an author with a mixed Celtic parentage of Southern Irish, one generation removed, and Welsh. That explains it!) The UK based society seeks to prevent cruelty to animals in Greece and I wish them every success. They deserve all animal lovers support. But, and here we come to my caveat, readers must carefully think through any instant reaction to the sight of animals subjected to inhumanity. I quickly lost count of the number of times that I had to 'mind my own business' when observing this or that particular example of cruelty and or neglect. On the other hand it is worth considering that until, say, thirty years ago, many, many Greeks lived in conditions of such poverty and deprivation that, were they to have been animals, it would have caused outcries of indignation from their Western neighbours. Another rejoinder is that the Greeks don't regard animals as having any soul, so mistreatment simply doesn't matter! I am not condoning the state of affairs but, prior to leaping up and down and berating a particular person, ponder that they regard children as sacrosanct. They find the type of sickening child abuse cases, it is impossible not to read about every day of the week in the British newspapers, as incomprehensible. Quite.

THE GREEK NATIONAL HOLIDAYS Listed below are the national holidays and on these days many areas and islands hold festivals, usually with a particular slant and emphasis.

1st January	New Year's Day/The Feast of Saint Basil
6th January	Epiphany/Blessing of the Waters – a cross is immersed in the sea, lake or river during a religious ceremony.
The period 27th Jan to 17th February	The Greek Carnival Season
25th March	The Greek National Anniversary/Independence Day
April – movable days	Good Friday/Procession of the 'Epitaph'; Holy Week Saturday/Ceremony of the Resurrection; Easter Sunday/open air feasts
1st May	May/Labour Day/Feast of the Flowers
1st to 10th July	Greek Navy Week
15th August	Assumption Day/Festival of the Virgin Mary, especially in the Cycladian island of Tinos (beware travelling at this time, anywhere in the area)
28th October	National Holiday/'Ochi' Day
24th December	Christmas Eve/Carols Evening
25th December	Christmas Day
26th December	St Stephen's Day
31st December	New Year's Eve carols, festivals

In addition to these national days, each island has its own particular festivals and holidays which are listed individually under each island.

HISTORY MYTHOLOGY.... 83

A word of warning to ferry-boat travellers will not go amiss here – **DO NOT travel to an island immediately prior to one of these festivals, NOR off the island immediately after the event.** It will be almost impossible to do other than stand, that is if one has not already been trampled to death in the various stampedes to and from the ferry-boats.

Even more useful names & addresses
Greek Animal Welfare Fund 11 Lower Barn Road, Purley, Surrey, CR2 1HY   Tel (01) 668 0548

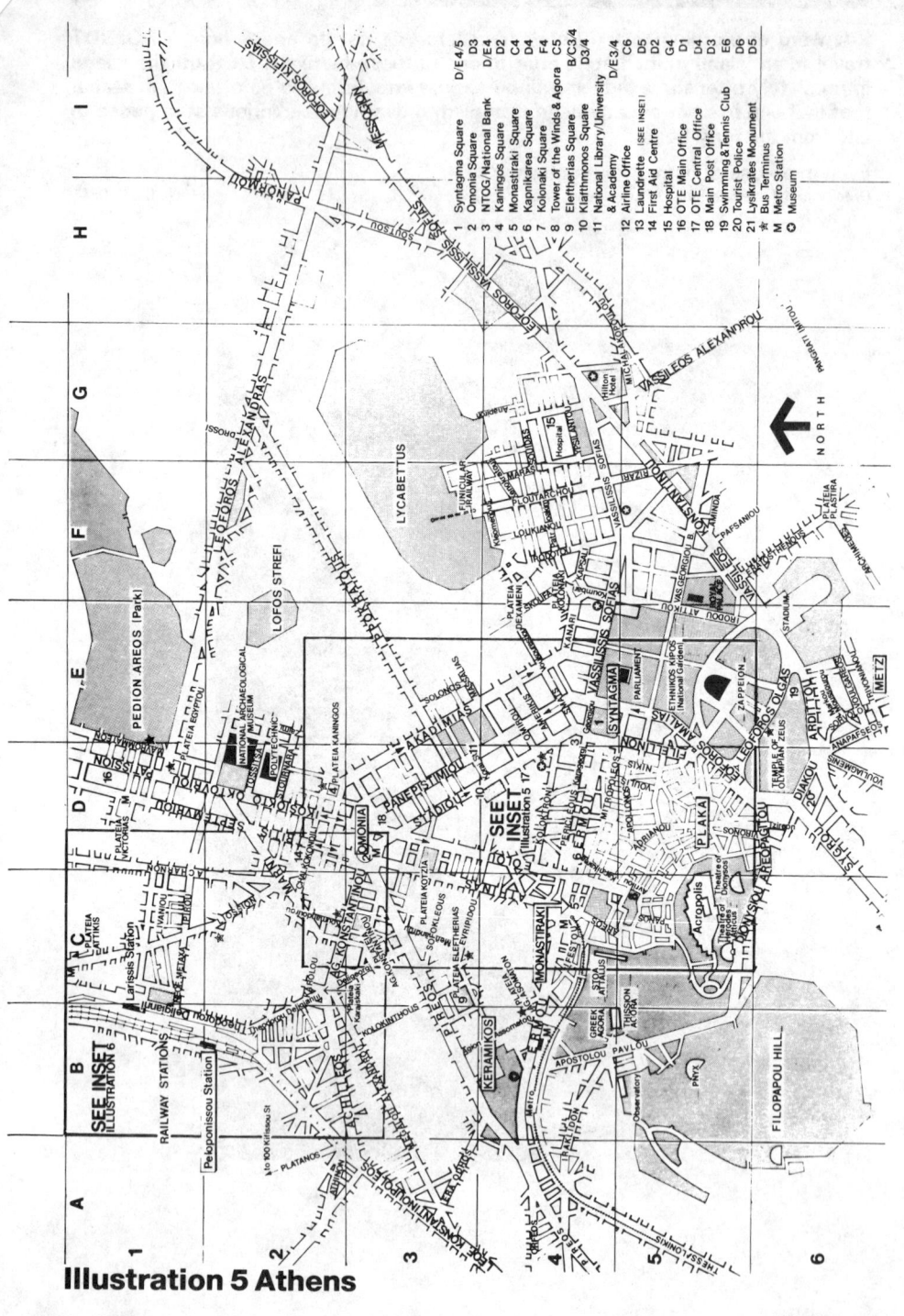

Illustration 5 Athens

PART TWO
9 ATHENS CITY (ATHINA, AΘHNAI)

There is no end of it in this city, wherever you set your foot, you encounter some memory of the past.
Marcus Cicero

Tel prefix 01. The capital of Greece and major city of Attica (Illustrations 5, 6 & 7).

Previously the pivotal point for travel to most of the Greek islands (with Piraeus Port the springboard), but less so since a number of flights have become available direct to the larger islands. Experienced travellers flying into Athens airport, often try to arrange their arrival for early morning and head straight to either the West airport (for a domestic flight), Piraeus Port, the railway station or bus terminal.

ARRIVAL BY AIR International flights other than *Olympic Airways* land at the:

East Airport The terminal building facilities include not only the usual snackbar and toilets, but several bank counters and an NTOG (Greek Tourist Board) counter. Public transport available includes:

East Airport The terminal building facilities include not only the usual snackbar and toilets, but several bank counters and an NTOG (Greek Tourist Board) counter. Public transport available includes:

Bus A: East Airport to Kifissou Bus Station, via Syntagma Sq, Omonia Sq, Vathis, Karaiskaki.
    Going to the Airport, the bus stop is at the Syntagma end of Leoforos Amalias (just beyond the British Airways Offices). The bus runs at the following times; 0500, 0620, 0700, 0750, 0840, 0930, 1010, 1050, 1130, 1210, 1250, 1330, 1410, 1450, 1535, 1625, 1715, 1805, 1850, 1940, 2030, 2120, 2210, 2300, 2400, 0100 & 0300hrs.
    Fare 100drs (From 2400-0600hrs, 150drs night fare).
    Blue and yellow doubledecker express bus.

Bus B: East Airport to Liossion Bus Station via Syntagma Sq, Omonia Sq, Vathis, Karaiskaki, Stathmos Larissis.
    Going to the Airport, the bus stop is as for Bus A. The bus runs at the following times; 0600, 0640, 0725, 0815, 0905, 0950, 1030, 1110, 1150, 1230, 1310, 1350, 1430, 1510, 1600, 1650, 1740, 1830, 1915, 2005, 2055, 2145, 2230, 2330, 1230, 0200hrs.
    Fare 100drs (From 2400-0600hrs, 150drs night fare).
    Blue and yellow doubledecker express bus.

Bus No. 121:   East Airport to Leoforos Vassilissis Olgas. Runs every 40 mins between 0650-2250hrs.
    Fare 30drs. Blue bus.

Bus No. 101:   East Airport via Leoforos Possidonos (coast road) to Klisovis, Piraeus. Every 40 mins between 0500-2245hrs.
    Fare 30drs. Blue bus.

Bus No. 19:   East Airport to Plateia Karaiskaki, Piraeus. Every 30mins from 0600-2400hrs, every 90mins from 2400-0600hrs.
    Fare 100drs. Yellow express bus.* (2400-0600hrs, 150drs night fare).

* At the airport, don't jump for the bus without obtaining tickets first from the office adjacent to the bus terminus.

One correspondent advised that, for those not wanting to trek into Athens centre, it is worth considering staying in a hotel close by the airport. One drawback is the proximity of the flight-path. A recommended hotel that is a short distance away and not in a direct line with the runway is the:-

Hotel Avra (Class C) 3 Nireos, Paleon Faliro   Tel 981 4064
Directions: Proceed north (in the direction of Piraeus) along the coastal avenue of Leoforos Vas. Georgiou B, which at Paleon Faliro becomes Leoforos Possidonos. A No. 101 bus travels the route. Proceed past the Marina to the area where the road cuts inland from the coastline, an overall distance of some 6km. Nireos St is a branch off the Esplanade Road.

The Avra is close to a beach and not outrageously expensive, in comparison to many other Athens and Piraeus hotels. Singles, sharing the bathroom, start at 1750drs & en suite 2500drs, while a double en suite costs 3100drs. These prices rise respectively, to 2100, 3000 & 3750drs, (1st June-31st Oct). Breakfast costs an extra 300drs.

Domestic and all Olympic flights land at the:-
West Airport Public transport available includes:

Bus A:	West Airport to Kifissou Bus Station via Syntagma Sq, Omonia Sq, Vathis, Karaiskaki. Going to the airport, the bus stop is the same as for the East Airport.
Bus B:	West Airport to Liossion Bus Station via Syntagma Sq, Omonia Sq, Vathis, Karaiskaki, Stathmos Larissis. The bus stop is the same as above.
	The A & B buses run all night; Every 20mins from 0600-2400hrs, every 90mins from 2400-0600hrs. Fare 100drs (2400-0600hrs, 150drs night fare). Yellow and blue double decker express buses.
Bus No. 133*	West Airport to Othonos St (Syntagma Sq). Every 15 mins from 0540-2400hrs. Fare 30drs. Blue bus.
Bus No. 122*	West Airport to Leoforos Vassilssis Olgas (Zappeion Gdns). Every 15mins from 0530-2330hrs. Fare 30drs. Blue bus.
Bus No. 167	West Airport to Akadimias and Sina St. Night bus 0030, 0115, 0200, 0300, 0400hrs. Fare 45drs. Blue bus.
Bus No. 19	West Airport to Plateia Karaiskaki, Piraeus. About every 30mins from 0600-2400hrs, about every 90mins from 2400-0600hrs. Fare 100drs. Yellow bus. (2400-0600hrs, 150drs night fare).

* Note Regular blue buses do not stop at the Air Terminal but on the main road, by the airport.

ARRIVAL BY BUS Inter-country coaches usually decant passengers at Syntagma Sq (*Tmr* 1D/E4/5), Stathmos Larissis Railway Station (*Tmr* B/C1) or close to one of the major city bus terminals.

ARRIVAL BY TRAIN See **Trains, A To Z**.

GENERAL (Illustrations 5 & 6) Even if a traveller is a European city dweller, Athens will come as a sociological and cultural shock to the system. In the summer it is a hot, dusty, dry, crowded, traffic bound, exhaust polluted bedlam, but always friendly, cosmopolitan and ever on the move.

On arrival in Athens, and planning to stay over, it is best to seek out the two main squares of Syntagma (*Tmr* 1D/E4/5) and Omonia (*Tmr* 2/D3). These can then be used as centres for the initial sally and from which to radiate out

There is no substitute for a city map which is issued free (yes, free) from the Tourist desk in the National Bank of Greece (*Tmr* 3/D/E4). See **NTOG, A To Z**.

Syntagama Square (Constitution or Parliament Sq) (*Tmr* 1D/E4/5) Many of the city buses, as well as airport bus connections, stop here or hereabouts. It is the city centre with the most elite hotels, airline offices, international companies, including the *American Express* headquarters, smart cafes and the Parliament building, all circumscribing the central, sunken square. In the bottom, right-hand (or south-east) corner of the plateia, bounded by Odhos Othonos and Leoforos Amalias, are some very clean, attendant-minded toilets. There is a charge for the use of these 'squatties'.

To orientate, the *Parliament* building and *Monument to the Unknown Warrior* lie to the east of the square. To the north-east, in the middle distance, is one of the twin hills of Athens, *Mt Lycabettus (Lykavittos, Lykabettos* & etc, etc). The other hill is the *Acropolis*, to the south-west, and not now visible from Syntagma Sq due to high-rise buildings. On the west side of the square are the offices of *American Express* and a battery of pavement cafes, with Ermou St leading due west to Monastiraki Sq. To the north are the two parallel, main avenues of Stadiou (a one-way street down to Syntagma) and Venizelou or Panepistimiou (a one-way street out of Syntagma) that run north-west to:

Omonia Square (Concorde or Harmony Sq) (*Tmr* 2D3) The 'Piccadilly Circus' or 'Times Square' of Athens, but rather tatty really, with a constant stream of traffic bludgeoning its way round the large central island which is crowned by an impressive fountain. Visitors trying to escape the human bustle on the pavements, by stepping off into the kerbside, should beware that they are not mown down by a bus, taxi or car.

There is constant activity night and day and the racial admixture of people, cheek by jowl, lends the square a cosmopolitan character all of its own. On every side are hotels. These vary from the downright seedy to the better-class tawdry, housed in rather undistinguished, 'neo-city-municipal' style, nineteenth century buildings, almost unique to Athens.

Various Metro train entrance/exits emerge around the square, spewing out and sucking in travellers. The Omonia underground concourse has a Post Office, telephones, a bank and, by the Dorou St entrance, a block of 'squatty' toilets, for which the attendant charges 10drs for two sheets of paper.

Shops, cafes and booths fill the gaps between the hotels and the eight streets that converge on the Square. To the north-east side of Omonia, on the corner of Dorou St, is a taxi rank and beyond, on the right, a now rather squalid, covered arcade brimful of reasonably priced snackbars. Through this covered passageway, and turning to the left along 28 Ikosiokto Oktovriou (28th October St)/Patission St, and then right down Veranzerou St, leads to:

Kaningos Square (*Tmr* 4D2) Serves as a bus terminal for some routes.

To the south of Omnia Sq is Athinas St, the commercial thoroughfare of Athens. Here almost every conceivable item imaginable can be purchased, including ironmongery, tools, crockery and clothing. Parallel to Athinas St, and for half its length, runs Odhos Sokratous, the city street market during the day and the red-light district by night.

Athinas St heads due south to:
Monastiraki Square (*Tmr* 5C4) This marks the northernmost edge of the area known as the *Plaka* (*Tmr* D5), bounded by Ermou St to the north, Filellinon St to the east and by the slopes of the Acropolis to the south.

Many of the alleys in this area follow the course of the old Turkish streets; most of the houses are mid-nineteenth century and represent the 'Old Quarter'.

Climbing the twisting maze of streets and steps of the lower, north-east slopes of the Acropolis requires the stamina of a mountain goat. The almost primitive, island-village nature of some of the houses hereabouts is very noticeable, due, it is said, to a law passed after Independence. The Act was sanctioned to alleviate a housing shortage and allowed anyone who could raise the roof of a dwelling, between sunrise and sunset, to complete the building which then became theirs. Some inhabitants of the Cyclades island of Anafi (Anaphe) were reputed to have been the first to benefit from this new law. Other islanders followed to specialise in restoration and rebuilding, thus bringing about a colony of expatriates within the Plaka district.

From the south-west corner of Monastiraki Sq, Ifestou St and its associated byways house the *Flea Market*, which climaxes on Sunday into stall upon stall of junk, souvenirs, junk, hardware, junk, boots, junk, records, junk, clothes, junk, footwear, junk, pottery and junk. Where Ifestou becomes Odhos Astigos, and curves round to join up with Ermou St, there are a couple of extensive second-hand bookshops with reasonably priced (for Greece that is), if battered, paperbacks for sale.

From the south-east corner of Monastiraki, Pandrossou St, one of the only enduring reminders of the Turkish Bazaar, contains a better class of antique dealer, sandal and shoemaker, and pottery store.

Due south of Monastiraki Sq is Odhos Areos. The raggle-taggle band of European and

Japanese drop-outs, selling junk trinkets from the pavement kerb, appear to have been replaced by a few local traders. Climbing Odhos Areos skirts the *Roman Agora*, from which various streets lead upwards, on ever upwards, and which contain a plethora of stalls and shops, specialising in leather goods, clothes and souvenirs. The further you climb, the cheaper the goods become. This interestingly enough does not apply to the tavernas and restaurants which seemingly become more expensive as one ascends.

The Plaka (*Tmr* D5) The 'chatty' area known as the Plaka is littered with eating places, a few good, some bad, some tourist rip-offs. The liveliest street, Odhos Kidathineon, is, at its lowest end, jam-packed with cafes, tavernas and restaurants and at night attracts a number of music-playing layabouts. The class, tone and price of the establishments improves as the street climbs in a north-eastwards direction. I have to admit to gently 'knocking' the Plaka over the years. Despite this, it has to be acknowledged that the area offers the cheapest accommodation and eating places in town and appears to have been cleaned up in recent years. Early and late in the year, once the hordes of overseas 'invaders' have dispersed, the Plaka once again becomes a 'village', a super place to visit. The shopkeepers revert to being human, the cost of shopping becomes inexpensive and the tavernas hark back to being 'Greek', as well as lively. In the last three weeks of February the *Apokria Festival*, a long running 'Halloween' style carnival, is centred on the Plaka. The streets are filled with dozens of revellers dressed in fancy dress, masks and funny hats who wander about, throwing confetti, wielding plastic clubs, spraying shaving foam and generally creating a marvellous atmosphere. For this event all the tavernas are decorated.

To the east of Monastiraki Sq is Ermou St, initially lined by clothes and shoe shops. One third of the way towards Syntagma Sq and Odhos Ermou opens out into a small square on which there is the lovely *Church of Kapnikarea* (*Tmr* 6D4). Continuing eastwards, the shops become smarter with a preponderance of fashion stores, whilst parallel to Ermou St is Odhos Ploutonos Kteka, which becomes Odhos Mitropoleos. Facing east, on the right, is the City's Greek Orthodox Cathedral, *Great Mitropolis*. Built circa 1850, from the materials of about seventy old churches, to the design of four different architects, the result, not unnaturally, was a building of a rather 'strange' appearance. In strict contrast, alongside, and to the south, is the diminutive, medieval *Little Mitropolis* Church or Agios Eleftherios. This dates back to at least the twelfth century, but incorporates materials, reliefs and building blocks probably originating from as early as the sixth century AD. A little further on is the intriguing and incongruous site of a small Byzantine church, dominated by a modern office block, the columns of which tower above the tiny building.

Leaving Syntagama Sq by the north-east corner, along Vassilissis Sofias, and turning left at Odhos Irodou Attikou, runs into:
Kolonaki Square (*Tmr* 7F4) The most fashionable square in the most fashionable area of Athens, around which most of the foreign embassies are located. The *British Council* is located on this square, as are some expensive cafes, restaurants and boutiques.

To the north of Kolonaki, across the pretty, orange tree planted Dexameni Sq, is the southernmost edge of:
Mt Lycabettus (*Tmr* F/G3) Access to the summit can be made on foot by a number of steep paths, the main one of which, a stepped footpath, advances from the north end of Loukianou St, beyond Odhos Kleomenous. A little to the east, at the top of Ploutarchou St, which breaks into a sharply rising flight of steps, is the cable car funicular railway. This climbs in a 213m long tunnel to emerge alongside a modern and luxuriously expensive restaurant, close by the nineteenth century chapel which caps the fir tree covered outcrop. There are some excellent toilets.

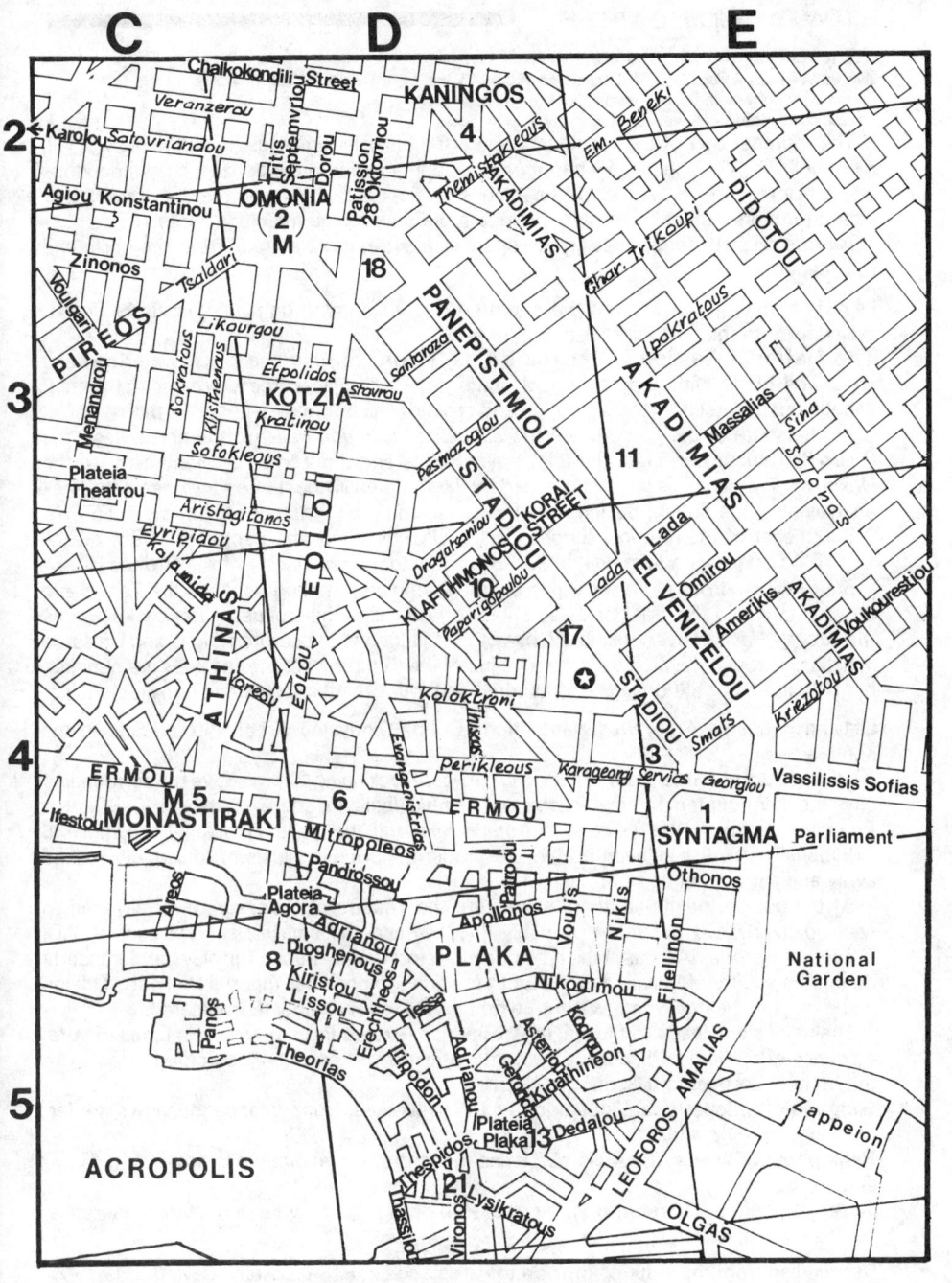

Illustration 6 Athens inset - The Plaka

The railway service runs continuously as follows:
Winter: Wed, Sat & Sun 0845-2400hrs; Thurs 1030-2400hrs; Mon, Tues & Fri 0930-2400hrs.
Summer: As for winter, but the opening hours might extend.
The trip costs 120drs one-way and 200drs for a return ticket.

The topmost part of the mountain, where the funicular emerges, is surprisingly small, if not doll-like. The spectacular panorama that spreads out to the horizon, the stupendous views from far above the roar of the Athens traffic, are best seen in the early morning or later afternoon. Naturally the night hours are the time to see the city's lights.

A more relaxed climb, passing the open air theatre, can be made from the north end of Lycabettus.

Leaving Plateia Kolonaki from the south corner and turning right at Vassilissis Sofias, sallies forth to the north corner of:

The National Garden (Ethnikos Kipos) (*Tmr* E5) Here peacocks, waterfowl and songbirds blend with a profusion of shrubbery, subtropical trees, ornamental ponds, various busts and cafe tables through and around which thread neat gravel paths.

To the south of the gardens are the *Zappeion Exhibition Halls*; to the north-west, the Greek Parliament buildings, the (old) Royal Palace and the Tomb, or Monument, to the Unknown Warrior. This latter is guarded by the traditionally costumed *Evzones*, the Greek equivalent of the British, Buckingham Palace Guards (*See* **Places of Interest, A To Z**).

South-east of the National Gardens is the *Olympic Stadium*, erected in 1896, on the site of the original stadium built in 330 BC, and situated in a valley of the Arditos Hills.

South-west across Leoforos Olgas are the Olympic swimming pool and the *Tennis and Athletic Club*. To the west of these sporting facilities is the isolated gateway known as the *Arch of Hadrian* overlooking the busy traffic junctions of Leoforos Olgas and Leoforos Amalias. Through the archway, the remains of the *Temple of Olympian Zeus* are outlined, but only fifteen of the original one hundred and four Corinthian columns remain standing.

Leaving Hadrian's Arch, westwards along Odhos Dionysiou Areopagitou, leads to the south side of:-

The Acropolis (Akropoli) (*Tmr* C5) A 10-acre rock rising 229m above the surrounding city and surmounted by the *Parthenon Temple* (built in approximately 450 BC), the *Propylaia Gateway*, the *Temple to Athena Nike* and the triple *Temple of Erechtheion*. Additionally, there has been added the modern Acropolis Museum, discreetly tucked away and almost out of sight.

At the bottom of the southern slopes are the *Theatre of Dionysos*, originally said to seat up to 30,000 but more probably 17,000, and the smaller, second century AD, *Odeion of Herodes Atticus*, which has been restored and is used for plays and concerts during the summer festival. It is thought provoking to consider that the Dionysos Odeion is the original theatre where western world drama, as we know it, originated.

The west slope leads to the **Hill of Areopagos (Areios Pagos)** where, in times of yore, a council of noblemen dispensed supreme judgements. Across Apostolou Pavlou St lie the other tree covered hills of:

Filopapou (Philopappos/Mouseion), or **Hill of Muses**, from whence the views are far-reaching and outstanding,

Pynx (Pynka), where The Assembly once met and a *son et lumiere* is now held, and the

Asteroskopeion (Observatory), or the **Hill of Nymphs**, whereon stands, surprise, surprise, an observatory.

Descending from the Asteroskopeion towards and across Apostolou Pavlou St is:

The Greek Agora (*Tmr* B/C4) The gathering place from whence the Athenians would have approached the Acropolis. This marketplace cum-civic centre is now little more than rubble, but the glory that once was is recreated by a model.

Nearby the *Temple of Hephaistos*, or *Thission* (*Theseion*), sits on a small hill overlooking the Agora. To one side is the reconstructed marketplace, *Stoa Attalus*, the cost of which was met from private donations raised by American citizens.

A short distance to the east of the Greek Agora is the site of:-
The Roman Forum (Agora) (*Tmr* C5) Close by is the *Tower of the Winds* (*Tmr* 8C5), a remarkable, octagonal tower, probably built in the first century BC and which served as a combination water clock, sundial and weather vane. Early descriptions say the building was topped off with a bronze weather vane represented by the mythological Triton complete with a pronged trident. The carved eight gods of wind can be seen, as can traces of the corresponding sundials, but no interior mechanism remains and the building is now sadly used as a store for various stone antiquities.

Not far away, to the north-west, is an area known as **The Keramikos** (*Tmr* B4), a cemetery or graveyard, containing the *Street of the Tombs*, a funeral avenue laid down about 400 BC.

In a north-easterly direction from Keramikos, along Pireos St, via Eleftherias Sq Bus Terminal (*Tmr* 9C3), turning right down Evripidou St, across Athinas and Eolou Sts, leads to:-
Klafthmonos Square (Klathmonos) (*Tmr* 10D3/4) Supposedly the most attractive Byzantine church in Athens, *Aghii Theodori*, is positioned in the west corner of the Square.

Looking north-east across Stadiou St, up Korai St and across Panepistimiou Ave, reveals an imposing range of neo-classical buildings (*Tmr* 11D/E3/4), fronted by formal gardens. These comprise the *University* flanked, on the left (*facing*), by the *National Library* and, on the right, by the *Academy*. Behind and running parallel to Stadiou and Penepistimiou, is Akadimias St, on which is another bus terminal. Just off Akadimias St, in Massalias St, is the *Hellenic-American Union*, many of the facilities of which are open to the general public. These include English and music libraries, as well as a cafeteria.

North-west of Klafthomonos Sq, to the left of Eolou St, is:-
Kotzia Square (*Tmr* D3) A very large plateia around which, on Sunday at least, circle a profusion of flower sellers' stalls.

The once paved area has been dug up by archaeologists who have unearthed a veritable treasure trove of ancient Athens city walls. The fate of the site is in the hands of the opposing and seemingly irreconcilable factions represented by the modernists, who have a vision of a vast underground car park, and the traditionalists, who quite rightly, wish to see the 'dig' preserved for posterity. This matter still remained unresolved early in 1989.

Fokionos Negri Actually a street, if not an avenue, rather than a square. It is somewhat distant from the city centre, almost in the suburbs to the north, and few, if any street plans of Athens extend far enough to include the full extent of the thoroughfare. To reach Fokionos Negri from Omonia Sq, proceed north along 28 Ikosiokto Oktovriou, which runs into Patission St, on past the *National Archaeological Museum* and *Green Park* (*Pedion Areos*), both on the right, to where Agiou Meletiou St runs across Patission St. Fokionos Negri starts out as a fairly narrow side-street to the right, but widens out into a tree lined, short, squat avenue with a wide, spacious, centre pedestrian way once gravelled but now extensively resurfaced. Supposedly the *Dolce Vita* or *Via Veneto* of Athens but not out of the ordinary, if quiet wealth is normal. Extremely expensive cafes edge the square halfway up on the right and it certainly becomes extremely lively after nightfall.

Trolley-buses 3, 5, 11, 12, 13, or 14 going north, trundle past the turning.

THE ACCOMMODATION & EATING OUT
The Accommodation Generally, in describing the islands, the 'haul' of accommodation

detailed includes even 'E' Class hotels, but in Athens I have erred on the side of caution, sticking with 'B', 'C' and some better 'D' class hotels and pensions. No doubt there are acceptable Class 'E' hotels but... Most of the Athens pensions and lower category hotels operate a night-time curfew, usually some time between 0100-0200hrs, and an earlier than usual morning 'chuck-out', often from 1000hrs to 1100hrs, so check.

On Adrianou St (*Tmr* D5), in the Plaka district, are a few, very cheap dormitories and students' hostels, where a certain amount of rooftop sleeping is allowed, costing upwards of 500drs per night. Unless set well back from the main road, a set of earmuffs or plugs is almost obligatory to ensure a good night's sleep.

On a cautionary note, in recent years the Greek authorities have been closing a number of the more 'undesirable', unlicensed hotels, so a particular favourite overnight stop from years gone by may no longer be in business.

Most of the detailed accommodation charges listed in this guide are priced at 1989 prices. *See* **Chapter Four** for a table outlining the various categories, with comments and guideline prices.
See **Arrival By Air, East Airport, Introduction**.

SYNTAGMA AREA (*Tmr* D/E4/5)
Festos Guest House (*Tmr* D/E5) 18 Filellinon St　　　　　　　　　　　　　　Tel 323 2455
Directions: From Syntagma Sq, walk up the rise of Odhos Filellinon past a number of cut-price ticket joints. The entrance is very nearly opposite Ag Nikodimos Church, on the right.

Ethnic guest house with dormitories, triples & quadruple rooms working out at between 750 & 1200drs per person. Hot showers cost an extra 100drs, but luggage is stored free. The bar not only serves drinks but simple snacks. For the indiscriminately young at heart.

Hotel Cleo (Cleopatra) (*Tmr* D4) (Class D) 3 Patroou St　　　　　　　　　　　Tel 322 9053
Directions: Leaving Syntagma Sq, walk down Mitropoleos St, towards Monastiraki Sq and take the fourth turning left.

Well recommended if threadbare. Ground floor dormitory, free baggage store. Double rooms en suite cost 1900drs, rising to 3400drs (1st May-30th Sept).
NB *The owners also have a guest house nearby in Apollonos St.*

Pension John's Place (*Tmr* D4) (Class C) 5 Patroou St　　　　　　　　　　　Tel 322 9719
Directions: As for *Hotel Cleo* above.

Not surprisingly, the affable, old Papa is named John. Well looked after accommodation with singles starting at 1600drs & doubles from 2250drs (1st Jan-30th April & 1st Oct-31st Dec), increasing to 1800drs & 2700drs (1st May-30th Sept). Naturally rooms share the bathroom facilities.

George's Guest House (*Tmr* D4) (Class B) 46 Nikis St　　　　　　　　　　　Tel 322 6474
Directions: From Syntagma Sq, walk west along Mitropoleos St and turn down the first left-hand turning. The guest house is on the right, beyond the first side-street.

Calls itself a *Youth Hostel with student prices*. It was recommended by four Texas college girls, met on the train to Patras, some years ago, and whose first stop in Greece this was. Shared bathroom and hot water, if you are quick. Double rooms only from 1510drs, rising to 2000drs (April- Sept).

Hotel Kimon (*Tmr* D5) (Class D) 27 Apollonos　　　　　　　　　　　　　　Tel 323 5223
Directions: Midway on Apollonos St, one block down from Mitropoleos St.

Old but renovated. Single rooms, sharing bathrooms, start off at 2200drs, increasing to 2500drs (1st June-30th Sept) & en suite 2660drs, rising to 2750drs. Double rooms, which have to share a bathroom, cost 2500drs, rising to 2900drs.

Hotel Plaka (*Tmr* D4) (Class B) 7 Kapnikareas/Mitropoleos Sts　　　　　　Tel 322 2097
Directions: From Syntagma Sq proceed west along Mitropoleos. Kapnikareas St lies between Evangenistrias and Eolou Sts and the hotel is on the left.

Listed because the hotel accepts *American Express* and or *Diners*, despite which the charges are not too exorbitant and the rooms excellent. All have en suite bathrooms with a single room costing 2345drs a night & a double 3335drs, increasing, respectively, to 3200drs & 4460drs (16th Mar-15th June) and 4135drs & 5735drs (16th June-15th Oct). Breakfast, which might have to be taken, is

ATHENS 93

charged extra at between 380drs & 430drs per head.

YMCA (XAN) (*Tmr* E4) 28 Omirou St   Tel 362 6970
Directions: From the north-east corner of Syntagma Sq, proceed along Panepistimiou St, take the third turning right and across Akadimias Avenue, on the right.
It has been closed for renovations but may be open in 1989... then again it may not.

YWCA (XEN) (*Tmr* E4) 11 Amerikis St.   Tel 362 4291
Directions: All as above, but second turning off Panepistimiou St and on the left.
Don't forget, women only. Apart from accommodation there is a cafe serving breakfasts (200drs), sandwiches, a hair dressing salon, library and laundry facilities. Singles from 1200drs and shared rooms 1100drs per head.

Pension Theseus (*Tmr* D4) (Class C) 10 Thiseos   Tel 324 5860
Directions: From the top, north-west corner of Syntagma Sq, proceed along Odhos Karageorgi Servios, which becomes Periklious St, as far as the right-hand turning of Odhos Thiseos.
This friendly pension is situated in a comparatively 'serene' street. All rooms share the bathrooms with a single costing 2660drs & a double 3235drs, which charges increase to 3235drs & 3990drs (1st May-31st Oct).

OMONIA AREA (*Tmr* 2D3) Any hotel or pension rooms facing out over Omonia Square must be regarded as very noisy.

Hotel Omonia (*Tmr* D3) (Class C) 4 Omonia Sq.   Tel 523 7210
Directions: Just stand on Plateia Omonia, swivel round and on the north side of the Square.
The reception is on the first floor, as is a cafe-bar and terrace, overlooking the square and its action. Modern but a 'worn international' look to the place. Clients may well have to take demi-pension terms. All rooms have en suite bathrooms. Singles start at 1800drs & a double room 2500drs, rising, respectively, to 2000drs & 2800drs (21st Mar-14th July & 15th Sept-31st Oct) and 2300drs & 3300drs (15th July-14th Sept). Breakfast costs 280drs and a meal from 1100drs.

Hotel Banghion (*Tmr* D3) (Class C) 18b Omonia Sq.   Tel 324 2259
Directions: As for *Hotel Omonia*, but on the south side of the square.
Elegant but aging. Rooms sharing a bathroom cost 1800drs for a single & 2820drs for a double room and with en suite bathroom 2650drs & 3600drs. These charges rise, respectively, to 2160/3420drs & 3180/4320drs (16th July-30th Sept). Breakfasts costs 350drs, increasing to 400drs.

Hotel Carlton (*Tmr* D3) (Class C) 7 Omonia Sq.   Tel 522 3201
Directions: As for the *Hotel Omonia*.
Very provincial and old fashioned. All rooms share bathrooms, with single rooms charged from 1800drs & double rooms 2000drs, increasing to 2000drs & 2600drs (1st April-15th Oct).

Hotel Europa (*Tmr* D2) (Class C) 7 Satovriandou St   Tel 522 3081
Directions: North of Omonia Sq and in the second main street along, tracking east/west. This is often listed as Chateaubriandou St but the local authorities either have, or have not been notified of the change. Whatever, the street is now a pedestrian precinct.
Another 'Greek provincial' hotel, the remarkably ancient lift of which creaks its way up and down to the various floors. The rooms are adequate but dingy, there are wardrobes and the floors are covered with brown linoleum. If matters are still as they were, to use the shower it is necessary to ask the concierge for the relevant key. This may have to be in mime, if a guest's Greek is as sketchy as the staff's knowledge of English. When produced, this key might well be adjudged large enough to open the doors of the Bastille. Weighted down by the 'instrument', the moment of truth is about to dawn. When the door is opened, sheer disbelief may well be the first reaction, especially if it is the first ever stopover in Athens, as it was mine many years ago. A cavernous and be-cobwebbed room reveals plumbing that beggars description. Enough to say the shower is most welcome even if the lack of a point to anchor the shower head, whilst trying to soap oneself down, requires interesting body contortions. The rate for a single room is 1400drs & for a double 2000drs, increasing to 1700drs & 2500drs (1st July-15th Oct), sharing the bathrooms and the shower...

Hotel Alma (*Tmr* D2/3) (Class C) 5 Dorou   Tel 524 0858
Directions: Dorou St runs north from the north-east corner of Omonia Sq.
Modern and the rooms with a balcony are on the seventh and eighth floors. Single rooms, sharing a bathroom, cost 2000drs & en suite 2640drs, while double rooms cost 2750drs & 3500drs.

Hotel Orpheus (*Tmr* C/D2) (Class C) 58 Chalkokondili St   Tel 522 4996
Directions: North of Omonia Sq.
    Stolid, studentish and provincial in character. Very well recommended and reasonably priced, with a mix of accommodation available. A single room sharing a bathroom costs 2000drs, a double sharing 2500drs & with an en suite bathroom 2800drs. There is a TV lounge, outdoor patio and bar. Continental breakfast is available for 250drs and an English breakfast costs 400drs. Bar prices are reasonable with a Nes meh ghala costing 90drs, an ouzo 60drs, Metaxa 3 star brandy 60drs and an Amstel beer 100drs. Overseas telephone calls can be made.

Hotel Eva (*Tmr* C2) (Class D) 31 Victoros Ougo   Tel 522 3079
Directions: West of Omonia, as far as Plateia Karaiskaki, and to the north, parallel with and two blocks back from Ag Konstantinou.
    Well recommended and all rooms have en suite bathrooms. Single rooms start at 1550drs & double rooms 3000drs, rising to 2000drs & 3900drs (1st June-30th Sept). Breakfast costs 350drs.

Hotel Marina (*Tmr* C3) (Class C) 13 Voulgari   Tel 523 7832/3
Directions: South-west from Omonia Sq, along Odhos Pireos and 4th turning to the right.
    Single rooms cost from 1535drs, double rooms 2080drs, both sharing bathrooms, while rooms with en suite bathrooms cost from 1900drs & 2710drs respectively. These rates rise (16th March-30th June & 16th Oct-31st Dec) to 1720drs & 2260drs (single & doubles sharing) and 2080drs & 3160drs (singles & doubles en suite) and again (1st July-15th Oct) to 1990/2890drs & 2530/3795drs. Breakfast is charged at 330drs.

Hotel Vienna (*Tmr* C3) (Class C) 20 Pireos   Tel 524 9143
Directions: South-west of Omonia Sq.
    New, clean and noisy. All rooms have en suite bathrooms with singles starting at 2350drs & doubles 3205drs, increasing to 2710drs & 4060drs (1st July-31st Oct). A breakfast costs 330drs.

Hotel Athinea (*Tmr* C2) (Class C) 9 Vilara   Tel 524 3884
Directions: Westwards along Ag Konstantinou and situated on one side of the small square of Agiou Konstantinou.
    Old but beautifully positioned, although cabaret night life may intrude. A restaurant and cake shop are close by, as is a taxi rank. All rooms have en suite bathrooms. A single room starts off at 1950drs & a double 2750drs, increasing to 2450drs & 3400drs (16th March-15th June & 16th Oct-15th Nov) and 2700drs & 3800drs (16th June-15th Oct). Breakfast is priced at 500drs.

Hotel Florida (*Tmr* C3) (Class C) 25 Menandrou   Tel 522 3214
Directions: Third turning left, south-west along Pireos St.
    Single rooms are charged from 900/1200drs & doubles 1750drs, both without a bathroom, whilst a double room en suite costs 2200drs. These charges rise, respectively, to 1165/1550drs & 2000/2750drs (1st June-30th Sept). Breakfast is charged at 300drs.

Hotel Alcestis (Alkistis) (*Tmr* C3) (Class C) 18 Plateia Theatrou   Tel 321 9811
Directions: From Pireos St, proceed south down either Sokratous or Menandrou Sts and across Odhos Sofokleous.
    Despite its chromium-plated appearance, all glass and marble with a prairie-sized lobby, it is a Class C hotel in a commercial square. Popular and all rooms have en suite bathrooms. Singles start off at 1535drs & doubles 2260drs, rising to 2350drs & 3160drs (11th March-30th June & 1st-31st Oct) and 2710drs & 3795drs (1st July-30th Sept). Breakfast costs 400drs & lunch/dinner 1300drs.

MONASTIRAKI AREA (*Tmr* C4)

Hotel Tembi(Tempi) (*Tmr* C/D4) (Class D) 29 Eolou (Aiolu/Aeolou)   Tel 321 3175
Directions: In a main street north of Ermou St, opposite the Church of Ag Irini.
    Pleasant rooms with singles sharing the bathroom starting at 1200drs, rising to 1450drs (1st May-31st Oct). Double rooms sharing cost from 1800drs & en suite 2400drs, advancing, respectively, to 2300drs & 2900drs. There is a laundry and book exchange.

Hotel Ideal (*Tmr* C/D4) (Class D) 39 Eolou/2 Voreou Sts.   Tel 321 3195
Directions: On the left of Eolou, walking northwards from Odhos Ermou, on the corner with Voreou St.
    A perfect example of a weather-worn, 19th century, Athens neo-classical building complete with an old fashioned, metal and glass canopy entrance and matchbox sized, wrought iron balconies. The accommodation lives up to all that the exterior promises! The management are helpful, there is a

telephone, TV room, a bar and luggage can be stored. Tourist information is freely available as are battered paperbacks for guests. The rooms are clean and the bathroom facilities are shared, but there is 24 hour hot water – they promise! Singles start at 1200drs & doubles 1800drs, rising to 1450drs & 2300drs (1st May-31st Oct).

Hotel Hermion (*Tmr* C/D4) (Class D) 66c Ermou St   Tel 321 2753
Directions: East of Monastiraki, adjacent to Kapnikarea Church/Square (*Tmr* 6D4).
    Old but clean, with the reception up the stairs. All rooms share bathrooms with the single room rate starting off at 1300drs & double rooms 1900drs, increasing, respectively, to 1500drs & 2400drs (1st May-31st Oct).

Hotel Attalos (*Tmr* C3/4) (Class C) 29 Athinas   Tel 321 2801
Directions: North from Monastiraki Sq.
    Recommended to us by a splendidly eccentric English lady artist who should know – she has been visiting Greece for some 20 years. Single rooms, sharing the bathroom, start from 1795drs & en suite 1895drs, while doubles cost 1895drs & 2260drs. These charges increase to (singles) 2125/2530drs & (doubles) 2530/3250drs (16th March-31st May) and 2125/2710drs & 3250/3795drs (1st June-15th Oct). Breakfast is charged at 380drs.

Hotel Cecil (*Tmr* C3/4) (Class D) 39 Athinas   Tel 321 7079
Directions: North from Monastiraki Sq and two buildings along from the Kalamida St turning, on the left-hand side. This is the other side of the road from a very small chapel, incongruously stuck on the pavement. The 'informative' sign outside the hotel is no help.
    Clean looking, single rooms costing 1350drs & a double 2100drs, both sharing the bathrooms.

PLAKA/METZ STADIUM AREAS (*Tmr* D5 & D/E6) The Plaka is rich in accommodation, as it is in most things!

Hotel Phaedra (*Tmr* D5) (Class D) 4 Adrianou/16 Herephontos   Tel 323 8461
Directions: Situated close by a multi-junction of various streets including Lysikratous, Galanou, Adrianou and Herephontos, opposite the Byzantine Church of Ag Ekaterini and its small, attractive gardens.
    Pretty area by day with splendid views but noisy by night. A clean, family hotel with a ground floor bar. All rooms share the bathrooms, with a single room costing 2000drs & a double 2400drs, which rates increase, respectively, to 2700drs & 3400drs (1st April-15th Oct). Breakfast costs 400drs.

Students' Inn (*Tmr* D5) (Class C) 16 Kidathineon St   Tel 324 4808
Directions: On the left of the liveliest stretch of Kidathineon St, walking up from the Adrianou St junction, and almost opposite the front garden of a Japanese eating house.
    Hostelish and classified as a pension but recommended as good value with hot showers 'on tap' (sorry) and an English-speaking owner. There is a rooftop, a passable courtyard, a snackbar, the use of a washing machine (which does not always work) and a baggage store costing 50drs per day. The clean but basic rooms, which all share the bathrooms, are complete with a rickety, oilcloth covered table and a mug. Single rooms cost 1500drs & doubles 2100drs. These rates increase to 1600drs & 2400drs (2nd May-15th Oct). Breakfast costs 350drs, but I would rather wander out to 'breathe in' the Plaka.

Left off Kidathineon Street, climbing towards Syntagma Sq, is Odhos Kodrou on which are two clean, agreeable hotels in a very pleasant area, the:

Hotel Adonis (*Tmr* D5) (Class B) 3 Kodrou/Voulis Sts   Tel 324 9737
Directions: As above and on the right.
    Actually a pension so the rates are not outrageous. All rooms have en suite bathrooms with singles starting off at 1900drs & doubles 2120drs, rising, respectively, to 2100drs & 2300drs (1st April-30th June & 1st-31st Oct) and 2600drs & 2900drs (1st July-30th Sept)
and the:

Acropolis House (*Tmr* D5) (Class B) 6-8 Kodrou   Tel 322 2344
Directions: As above and on the left.
    Comes highly recommended and is clean, evincing old-fashioned charm. Once again officially classified as a pension, with a choice of rooms sharing or complete with en suite bathrooms. Single rooms, sharing a bathroom, cost 2035drs & en suite 2350drs, whilst doubles, sharing, cost 2440drs & en suite 2710drs. These rates increase, respectively, to 2150/2505 & 2575/2845drs, (1st Oct-31st Dec) and 2835/3110drs & 3405/3720drs (1st July-30th Sept).

Closer to Kidathineon St, and on the right is the:
Kourous Pension (*Tmr* D5) (Class C) 11 Kodrou   Tel 322 7431
Directions: As above.

Rather more provincial than the two establishments detailed above, which lack of sophistication is reflected in the lower prices (and standards). All rooms share the bathrooms, with single room rates starting at 1600drs & a double 2250drs (1st Jan-30th April & 1st Oct-31st Dec), climbing to the dizzy heights (!) of 1800drs & 2700drs (1st May-30th Sept).

Hotel Solonion (*Tmr* D5) (Class E) 11 Sp Tsangari/Dedalou   Tel 322 0008
Directions: To the right of Kidathineon St (*facing Syntagma Sq*), between Dedalou St and Leoforos Amalias. Odhos Tsangari is a continuation of Asteriou St.

I did start out by pronouncing I would not list any E class hotels but... Run by a rather stern faced lady who is assisted by a varied collection of part-time assistants to run the old, faded but externally refurbished building. If a guest strikes lucky the night porter will be a delightful old boy who was once a merchant in the Greek community resident in Turkey, and caught up in the huge population resettlement of 1922/23. The accommodation is 'student provincial' quality, the rooms being high ceilinged with the rather dodgy floorboards overlaid and hidden beneath brown linoleum. The bathrooms are distinctly ethnic and Victorian in style but hot water is promised all day. On a fine day... it is possible to espy the Acropolis... well a bit of it. No single rooms are available. A double room, sharing the bathroom, costs from 2000drs, including one bath, which rises to 2400drs (1st May-31st Oct).

Close by the *Hotel Solonion* are the:-
Hotel Kekpoy (Cecrops) (*Tmr* D5) (Class D) 13 Sp Tsangari   Tel 322 3080
Directions: On the same side of the road as, and similar in style to, the *Solonion*, but a building or two towards Leoforos Amalias.

All rooms share the bathrooms, singles costing 1900drs & doubles 2400drs (1st May-31st Oct).
and:-
Hotel Phoebus (Fivos) *(Tmr* D5) (Class C) Asteriou/12 Peta Sts   Tel 322 0142
Directions: Back towards Kidathineon St, on the corner of Odhos Asteriou and Peta.

Rather more up-market than the three previously listed hotels and all rooms have en suite bathrooms. A single room is charged at 2575drs & a double room 3250drs. These rates rise, respectively, to 3090drs & 3900drs (1st June-30th Sept). Breakfast costs 410drs.

A few side streets towards the Acropolis is:-
Apartments Ava (*Tmr* D5) (Class A) 9-11 Lysikratous St   Tel 323 6618
Directions: As above.

I have no personal experience, but the establishment has been mentioned as a possibility and is in an excellent, central but quiet situation, although it is rather expensive. All rooms have en suite bathrooms, are heated and air conditioned. There are also suites with kitchen and refrigerator.

Hotel Delos (*Tmr* D6) (Class C) 12 Makri   Tel 922 0287
Directions: South of Dionysiou Areopagitou.

All rooms have an en suite bathroom. Single room charges start at 2710drs & a double room 3250drs, increasing to 3615drs & 4335drs (16th March-31st Oct).

New Clare's House (*Tmr* E6) (Class C) 24 Sorvolou St   Tel 922 2288
Directions: Rather uniquely, the owners have had a large compliments slip printed with a pen and ink drawing on the face and, on the reverse side, directions in Greek saying *Show this to the taxi driver*. This includes details of the location, south of the Stadium, on Sorvolou St between Charvouri and Voulgareos Sts. The pension is on the right, half-way down the reverse slope with the description *white building with the green shutters*. From Syntagma proceed south down the sweep of Leoforos Amalias, keeping to the main avenue hugging the Temple of Olympian Zeus and along Odhos Diakou. Where Diakou makes a junction with Vouligmenis and Ardittou Avenues, Odhos Anapafseos leads off in a south-east direction and Sorvolou St 'crescents' off to the left. Trolley buses 2, 4, 11 & 12 drop travellers by the Stadium. It is quite a steep climb up Sorvolou St, which breaks into steps, to the pretty and highly recommended area of Metz (highly regarded by Athenians that is). Plus points are that the narrow nature of the lanes, which suddenly become steps, keeps the traffic down to a minimum and the height of the hill raises it above the general level of smog and pollution.

The pleasant, flat-fronted pension is on the right and has a marble floor entrance hall. Inside, off to the left, is a large reception/lounge/bar/breakfast/common room and to the right, the lift. Apart from the usual hotel business, the establishment 'beds' some tour companies clients overnighting in Athens, and en route to other destinations. Thus the hotel can be fully booked, so it is best to make a forward booking or telephone prior to journeying out here. The self-confident English speaking owner presides over matters from a large desk in the reception area and is warily helpful. The friendly lady receptionists do not exactly go wild in an orgy of energy sapping activity, tending to indulge in a saturnalia of TV watching. Guests in the meantime can help themselves to bottles of beer and Coke from the bar, paying when convenient to them and the receptionist. Despite the inferred aura of excellence, the usual collection of faults can crop up from time to time including: cracked loo seats; no hot water, despite being assured that there is 24 hours hot water (and for longer no doubt were there more hours in the day!); missing locking mechanism on the lavatory door; toilets having to be flushed using a length of string and the television on the blink. I do not mean to infer that these irritating defects occur all at once – just one or two, every so often. Double rooms sharing a bathroom cost from 2900drs & en suite 4000drs, which charges increase during the summer months. Incidentally, where the well appointed bathrooms are shared, the pleasant bedrooms only have to go fifty-fifty with one other room. The charges, which include breakfast with warm bread every day, may at first impression (and for that matter second and third impression) appear on the expensive side. The 'pain' might be eased by the realisation that the 4th floor has a balcony and a self-catering kitchen, complete with cooker and a fridge, and the 5th floor a laundry room with an iron and 2 rooftop clothes lines. These facilities must of course be taken into account when weighing up comparative prices. The management creates an atmosphere that will suit the young, very well behaved student and the older traveller, but not exuberant, lager swilling rowdies. Hands are 'smacked' if guests lie around eating a snack on the front steps, hang washing out of the windows or make a noise, especially between 1330-1700hrs and after 2330hrs. You know, lights out boys and no smoking in the 'dorms'.

Clare's House was originally recommended by pension owner Alexis on the island of Kos. Certainly an old friend of ours, Peter, who 'has to put up with yachting round the Aegean waters during the summer months', almost always spends some of his winter at Clare's and swears by the place.

Before leaving the area, there is an inexpensive, intriguing possibility (accommodation that is) in a very quiet street edging the west side of the Stadium.

Joseph's House Pension (*Tmr* E6) (Class C) 13 Markou Moussourou   Tel 923 1204
Directions: From the region of Hadrian's Arch/the Temple of the Olympian Zeus (*Tmr* D6), proceed up Avenue Arditou in a north-easterly direction towards the Stadium. Odhos Markou Moussourou climbs steeply off to the right, immediately prior to the wooded hillside of Arditos. The pension is on the left, beyond Meletiou Riga St. On the other hand, it is just as easy to follow the directions to *Clare's House* and proceed east along Charvouri St until it 'bumps' into Markou Moussourou.

The bathrooms are shared, with single rooms charged at 1330drs throughout the year & doubles at 1775drs, which latter rate increases to 2215drs (1st May-30th Sept).

THISSION AREA (THESION) (*Tmr* B/C4/5) First south-bound Metro stop beyond Monastiraki and a much quieter area than, say, the Plaka.
Hotel Phedias (*Tmr* B4) (Class C) 39 Apostolou Pavlou   Tel 345 9511
Directions: South of the Metro station.

Modern and friendly. All rooms share en suite bathrooms with singles costing 2500drs & double rooms 3000drs. Breakfast is charged at 350drs per head.

Hotel Karayannis (*Tmr* C6) (Class C) 94 Leoforos Sygrou   Tel 921 5903
Directions: On the corner of Odhos Byzantiou and Leoforos Sygrou, opposite the side exit of the Olympic terminal office.

'Interesting', tatty and noisy, but very useful for weary travellers dumped late at night at the Olympic terminal. Rooms facing the main road should be avoided. The Athenian traffic, which roars non-stop and round the clock, up and down the broad avenue, gives every appearance of making the journey along Leoforos Sygrou via the hotel balconies, even on the third or fourth storeys. There are picturesque views of the Acropolis from the breakfast and bar rooftop terrace, even if they are through a maze of television aerials. Single rooms, with an en suite bathroom, cost 2090drs. Double rooms, sharing a bathroom, cost 2980drs & en suite 3080drs. Breakfast for one costs 330drs. Best to splash out for the en suite rooms as the hotel's shared lavatories are of a 'thought' provoking nature, possessing a number of the unique features detailed under the general description of Bathrooms in **Chapter Four**.

Whilst in this area it would be a pity not to mention the:-
Super-Bar Restaurant Odhos Faliron
Directions: As for the *Hotel Karayannis*, but one street to the west and parallel to Leoforos Sygrou.

Not inexpensive but very conveniently situated, even if it is closed on Sundays. Snackbar food, with 2 Nes meh ghala, a toasted cheese and ham sandwich and boiled egg costing 350drs. On that occasion I actually wanted toast...

HOSTELS
Youth Hostel 57 Kypselis St & Ag Meletiou 1   Tel 822 5860
Directions: Located in the Fokionos Negri area of North Athens. Proceed along 28 Ikosiokto Oktovriou/Patission St, from Omonia Sq, beyond Pedion Areos Park to Ag Meletiou St. Turn right and follow until the junction with Kypselis St. Trolley-buses 3, 5, 11, 13 & 14 make the journey.

This proclaims itself as *The Official Youth Hostel* and does fulfil the requirements of those who require very basic, cheap accommodation, albeit in dormitories. The overnight charge is 500-650drs and meals are available.

Taverna Youth Hostel (*Tmr* G2) 1 Drossi St/87 Leoforos Alexandra   Tel 646 3669
Directions: East of Pedion Aeros Park along Leoforos Alexandra, almost as far as the junction with Ippokratous St. Odhos Drossi is on the left. It is possible to catch Trolley-bus No. 7 from Panepistimiou Avenue or No. 8 from Kaningos Sq (*Tmr* 4D2) or Akadimias St.

Actually a taverna that 'sprouts' an 'unofficial Youth Hostel' for the summer months only.

If only to receive confirmation regarding the spurious Youth Hostels, it may be worth visiting the:-
YHA Head Office (*Tmr* D3/4) 4 Dragatsaniou   Tel 822 5860
Directions: The north side of Plateia Klafthmonos, in a street on the left-hand side of Stadiou St.

The office is open Mon-Fri, 0900-1400hrs. They advise of vacancies in the youth hostels and issue international youth hostel cards, as long as the application is accompanied by two full face photos. This latter is available in the Omonia Sq subway.

LARISSIS STATION AREA (*Tmr* B/C1) *See* Trains, A To Z.
Camping

Sample daily site charges are as follows:

Adults	From 150	to 550drs	Small tent	From 100	to 550drs
Children up to 4	Free	to 250drs	Large tent	From 150	to 550drs
Children 4 to 10 yrs of age	From 100	to 250drs	Camper Van	From 200	to 1000drs
Car	From 100	to 500drs			

Tent rental 100 to 800drs.

Sites include the following:-

Distance from Athens	Site name	Amenities
8km	**Athens Camping.** 198 Athinon Ave. On the road to Dafni (due west of Athens). Tel 581 4101/582 0353	Open all year, 25km from the sea. Bar, shop & showers.
10km	**Dafni Camping.** Dafni. On the Athens to Corinth National Road. Tel 581 1562/3	Open all year, 5km from the sea. Bar, shop, showers & kitchen facilities.

For the above: (Blue) Bus 853, Athens – Elefsina, departs from Koumoundourou Sq/Deligeorgi St (*Tmr* C2/3) (averagely) every 20 mins, between 0510-2215hrs.

14.5km	**Patritsia.** Kato Kifissia, N. Athens. Tel 801 1900 Closed 'temporarily' in 1987 & 1988, so who knows for 1989?	Open June-Oct. Bar, shop, showers, laundry & kitchen facilities.
16km	**Nea Kifissia.** Nea Kifissia, N. Athens. Tel 807 5544/807 5579	Open April-Oct, 20km from the sea. Bar, shop, showers, swimming pool & laundry.
18km	**Dionyssiotis Camping.** Nea Kifissia N. Athens. Tel 807 1494	Open all year.
25km	**Papa-Camping.** Zorgianni, Ag Stefanos. Tel 803 3446/361 6762	Open June-Oct, 25km from the sea. Laundry, bar & kitchen facilities.

ATHENS 99

For the above (sited on or beside the Athens National Road, north to Lamia): Lamia bus, from 260 Liossion St (*Tmr* C1/2), departs every hour from 0615 to 1915hrs & at 2030hrs.

35km	**Marathon Camping.** Kaminia, Marathon. NE of Athens. Tel 0294 5507	On a sandy beach & open all year round. Showers, bar restaurant & kitchen facilities.
35km	**Nea Makri.** 156 Marathonos Ave, Nea Makri. NE of Athens just south of Marathon. Tel 0294 92719/01 671 1987	Open April-Oct, 220m from the sea. Sandy beach, laundry, bar & shop.

For the above: A bus from Odhos Mavrommateon, Plateia Egyptou (*Tmr* D1), departs approximately every 45mins from between 0600-2215hrs.

26km	**Cococamp.** Rafina. East of Athens. Tel 0294 23413	Open all year. On the beach, rocky coast. Laundry, bar, showers, kitchen facilities, shop & restaurant.
29km	**Kokkino Limanaki Camping.** Kokkino Limanaki, Rafina. Tel 0294 31602/3/4	On the beach. Open April-Oct.
29km	**Rafina Camping.** Rafina. East of Athens. Tel 0294 23118/28436	Open May-Oct, 4km from sandy beach. Showers, bar, laundry, restaurant & shop.

For the above: The Rafina bus from Mavrommateon St, Plateia Egyptou (*Tmr* D1). Some thirty departures, between 0545-2230hrs.

20km	**Voula Camping.** 2 Alkyonidon St, Voula. (Just below Glyfada & the Airport). Tel 895 2712	Open all year, by a sandy beach. Showers, laundry, shop & kitchen facilities.
27km	**Varkiza Beach Camping.** Varkiza. Coastal road, Athens-Vouliagmeni-Sounion. Tel 897 3613/4	Open all year, by a sandy beach. Bar, shop, supermarket, taverna, laundry & kitchen facilities.
60km	**Sounion Camping.** Sounion Tel 0292 39358	Open all year, by a sandy beach. Bar, shop, laundry, kitchen facilities & a taverna.
76km	**Vakhos Camping.** Assimaki, nr Sounion. On the Sounion to Lavrio road. Tel 0292 39263	Open July-Sept, by a beach.

For the above: Buses from Mavrommateon St, Plateia Egyptou (*Tmr* D1), depart every hour between 0630-1730hrs & 1900hrs. *Note*: to get to **Vakhos Camping** catch the Sounion bus, via Markopoulo and Lavrio.

The Eating Out Apart from being such a matter of personal choice, in a city the size of Athens there are so many restaurants and tavernas from which to choose that only a few recommendations are made. In general, I can only suggest that readers steer clear of Luxury and Class A hotel dining rooms, restaurants offering international cuisine and tavernas with Greek music and or dancing*, all of which may be very good but are usually inordinately expensive.

'Gongoozling' from one of the chic establishments, such as a *Floka's*, edging one of the smart squares has become a comparatively expensive luxury, with a milky coffee (Nes meh ghala) or a bottle of beer costing anything up to 200drs, and an ouzo 250drs. In contrast it is possible to 'coffee' in the Plaka, at, say, *Kafeneion To Mainalon* (on the junction of Odhos Geronda, also named Monisasteriou, and Kidathineon St), where prices are much more reasonable, with a Nes meh ghala or an ouzo costing about 100drs. Incidentally, it is on an inside wall of *To Mainalon* that are preserved two price lists that vividly highlight the 'heady' effect of inflation in Greece. One of them dates back to 1965 and the other to 1968. They are priced in drachmae and lepta – one hundred lepta made up one drachma. A bottle of beer cost 2.50drs in 1965 and 3drs in 1968, a good brandy 3drs and 3.50drs, respectively, and an ouzo 3drs in both years. Thought provoking!

In Athens, and the larger, more cosmopolitan, provincial cities, it is usual taverna practice to round off prices, which proves a little disconcerting at first.

With despair, it is noted that some restaurants and tavernas climbing the slopes of the Acropolis (up Odhos Markou Avriliou, south of Eolou St) are allowing 'Chinese menu' style collective categories (A, B, & C) to creep into their listings.

* Note the reference to Greek dancing and music is not derogatory – only an indication that it is often the case that standards of cuisine may not be any better and prices usually reflect the 'overheads' attributable to the musicians' wages. But See **Palia** & **Xynou Tavernas**.

100 CANDID GUIDE TO ATHENS

PLAKA AREA (*Tmr* D5) A glut of eating houses ranging from the very good and expensive, the very expensive and bad, to some inexpensive and very good.

Taverna Thespis 18 Thespidos St　　　　　　　　　　　　　　　　　　　　Tel 323 8242
Directions: On the right of a lane across the way from Kidathineon St, towards the bottom or south-east end of Adrianou St.

Recommended and noted for friendly service. The house retsina is served in metal jugs. A two hour, slap-up meal of souvlakia, Greek salad, fried zucchini, bread and two carafes of retsina costs some 1600drs for two.

Plaka Village 28 Kidathineon
Directions: On the left (*Adrianou St behind one*), in the block edged by the streets of Adrianou and Kidathineon.

Once an excellent souvlaki pita snackbar but.... the offerings are now so-so, added to which to sit down costs extra. Price lists do not make this plain and the annoying habit can cause, at the least, irritation. (This practice is also prevalent in the Omonia Square 'souvlaki arcade'). Even more alarming is the 'take it or leave it' attitude that also extends to customer's money. The staff err towards 'taking' it, having to be badgered to return any change. The home-made tzatziki is good, the service is quick and they remain open Sunday lunchtimes. A souvlaki cost 100drs and a large bottle of beer 150drs.

Committed souvlaki pita eaters do not have to despair as any number of snackbars are concentrated on both sides of Mitropoleos St, at the Monastiraki Square end. Perhaps the most inexpensive souvlakis in the area are to be found by turning right at the bottom of Kidathineon St and wandering down Adrianou, in the direction of Monastiraki Sq.

ΟΤΖΕΡΙ Ο ΚΟΤΚΛΗΣ (or **PEPAVI**) 14 Tripodon St　　　　　　　　　　　Tel 324 7605
Directions: Up the slope from the Thespidos/Kidathineon junction, one to the left of Adrianou (*facing Monastiraki Sq*), and on the left.

Recognising the establishment is not difficult as the 1st floor balcony is still embellished with two, large, antique record player horns mounted on the wrought iron balustrade. A large, stuffed heron (yes a bird) has disappeared, the owners of the taverna maintaining that it has flown away to Mykonos! The 'HMV' style trumpets easily distinguish the old ouzerie/wine shop.

The taverna, standing on its own, evokes a provincial country atmosphere. It is necessary to arrive early as Pepavi is well supported by the locals, a popularity vouchsafed by the taverna being full prior to 2000hrs. The patronage is not surprising considering the inexpensive excellence of one or two of the dishes. These include salvers of dolmades and meatballs, as well as 'flaming sausages'. The latter cook away on stainless steel plates set down in front of the diner. They are served with a large plateful of hors d'oeuvres, amongst which are a meatball, beans, lettuce, feta, chilli, new potatoes and Russian salad, at a cost of 1000drs for two. Great value, very filling indeed but watch the napkins don't go up in flames and bear in mind that the house wine is pretty rough.

Eden Taverna 3 Flessa St.
Directions: Off Adrianou St, almost opposite Odhos Nikodimou, and on the left.

Mentioned because their menu includes many offerings that excellently cater (sorry) for vegetarian requirements. Open 1200hrs-2400hrs every day, except Tuesdays.

Palia Plakiotiki Taverna (Stamatopoulos) (*Tmr* D5) 26 Lissiou St　　Tel 322 8722
Directions: Proceed up Lissiou St, which parallels Adrianou St, in the general direction of Monastiraki Sq. The open-air taverna is behind a perimeter wall to the right, on a steep slope at the junction with Erechtheos St.

Claims to be one of Athens' oldest tavernas. The large terraced area is laid out with clean gravel chippings. Not particularly cheap but a super place at which to have an 'atmospheric' evening as there is a resident group. (Note this recommendation, despite my usual caveats regarding places at which music 'is on score'. Those remarks are usually attributed to establishments that advertise 'live' bouzouki). Here it is a major attraction in the shape of a huge, spherical man, with a name to match, Stavros Balagouras. He is the resident singer/accordionist/electric pianist and draws tourists and Greeks alike with his dignified and heartfelt performance. Besides traditional, national songs there is year-round dancing on the one square metre floor space, if customers are so moved! The taverna is particularly Greek and lively at festival times, added to which the food is good and much cheaper than similar establishments. Cheese and meat dishes, with salad and wine, cost about 1500drs for two. The dolmades are stuffed with meat and served in a lemon sauce so cost 350drs and meat dishes average 450/500drs. The wine is rather expensive with a bottle of Cambas red charged at 350drs and a large bottle of retsina 292drs. A bottle of Lowenbrau costs a reasonable 92drs. and the bread and head tax works out at only 15drs.

Michiko Restaurant 27 Kidathineon St   Tel 324 6851
Directions: On the right, beyond the junction with Asteriou St proceeding in a north-east direction (*towards Syntagma Sq*), close to a small square and church.
   Japanese dishes, if you must, and extremely expensive.

Xynou/Xynos 4 Arghelou Geronta (Angelou Geronta)   Tel 322 1065
Directions: Left off the lower, Plaka Square end of Kidathineon St (*facing Syntagma Sq*) and on the left, towards the far point of the short pedestrian way. The unprepossessing entrance door is tucked away in the corner of a recess and is easily missed.
   One of the oldest, most highly rated Plaka tavernas and well patronised by Athenians. Evenings only and closed on Saturdays and Sundays. A friend advises me that it is now almost obligatory to book in advance, although I have managed to squeeze a table for two early on in the evening. Mention of its popularity with Athenians prompts me to stress these are well-heeled locals – you know shipowners, ambassadors and aging playboys. Added to which the Xynou is definitely on the 'hotel captains' list of recommended establishments and the tourists who eat here tend to look as if they have stepped off the stage-set of Dallas. It is not surprising that the cognoscenti gather because, despite being in the heart of Athens, the premises evoke a rural ambience. The single storey, shed-like, roof tiled buildings edge two sides of a high wall enclosed gravel area, on which are spread the chairs and tables. The food is absolutely excellent and, considering the location, the prices are not outrageous. A meal of two plates of dolmades in lemon sauce, a plate of moussaka, a lamb fricassee in lemon sauce, a tomato and cucumber salad, a bottle of kortaki retsina and bread for two costs 1530drs. It seems a pity that the bread has to be charged at 50drs, but the ample wine list does include an inexpensive retsina. Three guitarists serenade diners, the napkins are linen and the service is first class. Readers are recommended to try Xynou's, at least once, for an experience that will not be easily forgotten.

To Fragathiko Taverna (*Tmr* D5)
Directions: On the left of Adrianou St (*proceeding towards Kidathineon St*) at the junction of Adrianou and Ag Andreou Sts.
   Clean, reasonably priced and popular with the younger generation, some of whom may not be entirely wholesome, but their enthusiasm is not surprising considering the inexpensively priced dishes on offer. These include moussaka special 325drs; moussaka special served with 4 kinds of vegetable 425drs; lamb special served with 4 kinds of vegetable 425drs and a vegetarian dish costing 240drs.

Plateia Agora is a lovely, elongated, chic Plaka Square formed at the junction of the bottom of Eolou and the top of Adrianou and Kapnikarea Sts. The square spawns a number of cafe-bar restaurants, including the *Posidion* and *Appollon*, the canopies, chairs and tables of which edge the pavement all the way round the neat, paved plateia. Don't forget that prices reflect the square's modishness with a bottle of beer or a coffee at the *Posidion* costing 250drs. There is a spotless public lavatory at the top (Monastiraki) end. The *Appollon* has a particularly wide range of choice and clients can sit at the comfortable tables for an (expensive) hour or so over a coffee, a fried egg breakfast or a full blown meal, if anyone can afford the same. On this tack it is becoming commonplace for some of the smarter places such as the *Posidion* to display unpriced menus. Hope your luck is in and the organ grinder wanders through the square.

From the little square formed by a 'junction of the ways', adjacent to the Lysikrates Monument (*Tmr* 21D5), Odhos Vironos falls towards the south Acropolis encircling avenue of Dionysiou Areopagitou.
Snackbar Odhos Vironos
Directions: As above and on the right (*Plaka behind one*) of the street.
   More a small 'doorway' souvlaki pita shop but small is indeed splendid.

Restaurant Olympia 20 Dionysiou Areopagitou
Directions: Proceed along Dionysiou Areopagitou, from the junction with Odhos Vironos, in a clockwise direction. The restaurant is on the right, close to the junction with Thassilou Lane (that incidentally climbs and bends back up to the top of Odhos Thespidos), hard up against the foot of the Acropolis. Between Thassilou Lane and the sun-blind-shaded lean-to butted on to the side of the restaurant, is a small grassed area and an underground public toilet.

The prices seem reasonable and the place appears to portend good things but....I can only report the promise was in reality, disappointing. The double Greek salad was in truth only large enough for one, the moussaka was 'inactive', the kalamares were unacceptable and the roast potatoes (yes roast potatoes) were in actuality nothing more than dumpy wedges. Oh dear! They do serve a kortaki retsina.

Odhos Panos, Plaka is a small street with a beautiful view of the Acropolis. As importantly it has a couple of very nice, reasonably priced, little tavernas with pavement tables, and the inexpensive pavement cafe, the *Trianon*.

STADIUM (PANGRATI) AREA (*Tmr* E/F6)
Karavitis Taverna (ΚΑΡΑΒΙΤΗΣ) 4 Pafsaniou (Paysanioy).
Directions: Beyond the Stadium (*Tmr* E/F6) going east (*away from the Acropolis*) along Vassileos Konstantinou, and Pafsaniou is the 3rd turning to the right. The taverna is on the left.

A small, leafy, tree shaded gravel square fronts the taverna, which is so popular that there is an extension across the street, through a pair of 'field gates'. Our friend Paul will probably berate me (if he was less of a gentleman) for listing this gem. Largely unknown to visitors but extremely popular with Athenians, more especially those who, when college students, frequented this jewel in the Athens taverna crown. A meal for four of a selection of dishes including lamb, beef in clay, giant haricot beans, garlic flavoured meatballs, greens, tzatziki, 2 plates of feta cheese, aubergines, courgettes, bread and 3 jugs of retsina, from the barrel, costs some 2400drs. Beat that! But some knowledge of Greek is an advantage and the taverna is only open in the evening.

Instead of turning off Vassileos Konstantinou at Odhos Pafsaniou, take the next right proceeding further eastwards.

ΜΑΓΕΜΕΝΟΣ ΑΥΛΟΣ **(The Magic Flute)** Odhos Aminda (Amynta).
Directions: As above and the restaurant is 20m up on the right.

Swiss dishes, including *fondue*, schnitzels and salads. Despite being rather more expensive than its near neighbours, it is well frequented by Athenians, including the composer Hadzithakis (so I am advised).

Virinis Taverna, Archimedes St
Directions: Prior to the side-streets that lead to the two restaurant/tavernas last detailed, the second turning to the right off Vassileos Konstantinou (beyond the Stadium (*Tmr* E/F6), proceeding in an easterly direction) is Odhos Eratosthenous. This climbs up to Plateia Plastira, to the right of which is Archimedes St. The taverna is about a 100m along on the left. Incidentally, if returning to the centre of Athens from hereabouts, it is possible to continue along Archimedes St and drop down Odhos Markou Moussourou back to Vassileos Konstantinou.

A good selection of bistro dishes at reasonable prices, including, for instance, beef in wine sauce at a cost of 350drs. It has been indicated that I might find the place rather 'up market', as there aren't any souvlaki pita on offer. Cheeky! It's only that over the years, I have learnt through costly experience that, in Greece, gingham tablecloths and French style menus tend to double the prices!

SYNTAGMA AREA (*Tmr* D/E4/5)
Corfu Restaurant 6 Kriezotou St   Tel 361 3011
Directions: North of Syntagma Sq and first turning right off Panepistimiou (El Venizelou).

Extensive Greek and European dishes in a modern, friendly restaurant.

Delphi Restaurant 15 Nikis St   Tel 323 4869
Directions: From the south-west corner of Syntagma Sq, east along Mitropoleos and the first turning left.

Modern, with reasonably priced food from an extensive menu as well as friendly service.

Sintrivani Restaurant 5 Filellinon St.
Directions: South-west corner of Syntagma Sq and due south.

Garden restaurant serving a traditional menu at reasonable prices.

Vassillis Restaurant 14A Voukourestiou.
Directions: North of Syntagma Sq and the second turning to the right off Panepistimiou St, along Odhos Smats and across Akadimias St.

Variety, in traditional surroundings.

Ideal Restaurant 46 Panepistimiou St.
Directions: Proceed up Panepistimiou from the north-east corner of Syntagma Sq and the restaurant is on the right.

Good food at moderate prices.

YWCA 11 Amerikis St.
Directions: North-west from Syntagma Sq along either Stadiou or Panepistimiou St and second or third road to the right, depending which street is used.
    Cafeteria serving inexpensive sandwiches.

There are many cafes in and around Syntagma Square. Recommended, but expensive, is the:-
Brazilian Coffee Cafe
Directions: Close by Syntagma Sq, in Voukourestiou St.
    Serves coffee, tea, toast, butter and jam, breakfast, ice-creams and pastries.

OMONIA AREA (*Tmr* D3)
Ellinikon Taverna (*Tmr* D2/3) Dorou St.
Directions: North of Omonia Sq, along Dorou St and almost immediately on the left down some steps to a basement.
    A cavernous, 'greasy spoon' well frequented by workmen and sundry officials, as well as a sprinkling of tourists. Inexpensive fare and draught retsina available.

Taverna Kostoyannus 37 Zaimi St.
Directions: Leave Omonia northwards on 28 Ikosiokto Oktovriou, turn right at Odhos Stournara to the nearside of the Polytechnic School, and Zaimi St is the second road along. The taverna is to the left, approximately behind the National Archaeological Museum.
    Good food, acceptable prices and comes well recommended. As in the case of many other Athenian tavernas, it is not open for lunch or on Sundays.

Snackbars
Probably the most compact, reasonably priced 'offerings', but in grubby surroundings, lurk in the arcade between Dorou St and 28 Ikosiokto Oktovriou, off Omonia Sq. Here are situated cafes and stalls selling almost every variety of Greek convenience fast food. A 'standard' souvlaki costs 70-80drs and a 'spezial', or de luxe, 90-100drs, BUT do not sit down unless you wish to be charged an extra 15-20drs per head. A bottle of beer is charged at about 100drs.

Cafes
Everywhere of course, but on Omonia Sq, alongside Dorou St and adjacent to the *Hotel Carlton*, is a magnificent specimen of the traditional kafeneion.
    Herein, Athenians sip coffee and tumble their worry beads, as they must have done since the turn of the century.

Bretania Cafe
Directions: Bordering Omonia Square, on the left-hand side (*Acropolis behind one or, more easily, facing the Hotel Omonia*) of the junction with Athinas St.
    An excellent, very old-fashioned, 'sticky' sweet cake shop which is rather more a galaktozacharoplasteion than a cafe. Renowned for its range of sweets, yoghurt and honey, cream and honey, rice puddings and so on, all served with sugar sweet bread and drinks until 0200hrs every morning. A speciality is 'Flower of the Milk', a cream and yoghurt dish costing 200drs per head.

Continuing on down Athinas St, beyond Plateia Kotzia, leads past the covered meat market building on the left and a number of:-
'Meat Market' Tavernas
Directions: As above and towards the rear of the building. It has to be admitted that it is necessary for prospective diners to pick their way through piles of bones and general market detritus after dark.
    Open 24 hours a day and a find for those who like to slum it, in less expensive establishments of some note.

LYCABETTUS (LYKAVITOS) AREA (*Tmr* F/G4)
As befits a high priced area, these listings are very expensive.

Je Reviens Restaurant 49 Xenokratous St.
Directions: North-east from Kolonaki Sq, up Patriachou Ioakim St to the junction with Odhos Marasli on which turn left and climb a flight of steps until they cross Xenokratous St.
    French food, creditable but expensive. Open midday and evenings.

L'Abreuvoir 51 Xenokratous St.
Directions: As for *Je Reviens*, as are the comments but even more expensive.

104 CANDID GUIDE TO ATHENS

Al Convento Restaurant (*Tmr* G4) 4 Anapiron   Tel 723 9163
Directions: North-east from Kolonaki Sq, along Patriachou Ioakim to Marasli St. Turn left and then right along Odhos Souidias and Anapiron St is nearly at the end.

Bonanza Restaurant 14 Voukourestiou.
Directions: From the north-west corner of Plateia Kolonaki, take Odhos Skoufa, which crosses Voukourestiou St.

Once known as the *Stage Coach*. Not only Wild West in decor, air-conditioned and serving American style food but very expensive with steaks as a house speciality. Why not go to the good old US of A? Lunch and evening meals, open 1200 to 1600hrs and 1900 to 0100hrs.

THE A TO Z OF USEFUL INFORMATION

AIRLINE OFFICE & TERMINUS (*Tmr* 12D/E4/5) The head offices (*Tmr* 12C6) are still at 96 Leoforos Sygrou but the terminus for clients and ticket purchases are on Syntagma Square. The various airport buses drop passengers close to the latter.

Aircraft timetables. See **Chapter Three** for general details of the island airports

BANKS (Trapeza – ΤΡΑΠΕΖΑ) Note that if a bank strike is under way (apparently becoming a natural part of the tourist season 'high jinks'), the National Bank on Syntagma Sq stays open and in business. However, in these circumstances, the place becomes even more than usually crowded. Athens' banks include the:

National Bank of Greece (*Tmr* 3D/E4) 2 Karageorgi Servias, Syntagma Sq.
All foreign exchange services: Mon to Thurs 0800-1400hrs & 1530-1900hrs; Fri 0800-1330hrs & 1500-1900hrs; Sat 0900-1500hrs; Sun & holidays 0900-1300hrs.

Ionian & Popular Bank (*Tmr* D/E/4/5) 1 Mitropoleos St.
Only open normal banking hours.

Commercial Bank of Greece (*Tmr* E4) 11 Panepistimiou (El Venizelou).
Normal banking hours.

American Express (*Tmr* D/E4/5) 2 Ermou St, Syntagma Sq.   Tel 324 4975/9
Carries out usual Amex office transactions and is open Mon to Thurs 0830-1400hrs; Fri 0830-1330hrs & Sat 0820-1230hrs.

There are several banks in the concourse of the East Airport terminal building.

BEACHES Athens is not on a river or by the sea, so to enjoy a beach it is necessary to leave the city and travel to the suburbs. Very often these beaches are operated under the aegis of the NTOG (Greek Tourist Board), or private enterprise in association with a hotel. The NTOG beaches usually have beach huts, cabins, tennis courts, a playground and catering facilities. Entrance charges vary from 25-100drs.

There are beaches and or swimming pools at:

Paleon Faliron/ Faliro	A seaside resort	Bus No. 126: Departs from Odhos Othonos, south side of Syntagma Sq (*Tmr* E5).
Alimos	NTOG beach	Bus No. 133: Departs from Odhos Othonos, south side of Syntagma Sq (*Tmr* E5).
Glyfada(Gilfada)	A seaside resort	Bus Nos. 121, 128, 129: Departs from Leoforos Olgas, south side of the Zappeion Gardens (*Tmr* E5/6).
Voula	NTOG beach Class A	Bus No. 122: Departs from Leoforos Olgas, south side of the Zappeion Gardens (*Tmr* E5/6).
Voula	NTOG beach Class B	Bus No. 122: As above.
	Admission costs: adults 60drs, children 40drs.	
Vouliagmeni	A luxury seaside resort & yacht marina. NTOG beach	Bus Nos. 110, 118, 153: Departs from Leoforos Olgas, south side of the Zappeion Gardens (*Tmr* E5/6). Admission costs: adults 100drs, children 50drs.
Varkiza	A seaside resort & yacht marina. NTOG Beach	Bus Nos. 115, 116, 117: Departs from Leoforos Olgas, south side of the Zappeion Gardens (*Tmr* E5/6). Admission costs: adults 100drs, children 50drs.
	All blue bus fares cost 30drs.	

There are beaches all the way down to Cape Sounion (Sounio) via the coast road. *See* **Bus timetables, A To Z**.

BOOKSELLERS Apart from the second-hand bookshops in the Plaka Flea Market (*See* **Monastiraki Square, Introduction**), there are three or four on Odhos Nikis (west of Syntagma Sq) and Odhos Amerikis (north-west of Syntagma Sq), as well as one on Lysikratous St, opposite the small church (*Tmr* 21D5).

Of all the above it is perhaps invidious to select one but here goes...
The Compendium Bookshop (& Computers) 28 Nikis St. Tel 322 1248
Directions: On the left of Nikis St *(facing Syntagma Sq)*.
Well recommended for a wide range of English language publications. As well as new books they sell some good condition, 'used' books. The owner, Rick Schulein, is happy to buy books back into stock that he has sold to a client. The *Transalpino* travel office is in the basement.

BREAD SHOPS In the more popular shopping areas. For instance, descending along Odhos Adrianou, in the Plaka (*Tmr* D5), from the Odhos Thespidos/Kidathineon end, advances past many shops, general stores and a bread shop (or two).

BUSES & TROLLEY-BUSES These run variously between 0500 and 0030hrs (half an hour past midnight), are usually crowded but excellent value with a 'flat rate' charge of 30Drs. Travel between 0500 and 0800hrs is free, not only on the buses but the Metro as well. Also *See* **Access to the Stations, Trains, A To Z**.

Purchase of Tickets Tickets for both bus & trolley buses have to be purchased at kiosks (peripteros) and inserted in a machine on boarding.

Buses The buses are blue (and green) and bus stops are marked *Stasis* (ΣΤΑΣΙΣ). Some one-man-operated buses are utilised.

Trolley-Buses Yellow coloured vehicles and bus stops. Entered via a door at the front marked *Eisodos* (ΕΙΣΟΔΟΣ), with the exit at the rear, marked *Exodos* (ΕΞΟΔΟΣ).

Major city terminals & turn-round points: include:
Kaningos Sq: (*Tmr* 4D2) North-east of Omonia Sq.
Stadiou/Kolokotroni junction: (*Tmr* D/E4). This has replaced the Korai Sq terminus, now that Korai has been pedestrianised.
Kifissou St: West-north-west of Omonia Sq. The depot on this major highway lies between the junctions of Lenorman and Leoforos Athinon.
Liossion St: (*Tmr* C2) North-west of Omonia Sq.
Eleftherias Sq: (*Tmr* 9C3) North-west of Monastiraki Sq.
Leoforos Olgas: (*Tmr* D/E5/6) South of the National Garden.
Mavrommateon St*: (*Tmr* D/E1) West of Pedion Areos Park, north of Omonia Sq.
* This tree shaded, north-south street is lined with bus departure points.

Egyptou Place (Aigyptou/Egiptou): (*Tmr* D1) Just below the south-west corner of Pedion Areos Park, alongside 28 Ikosiokto Oktovriou.
Ag Asomaton Square: (*Tmr* B/C4) West of Monastiraki Sq.
Koumoundourou St: (*Tmr* C2/3) West of Omonia Sq, third turning off Ag Konstantinou.
(Also *See* **KTEL** & **OSE** terminals listed at the end of this section).

Trolley-bus timetable Some major city routes include:

No. 1:	Plateia Attikis (Metro station) (*Tmr* C1), Leoforos Amalias, **Stathmos Larissis** (railway station), Karaiskaki Place, Ag Konstantinou, **Omonia Sq**, **Syntagma Sq**, Kallithea suburb (SW Athens). Every 10 mins, from 0505-2350hrs.
No. 2:	Kaissariani Pangrati (*Tmr* G6), Leoforos Amalias (Central), **Syntagma Sq**, **Omonia Sq**, 28 Ikosiokto Oktovriou/Patission St, Kipseli (N Athens). Between 0630-0020hrs.
No. 10:	Paleon Faliro, N. Smirni (S Athens), Leoforos Sygrou, **Syntagma Sq**, Kolokotroni junction (*Tmr* D/E4). Between 0500-2345hrs.

Other routes covered by trolley-buses include:

No. 3:	Patissia to Erythrea (N to NNE Athens suburbs). Between 0625-2230hrs.
No. 4:	Odhos Kypselis (*Tmr* E1, North of Pedion Areos Park), **Omonia Sq**, **Syntagma Sq**, Leoforos Olgas to Ag Artemios (SSE Athens suburbs). Between 0630-0020hrs.
No. 5:	Patissia (N Athens suburb), **Omonia Sq**, **Syntagma Sq**, Leoforos Vas. Amalias, Koukaki (S Athens suburb). Between 0630-0015hrs.
No. 6:	Ippokratous St (*Tmr* E3), Panepistimiou St, **Omonia Sq**, N Filadelfia (N Athens suburb). Every 10mins, from 0500-2320hrs.
No. 7:	Panepistimiou St (*Tmr* D/E3/4), 28 Ikosiokto Oktovriou/Patission St, Leoforos Alexandras (N of Lycabettus). Between 0630-0015hrs.
No. 8:	Leoforos Alexandras, 28 Ikosiokto Oktovriou/Patission St, Akadimias. Between 0630-0020hrs.

No. 9:	Odhos Kypselis (*Tmr* E1, North of Pedion Areos Park), 28 Ikosiokto Oktovriou/Patission St, Stadiou St, **Syntagma Sq**, Petralona (W Athens suburb – far side of Filopapou). Every 10mins, from 0455-2345hrs.
No. 10:	Stadiou/Koloktoroni junction (*Tmr* D/E4), **Syntagma Sq**, Leoforos Sygrou, Nea Smirni (S Athens suburb), Paleon Faliro. Every 10mins, from 0500-2345hrs.
No. 11:	Koliatsou (NNE Athens suburb), 28 Ikosiokto Oktovriou/Patission St, Stadiou St, **Syntagma Sq**, Filellinon St, Plastira Sq, Eftichidou St, N Pangrati (ESE Athens suburb). Every 5mins, from 0500-0010hrs.
No. 13:	N. Psychiko, Leoforos Kifissias, Leoforos Vas. Sofias, **Syntagma Sq**, Panepistimiou, 28 Ikosiokto Oktovriou/Patission St, Labrini. Every 10mins, from 0500-2400hrs.
No. 14:	N. Psychiko, Leoforos Kifissias, Leoforos Alexandras, 28 Ikosiokto Oktovriou/Patission, Plateia Papadiamandi.
No. 15:	Vafeiochoriou, Moustoxydi St, Leoforos Alexandras, 28 Ikosiokto Oktovriou/Patission, Stadiou St, **Syntagma Sq**, Filellinon St, Leoforos Vas. Amalias.

Bus timetable Bus numbers are subject to a certain amount of confusion, but here goes! Some of the routes are as follows:

No. 022 & 23:	Nea Kypseli, 28 Ikosiokto Oktovriou/Patission St, Akadimias, Kanari, Marasli, Plateia Elenas Venizelou (SE Lycabettus). Every 10mins, from 0520-2330hrs.
No. 024*:	Kasomouli, Leoforos Amalias (*Tmr* D/E5), **Syntagma Sq**, Panepistimiou St, **Omonia Sq**, Liossion St, Ag Anargyroi. Every 20mins, from 0530-2400hrs.

* This is the bus that delivers passengers to 250 Liossion St (Tmr C2), one of the main bus terminals.

No. 040:	Filellinon St (close to **Syntagma Sq** – *Tmr* D/E4/5), Leoforos Amalias, Leoforos Sygrou to Omiridou Skylitsi, Akti Xaveriou (**Piraeus**). Every 10mins, 24 hours a day. A green bus.
No. 047:	Menandrou St (SW of **Omonia Sq**), **Stathmos Larissis** (railway station), Lofos Skouze (NNW Athens).
No. 049:	Athinas St (*Tmr* C/D3), (S of Omonia Sq), Sofokleous, Pireos, Labrini, Leoforos Vas. Georgiou, Filonos St to Plateia Themistokleous, **Piraeus**. Every 10mins, 24 hours a day. A green bus.
No. 051*:	Menandrou St, off Ag Konstantinou (*Tmr* C2/3, W of **Omonia Sq**), Lenorman St, Palamidiou, Kifissou St. Every 10mins, from 0500-2400hrs.

* This is the bus that connects to the 100 Kifissou St (Tmr A2), a main bus terminal.

No. 115:	Leoforos Olgas (*Tmr* D/E5/6), Leoforos Sygrou, Leoforos Possidonos (coast road) to Vouliagmeni & Varkiza (S Athens coastal suburbs). Every 20mins, 24 hours a day.
No. 116, 117	Leoforos Olgas, Varkiza (S Athens coastal suburb).
No. 118:	Leoforos Olgas, Leoforos Sygrou, Leoforos Possidonos (coast road) to Vouliagmeni (S Athens coastal suburb). Every 20mins, from 1245-2015hrs.
No. 121,128, 129:	Leoforos Olgas (*Tmr* E6), Glyfada (SSE Athens coastal suburb).
No. 122:	Leoforos Olgas, Leoforos Sygrou, Leoforos Possidonos (coast road) to Voula (S Athens coastal suburb). Every 20mins, from 0530-2400hrs.
No. 132:	Othonos St **Syntagma Sq** – *Tmr* D/E4/5), Filellinon St, Leoforos Amalias, Leoforos Sygrou to Edem (SSE Athens suburb). Every 20mins, from 0530-1900hrs.
No. 153:	Leoforos Olgas, Vouliagmeni (SSE Athens coastal suburb).
No. 224:	Mitropetrova (Polygono N Athens suburb), 28 Ikosiokto Oktovriou/Patission St, Leoforos Alexandras, Kaningos Sq, Akadamias St, Vassilissis Sofias, Leoforos Vas. Alexandrou, Leoforos Ethnikis Antistaseos, Kaisariani (E Athens suburb). Every 20mins, from 0500-2400hrs.
No. 230:	Goudi, Leoforos Alexandras, Ippokratous St, Akadimias St, **Syntagma Sq**, Dionysiou Areopagitou, Thission. Every 10mins, from 0500-2320hrs.
No. 405:	Yp. Ethnikis Amynas, Leoforos Alexandras, **Stathmos Larissis** (railway station).
No. 527:	Kaningos Sq, (*Tmr* 4D2) Akadimias St, Leoforos Alexandras, Leoforos Kifissias, A. Pefki-Marousi. Every 15mins, from 0615-2215hrs.
No. 538, 539:	Kaningos Sq, Kifissia (NNE Athens suburb).
No. 603:	Akadimias St (*Tmr* D/E 3/4) to Psychiko (NE Athens suburb).
No. 610:	Akadimias St to Filothei (NE Athens suburb).
No. 853, 862,:	Plateia Eleftherias (*Tmr* 9B/C 3/4), Iera Odos, Elefsina (Elefsis – West of Athens, beyond Dafni).
No. 873:	Deligiorgi (Omonia Sq), Dafni (W Athens suburb).

Attica buses & timetable (orange buses) include:
Athens – Rafina: depart from 29, Mavrommateon St (*Tmr* D/E1).One-way fare 160drs.
Athens – Nea Makri: depart from 29, Mavrommateon St. One-way fare 200drs.
Athens – Marathon: depart from 29, Mavrommateon St. One-way fare 250drs.
Athens – Lavrio*: depart from 14, Mavrommateon St. One-way fare 330drs.
Athens – Oropos: depart from 14, Mavrommateon St. One-way fare 320drs.
* See Athens – Sounion details following.
All above depart every 45 minutes between 0600-2215hrs.

Athens –	Sounion – West coast road: depart from 14 Mavrommateon St Every half hour between 0600-1830hrs.
Return	0540, 0630, then every half hour between 0800-2000hrs & 2100hrs. One-way fare 420drs, duration 1 ½hrs.
Athens –	Sounion – via Markopoulo & Lavrio: depart from 14 Mavrommateon St. Every hour between 0600-1730hrs.
Return	Every hour between 0730-2130hrs. One-way fare 390drs, duration 1½hrs.
Athens –	Vravron: Take either the Sounion bus, via Markopoulo, or the Lavrio bus, get off at Markopoulo & catch a local bus to Vravron. One-way fare 260drs.

The rest of Greece is served by:
1) KTEL A pool of bus operators working through one company from two terminals. 260 Liossion St* and 100 Kifissou St**

* **Liossion St** (*Tmr* C2) is to the east of Stathmos Peloponissou Railway Station. This terminus serves Halkida, Edipsos, Kimi, Delphi, Amfissa, Kamena Vourla, Larissa, Thiva, Trikala (Meteora), Livadia, Lamia.
Refer to bus route No. 024 for transport to this terminus.

** **Kifissou St** (*Tmr* A2) is to the west north-west of Omonia Sq, beyond the 'steam railway' lines, across Leoforos Konstantinoupoleos and up either Leoforos Athinon and turn right, or Odhos Lenorman and turn left. This terminus serves Patras, Pirgos (Olympia), Nafplio (Mikines), Adritsena (Vasses), Kalamata, Sparti (Mistras), Githio (Diros), Tripolis, Messolongi, Igoumenitsa, Preveza, Ioanina, Corfu, Zakynthos, Cephalonia, Lefkas, Kozani, Kastoria, Florina, Grevena, Veria, Naoussa, Edessa, Seres, Kilkis, Kavala, Drama, Komotini, Korinthos, Kranidi, Xilokastro.
Refer to Bus route No. 051 for transport to this terminus.

2) OSE (The State Railway Company) Their buses terminus alongside the main railway stations of Stathmos Peloponissou and Larissis. Apart from the domestic services, there is a terminal for other European capitals, including Paris, Istanbul and Munich, at Stathmos Larissis Station.

CAMPING *See* **The Accommodation**.

CAR HIRE As any other capital city, numerous offices, the majority of which are dotted about the smarter areas and squares, such as Syntagma Sq and Leoforos Amalias. Apart from the international firms of *Avis* and *Hertz* typical is: **Pappas**, 44 Leoforos Amalias Tel 322 0087.
There are any number of car hire (and travel) firms in and around the airport, bus and train locations, as well as on the right of Leoforos Sygrou, descending from the 'spaghetti junction' south of the Temple of Olympian Zeus (*Tmr* D6).

CAR REPAIR Help and advice can be obtained by contacting: **The Automobile & Touring Club of Greece (ELPA)**, (*Tmr* I/3) 2 Messogion St Tel 779 1615. For immediate, emergency attention dial 104.
There are dozens of back street car repairers, breakers and spare part shops parallel and to the west of Leoforos Sygrou, in the area between the Temple of Olympian Zeus and the Olympic Airline terminal.

CINEMAS There are a large number of cinemas in Athens. Do not worry about a language barrier as the majority of the films have English (American) dialogue with Greek subtitles. From the end of May to September, there are only outdoor cinemas, most of which are bunched together on the streets of Stadiou, Panepistimiou and Patission.
Aigli in the Zappeion is a must and is situated at the south end of the National Garden.
Cine Paris in Kidathineon St, Plaka is the best as it is clean, free from traffic noise and there is a spectacular view of the Acropolis lit up at night.
Note that the outdoor cinemas only show old films which are generally poor quality with scratches, hisses, jumps, long black gaps and or loss of sound. There are two performances an evening, the first at about 2100hrs and the second at 2300hrs. I advise cinema-goers to attend the first performance. Although the first few minutes of the film may be difficult to see (the last moments of daylight), the sound is almost always turned down in the second performance, which can be very frustrating!
From September to May, it is the turn of the indoor cinemas of which there are a great number. In contrast to their outdoor 'cousins', the films shown are up-to-date, new releases. Recommended are:-
Radio City – Koliatsu Sq, Patission.
and
The Studio – Plateia Amerikis, Patission - very comfortable and shows more alternative films.

CLUBS, BARS & DISCOS Why leave home? But if you must, there are enough to go round.

COMMERCIAL SHOPPING AREAS During daylight hours a very large street market ranges along Odhos Athinas (*Tmr* C3/4), Odhos Sokratous and the associated side streets from Ermou St, almost all the way up to Omonia Sq. After dark the shutters are drawn down, the stalls canvassed over and the 'ladies of the night' appear.

Plateia Kotzia (*Tmr* C/D3) spawns a flower market on Sundays, whilst the Parliament Building side of Vassilissis Sofias (*Tmr* E4) is lined with smart flower stalls that open daily.

Monastiraki Sq (*Tmr* 5C4) and the various streets that radiate off are abuzz, specialising in widely differing aspects of the commercial and tourist trade. Odhos Areos contains a plethora of leather goods shops; the near end of Ifestou Lane is edged by stall upon stall of junk and tourist 'omit-abilia' (forgettable memorabilia); Pandrossou Lane contains a better class of shop and stall selling sandals, pottery and smarter 'memorabilia', while the square itself has a number of handcart hawkers.

The smart department stores are conveniently situated in or around Syntagma Sq, and the main streets that radiate off the square, including Ermou, Stadiou and Panepistimiou, as well in and around Omonia Square. Anyone tempted to buy may well be surprised at the comparatively expensive prices.

Tapestries are an extremely good buy. A reliable shop is sited close to and on the far side (*From Syntagma Sq*) of Kapnikarea Church (*Tmr* 6 D4), on Ermou St.

In the area south of Syntagma Sq, on the junction of Apollonos and Pendelis Sts, close by Odhos Voulis, are three small, obliging fruit and greengrocery shops. Apollonos St is useful to shoppers because, close by the junction with Odhos Nikis and on the right-hand side, is a combined fruit and butcher's shop. Next door is a stick souvlaki snackbar and across the road an ironmongers.

See **Bread Shops** & **Trains, A To Z** for details of other markets and shopping areas.

EMBASSIES

Australia: 37 Dem. Soutsou.	Tel 641 1712
Belgium: 3 Sekeri St.	Tel 361 7886
Canada: 4 Ioannou Gennadiou St.	Tel 723 9511
Denmark: 15 Philikis Etairias Sq.	Tel 724 9315
Finland: 1 Eratosthenous & Vas. Konstantinou Sts.	Tel 751 9795
France: 7 Vassilissis Sofias.	Tel 361 1663
German Federal Republic (West Germany): 10 Vass Sofias.	Tel 369 4111
Great Britain: 1 Ploutarchou & Ypsilantou Sts.	Tel 723 6211
Ireland: 7 Vassileos Konstantinou.	Tel 723 2771
Netherlands: 5-7 Vassileos Konstantinou.	Tel 723 9701
New Zealand: 15-17 Tshoa St.	Tel 641 0311
Norway: 7 Vassileos Konstantinou St.	Tel 724 6173
South Africa: 124 Kifissias/Iatridou.	Tel 692 2125
Sweden: 7 Vassileos Konstantinou St.	Tel 722 4504
USA: 91 Vassilissis Sofias.	Tel 721 2951

FERRY-BOAT & FLYING DOLPHIN TICKET OFFICES Apart from the headquarters, most, if not all, ferry-boat ticket offices are located in Piraeus Port, as is the main *Ceres Flying Dolphin* booking office. Incidentally, the latter are the hydrofoils that service the Argo-Saronic and Sporades islands. There is also a *Ceres* first floor office in the building immediately to the left of the *National Bank* (*Tmr* 3D/E4) (*Syntagma Sq behind one*). Despite the staff being disinterested, they are able to hand over a comprehensive timetable and prices.

HAIRDRESSERS No problems, with sufficient in the main shopping areas.

LAUNDERETTES There are others but a good, central recommendation must be:
Coin-op (*Tmr* 13D5) Angelou Geronda.
Directions: From Kidathineon St (*proceeding towards Syntagma Sq*), at the far end of Plateia Plaka turn right down Angelou Geronda, towards Odhos Dedalou, and the launderette is on the right

A machine load costs 300drs, 9 mins of dryer time 150drs and a measure of powder 50drs. In respect of the detergent, why not pop out to Kidathineon St and purchase a small packet of *Tide* for some 80drs? For customers who are busy and are prepared to leave the laundry behind, the staff supervise the wash and dry operation at an extra cost of 600drs. Open daily between 0900-1900/2000hrs. Note that my lavatorial obsession would not be satisfied without mentioning the Public toilet sited on Plateia Plaka.

Other launderettes are situated in Odhos Psarion, north of Plateia Karaiskaki (*Tmr* B/C2), and in Didotou St (*Tmr* E3), close to the junction with Odhos Zoodochos Pigis. The more usual Athens style is for customers to leave their washing at any one of the countless laundries, collecting it next day dry, stiff and bleached (if necessary).

ATHENS 109

LOST PROPERTY The main office is situated at 33 Ag Konstantinou (Tel 523 0111), the Plateia Omonia end of Ag Konstantinou. The telephone number is that of the Transport police who are now in charge of lost property (or *Grafio Hamenon Adikimenon*). Another 'lost & found' telephone number is 770 5771. It is still true to say that you are far more likely to 'lose' personal belongings to other tourists, than to Greeks.

LUGGAGE STORE There is one at No. 26 Nikis St (*Tmr* D5) advertising the service at a cost of 100drs per day per piece, 350drs per week and 1000drs per month. Many hotels, guest houses and pensions 'mind' a clients' bags, quite a number at no charge.

MEDICAL CARE
Chemists/Pharmacies (Farmakio – ΦΑΡΜΑΚΕΙΟ) Identified by a green or red cross on a white background. Normal opening hours and a rota operates to give a 'duty' chemist cover.
Dentists & Doctors Ask at the **First Aid Centre** for the address of the School of Dentistry, where free treatment is available. Both dentists and doctors advertise widely and there is no shortage of practitioners.
First Aid Centre (KAT) (*Tmr* 14D2) 21 Tritis Septemvriou St, beyond the Chalkokondili turning and on the left. Tel 150
Hospital (*Tmr* 15G4) Do not proceed direct to a hospital (or *Go*) but initially attend the **First Aid Centre**. When necessary they direct patients to the correct destination.
Medical Emergency: Tel 166

METRO/ELEKTRIKOS (ΗΣΑΜ) The Athens underground, or subway system, operates below ground in the heart of the city and overground for the rest of the journey. It is a simple, one track layout from Kifissia (NE Athens suburb) to Piraeus (SW of Athens), and represents marvellous value at 30drs. The service operates every 10 mins between 0500 and 2400hrs and travel before 0800hrs is free, as it is on the buses. Keep an eye open for the old-fashioned wooden carriages.
Purchase of Tickets Passengers must have the requisite coins to obtain a ticket from the machine, prior to gaining access to the platforms. Everyone is most helpful and will, if the ticket machine 'frightens' a chap, show how it should be operated. Take care, select the ticket value first, then put the coins in the slot and don't forget to keep the ticket so as to be able to hand it in at the journey's end. The station ticket office men will not give change or tickets, unless ten are purchased at a time.
Station Stops There used to be 21 stations, but there are two new stations – KAT, between Maroussi & Kifissia, and Tavros, between Kalithea & Petralona. Others include Kifissia (NE suburb), Stathmos Attiki (for the main railway stations), Plateia Victorias (N Athens), Omonia Sq, Monastiraki Sq (for the Plaka), Plateia Thission (for the Acropolis) and (Piraeus) Port.
Incidentally, from the outside, the Piraeus terminus is rather difficult to locate, the entrance being in the left-hand corner of what appears to be an oldish, waterfront building.
See **Access to the stations**, **Trains**, **A To Z**.

MUSIC & DANCING *See* **Clubs, Bars & Discos, A To Z,** & **The Eating Out**.

NTOG (EOT) The headquarters of the National Tourist Organisation (NTOG) or, in Greek, the EOT (Ellinikos Organismos Tourismou – ΕΛΛΗΝΙΚΟΣ ΟΡΓΑΝΙΣΜΟΣ ΤΟΥΡΙΣΜΟΥ) is on the 5th floor at 2 Amerikis St (*Tmr* E4), close by Syntagma Sq. But this office does not handle the usual tourist enquiries, although the commissionaires manning the desk do hand out bits and pieces of information.
  The information desk, from whence a free Athens map, advice, information folders, bus and boat schedules and hotel facts may be obtained, is situated inside and on the left of the foyer of the: *National Bank of Greece* (*Tmr* 3D/E4) 2 Karageorgi Servias, Syntagma Sq Tel 322 2545 *See* **Banks, A To Z** for directions. Do not hope to obtain anything other than pamphlets and a snatch of guidance, as it would be unrealistic to expect personal attention from staff besieged by wave upon wave of tourists of every creed, race and colour. In fact the staff are generally very unfriendly and unhelpful. The Athens hotel information sheets handed out now include a list of Class D & E establishments. The desks are open as follows:- Mon-Thurs 0800-1400hrs & 1500-1900hrs; Fri 0800-1330hrs & 1500-1900hrs; Sat 0900-1500hrs; Sun & holidays 0900-1300hrs.
  There is now a sign requesting, if there are long queues, that enquirers use the tourist information office inside the *General Bank*, situated at the junction of Ermou St and Syntagma Sq. In total contrast to the National Bank, the staff at this desk are extremely helpful.

110 CANDID GUIDE TO ATHENS

There is also an NTOG office sited at the East Airport but it has rarely, if ever, been observed open, no matter what time of day or night! The leaflets are within easy grasp.

OPENING HOURS *See* **Chapter Seven**.

OTE There are offices at: No. 85, 28 Ikosiokto Oktovriou/Patission St (*Tmr* 16D1) (open 24hrs a day); 15 Stadiou St (*Tmr* 17D4) (open Mon to Fri 0700-2400hrs, Sat & Sun 0800-2400hrs); 53 Solonos (*Tmr* E3) and 7 Kratinou (Plateia Kotzia) (*Tmr* C/D3) (open between 0800 and 2400hrs). There is also an office at 45 Athinas St (*Tmr* C/D3).

PLACES OF INTEREST Most areas are described in the **Introduction**.

Parliament Building (*Tmr* E4/5) Syntagma Sq. Here it is possible to watch the Greek equivalent of the British 'Changing the Guard at Buckingham Palace'. The special guards (*Evzones*) are spectacularly outfitted with tasselled red caps, white shirts (blouses do I hear?), coloured waistcoats, a skirt, white tights, knee-garters and boots topped off with pom-poms. The ceremony officially kicks off at 1100hrs on Sunday morning but seems to falter into action at about 1045hrs. Incidentally, there is a band thrown in for good measure.

Museums The seasons are split as follow: Winter (1st Nov-31st March) & Summer (1st April-31st Oct). Museums are closed on: 1st Jan, 25th March, Good Friday, Easter Day & Christmas Day. Sunday hours are kept on Epiphany, Ash Monday, Easter Saturday, Easter Monday, 1st May, Whit Sunday, Assumption Day, 28th October & Boxing Day. They are only open in the mornings on Christmas Eve, New Year's Eve, 2nd January, Easter Thursday & Easter Tuesday. Museums are closed on Tuesdays, unless otherwise indicated. Only students with ISIC cards will achieve a reduction in fees.

Acropolis (*Tmr* C5). The museum exhibits finds made on the site. Of special interest are the sixth century BC statues of Korai women. Entrance charges are included in the admission fee to the Acropolis, which costs 600drs per head and is open Summer months: weekdays 0800-1930hrs; Sat, Sun & holidays 0830-1800hrs. The Museum hours follow suit except on Mondays when it does not open until 1100hrs.

Benaki (*Tmr* E/F4) On the corner of Vassilissis Sofias and Koubari (Koumbari) St, close by Plateia Kolonaki. A very interesting variety of exhibits made up from private collections. Particularly diverting is a display of costumes. Open Summer months: daily 0830-1400hrs & closed Tues. Entrance 200drs.

Byzantine (*Tmr* F4/5) 22 Vassilissis Sofias. As one would deduce from the name – Byzantine art. Open Summer hours: daily 0835-1500hrs; closed Mon. Entrance costs 300drs.

Goulandris 13 Levidou St, Kifissia, N Athens. Natural History. Open Summer months: daily 0900-1400hrs; closed Fri. Entrance costs 150drs.

Goulandris (*Tmr* F4) 4 Neophitou Douka St (off Vassilissis Sofias). The second or 'other' Goulandris Museum. The situation is not helped by the little quirk of some people referring to the Natural History Museum as 'Goulandris'. Help! This Goulandris, that is the *Cycladic & Ancient Greek Art Goulandris Museum*, is open daily in the Summer months: weekdays 1000-1600hrs; Sat 1000-1500hrs; closed Tues, Sun & holidays. Entrance costs 150drs.

Kanellopoulos (*Tmr* C5) On the corner of Theorias and Panos Sts, in the Plaka, and located at the foot of the northern slope of the Acropolis, at the Monastiraki end. A smaller version of the *Benaki Museum* open Summer months: daily 0830-1500hrs; closed Mon. Entrance costs 200drs.

Keramikos (*Tmr* B4) 148 Ermou St. Finds from Keramikos cemetery. Open Summer months: daily 0830-1500hrs; closed on Mon. Entrance to the site and museum costs 200drs.

National Gallery & Alexandros Soutzos (*Tmr* G4) 46 Vassileos Konstantinou/Sofias. Mainly 19th and 20th century Greek paintings. Open Summer months: weekdays 0900-1500hrs; Sun & holidays 1000-1400hrs; closed on Mon. Admission costs 30drs.

National Historical & Ethnological (*Tmr* D4) Kolokotroni Sq, off Stadiou St. Greek history and the War of Independence. Open Summer months: weekdays 0900-1330hrs; Sat, Sun & holidays 0900-1300hrs; closed Mon. Entrance costs 100drs.

National Archaeological (*Tmr* D/E2) 1 Tossitsa St, off 28 Ikosiokto Oktovriou/Patission St. The largest and possibly the most important Greek museum, covering a wide variety of exhibits. A must if you are a museum buff. Open Summer months: weekdays 0800-1700hrs; Mon 1100-1700hrs; Sat, Sun

& holidays 0830-1500hrs. Entrance costs 500drs, which includes entrance to the *Santorini* and *Numismatic* exhibitions (*See* below).
Also housed in the same building are the:
Numismatic Displaying, as would be imagined, a collection of Greek coins, spanning the ages. Open Summer months: weekdays 0830-1500hrs; closed on Mon. Admission is free.
as well as the:
Epigraphical Collection, Santorini & *The Casts & Copies Exhibition*: Open Summer months: as for the *Numismatic Exhibition*.
Popular (Folk) Art (*Tmr* D5) 17 Kidathineon St, The Plaka. Folk art, folklore and popular art. Open Summer months: daily 1000-1400hrs; closed on Mon. Entrance costs 200drs.
War (*Tmr* F4/5) 2 Rizari St, off Leoforos Vassilissis Sofias. Warfare exhibits covering a wide variety of subjects. Open Summer months: daily 0900-1400hrs; closed on Mon. Entrance is free.

Theatres & Performances For full, up-to-date details enquire at the NTOG enquiry desk (*Tmr* 3D/E4) (*See* **NTOG, A To Z**). They should be able to hand out a pamphlet giving a precise timetable for the particular year. As a guide the following are performed year in and year out:
Son et Lumiere. From the *Pynx* hillside, a *Son et Lumiere* features the Acropolis. This show is produced from early April to the end of October. The English performance starts at 2100hrs every evening, except when the moon is full, and takes 45 minutes. There are French versions at 2215hrs daily, except Tues & Fri when a German commentary is provided at 2200hrs.

Tickets and information are available from the *Athens Festival booking office* (*See Athens Festival*) or at the Pynx, prior to the outset of the show. Tickets cost 500drs (students 200drs), and are also available at the entrance of the Church, Ag Dimitros Lombardiaris, on the way to the show. Catch a Bus No. 230 along Dionysiou Areopagitou St, getting off one stop beyond the *Odeion (Theatre) of Herodes Atticus* and follow the signposted path on the left-hand side.

Athens Festival This prestigious event takes place in the restored and beautiful Odeion of Herodes Atticus. This was built in approximately AD 160 as a Roman theatre, seating about 5000 people and situated at the foot of the south-west corner of the Acropolis. This Festival lasts from the middle of June to the middle of September, and consists of a series of plays, ballet, concerts and opera. The performances usually commence at 2100hrs and tickets, which are on sale up to 10 days before the event, are obtainable from the Theatre one hour prior to the commencement of the show or from the Athens Festival booking office (*Tmr* D/E4) at 4 Stadiou St, Tel 322 1459.

Dora Stratou Theatre (*Tmr* A6) A short stroll away on *Mouseion* or *Hill of Muses*. On the summit stands the *Monument of the Filopapou (Philopappos)* and, nearby, the Dora Stratou Theatre, where an internationally renowned troupe of folk dancers, dressed in traditional costumes, perform a series of Greek dances and songs. The theatre group operates daily from about the middle of May to the end of September. The show starts at 2225hrs, that is except Wed & Sun when they perform at 2015 & 2225hrs. Ticket prices vary from 750-950drs (students reduced rates) and are available between 0900-1400hrs (Tel 324 4395) & 1900-2300hrs (Tel 921 4650).

Performances are timed to coincide with the ending of the *Son et Lumiere*, on the *Pynx*.

Lycabettus Theatre On the north-east side of Lycabettus Hill. Concerts and theatrical performances take place at the hillside sited open-air theatre, between the middle of June and the first week of September, from 2100hrs. Tickets can be purchased from the theatre box office, one hour before the event, or from the *Athens Festival booking office*, referred to previously under *Athens Festival*.

Wine Festival Held daily at Dafni, between 1900-0030hrs, from the 1st July to 20th August. Ticket price 300drs per head, students 150drs. Information and tickets from the *Athens Festival office*.

POLICE *See* **Tourist Police, A To Z**.

POST OFFICES (Tachidromio – ΤΑΧΤΔΡΟΜΕΙΟΞ) The Central Post Office at 100 Eolou St (*Tmr* 18D3), close by Omonia Sq, is open between Mon-Fri 0730-2000hrs; Sat 0730-1415hrs. The main Syntagma Post Office has been newly refurbished and opens Mon-Fri between 0730-2000hrs; Sat 0730-1415hrs & Sun 0900-1330hrs. Branch offices are situated at the Omonia Sq underground Metro concourse and on Dionysiou Areopagitou St, at the corner of Tzireon St (*Tmr* D6).

The telephone and telegraph system is run by a separate state organisation. For details of the telephone service *See* **OTE, A To Z**.

SPORTS FACILITIES

Golf. There is an 18 hole course, the *Glifida Golf Club* (Tel 894 6820) close by the East Airport. Changing rooms, restaurant and refreshment bar.

Horse Riding. A number of stables including the *Hellenic Riding Club* (Tel 681 2506), Maroussio (NNE Athens suburb) & the *Athens Riding Club* (Tel 661 1088), Gerakas (ENE Athens suburb).

Swimming. There is a *Swimming (& Tennis) Club* on Leoforos Olgas (*Tmr* 19E6), across the way from the Zappeion National Gardens. *The Hilton Hotel* (*Tmr* G4) has a swimming pool but, if you are not staying there, use of it costs the price of an (expensive) meal. See **Beaches, A To Z**.

Tennis. There are courts at most of the NTOG beaches (See **Beaches, A To Z**), as well as at the *Ag Kosmas Athletics Centre* (Tel 894 8900), close by the West airport.

TAXIS (ΤΑΞ) Used extensively and, although they seem to me to be expensive, are 'officially' the cheapest in Europe. The Athens drivers are, now, generally without scruples. The metered fares cost about 34drs per kilometre in the centre and 58drs per kilometre in the suburbs, with a minimum fare of 200drs. But these are subject to various surcharges, including 20drs for each piece of baggage, 250drs per hour of waiting time and 50drs for collection from, or delivery to, public transport facilities. After 0100hrs charges are doubled. Prospective fares, standing at a taxi rank, must be picked up but taxis are not obliged to stop when cruising, for which there is an extra 'flag falling' charge of 25drs. The sign ΕΛΕΘΕΡΟΝ indicates a cab is free for hire. Passengers must ensure that the meter is zeroed at the start of any journey.

Sample fares include: Syntagma/Omonia Square to the East airport 650drs and to the West airport 550drs; the East airport to Piraeus 650drs and the West airport to Piraeus 500drs. The Syntagma taxi station telephone number is 323 7942.

TELEPHONES See **OTE**.

TOILETS Apart from the facilities sited at the various bus termini and the railway stations, there is a super public toilet on the south-east corner of Syntagma Sq, as there is a pretty grim 'squatty' in the Omonia Sq Metro concourse (which latter costs 20drs). The Plaka is well 'endowed' with one at Plateia Plaka, (on Odhos Kidathineon) and another on the Plateia Agora, at the other end of Odhos Adrianou. Visitors to Mt. Lycabettus will not be 'caught short' and the toilets there are spotless.

TOURIST OFFICE/AGENCIES See **NTOG & Travel Agents & Tour Offices, A To Z**.

TOURIST POLICE (*Tmr* 20D6) Despite the reorganisation of the service, the Athens headquarters remains in operation. This is situated at 7 Leoforos Sygrou (Sygrou/Syngrou/Singrou Av) (Tel 923-9224) and is open daily 0800-2100hrs. Tourist information in English is available on the telephone number 171.

There are also Tourist police offices close by and just to the north of Larissis Railway Station (open 0700-2300hrs, tel 821 3574) and the East airport (open 24 hours a day, tel 981 4093/969 9500).

TRAINS (Illustration 7) They arrive at (or depart from) either (a) Larissis Station (Stathmos No. 1) or (b) Peloponissou Station (Stathmos No. 2).

Advance Booking Office . Information and advance booking for both stations is handled at: No. 6 Sina (*Tmr* E3, tel 363 4402/4406) off Akadimias St; No. 1 Karolou (Satovriandou (*Tmr* C2, tel 524 0601/6) west of Omonia Sq & No. 17 Filellinon (*Tmr* D/E5, tel 323 6747/6253).

Toilets The station toilets usually, well always, lack toilet paper.

Sustenance (on the train) An attendant brings inexpensive drinks and snacks around, from time to time, and hot snacks are available from platform trolleys at the major railway stations.

Railway Head office (*Tmr* C2) Hellenic Railways Organisation (OSE), 1-3 Karolou St. Tel 522 2491 This office is one back from the far end of Ag Konstantinou, west from Omonia Sq.

Provisions Shopping in the area of the railway stations is made easy by the presence of the Street Market on Odhos Chiou (See **Larissis Station, Trains**).

Access to the stations

Bus/Trolley-bus. From the Airport, travel on the buses B & Ḃ which proceed directly to the Railway stations. The only trolley-bus which proceeds past the stations is No. 1.

From Piraeus Port catch the No. 40 (green) bus that 'routes' along Leoforos Vassileos Konstantinou (parallel to the quay) as far as Syntagma Sq, or the No. 049 from Plateia Themistokleous to Athinas

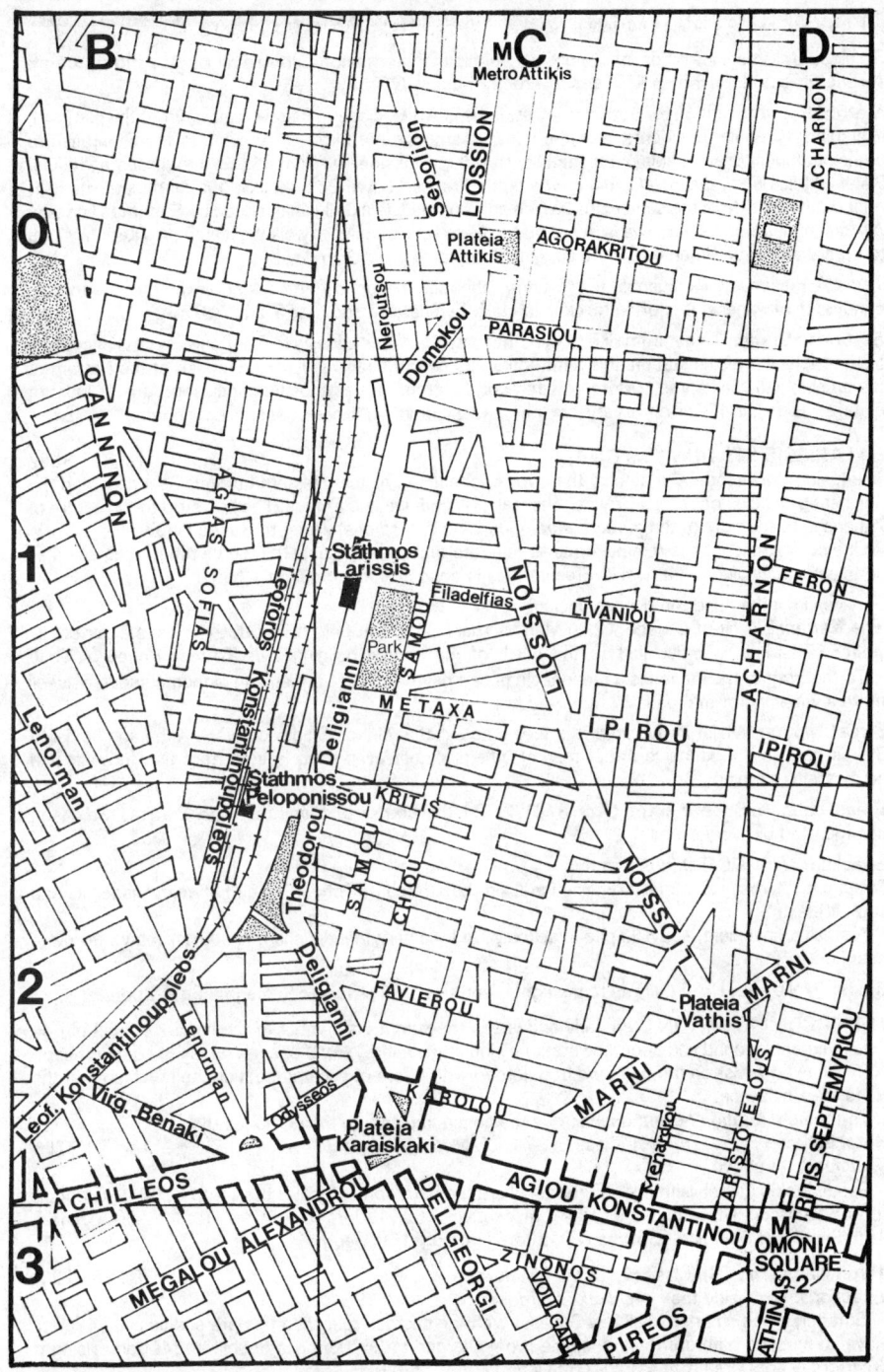

Illustration 7 Athens inset - The Railway Stations

St, close by Omonia Sq. For other possibly conflicting information *See* **Arrival by Air, Introduction;** **Airline offices & terminus** & **Buses & Trolley-buses, A To Z.**

Metro The metro station for both railway stations is Attiki, close to Plateia Attikis. From the platform, assuming a traveller has come from the south, dismount and turn right down into the underpass to come out the far or west side of the station, on Odhos Liossion. Turn left and walk to the large irregular Plateia Attikis (*with the Hotel Lydia on the right*). Proceed down Domokou St (the road that exits half-right on the far side of the square) and which spills onto Plateia Deligianni, edged by Stathmos Larissis. A more long-winded alternative is to get off the Metro at Omonia Sq, walk west along Ag Konstantinou to Karaiskaki Sq and then up Odhos Deligianni, or catch a No. 1 trolley-bus.

Taxis A reasonable indulgence, if in a hurry, although it must be noted that, in the crowded traffic conditions of Athens, it is often quicker to walk than catch a cab. *See* **Taxis, A To Z.**

Station to Station To get from one to the other, say Stathmos Larissis to Peloponissou, it is necessary to turn right out of the station and climb the steps over the railway line, turning left at the bottom of the far side and walk some 100m to the forecourt in front of Stathmos Peloponissou. Almost, but not quite adjacent, if 150m on a very hot day, laden down with cases seems contiguous.

(A) LARISSIS STATION (*Tmr* B/C1)   Tel 821 3882
The main, more modern station of the two. Connections to the Western European services and the northern provinces of Central Greece, Thessaly, Macedonia and Thrace. The bus stop to the centre of Athens is to the right of the station (*station building behind one*). Refer to **Buses** below.

One correspondent has reminded me to reiterate that it is advisable to reserve return train seats as soon as is possible after arrival in Greece. This is done at the International 'hatch'.

Services in and around the building include:
The National Bank of Greece. Open Mon to Thurs 0830-1400hrs & Fri 0830-1330hrs. **Tourist police.** There is an office just to the north of the station building. *See* **Tourist Police, A To Z.**

To the front of the station is a reasonable priced pavement cafe-bar and an elongated square – well more a widening of the road.

Street Market Whilst in this area it is worth noting that Odhos Chiou, between Kritis and Favierou Sts, is host to an extensive street market where almost everything is sold from fish to meat and hardware to clothing.

Bread shop & Supermarket (*Tmr* B/C1/2) On the corner of Samou St and Eratyras St. A bit disorganised but very useful.

Snackbar (*Tmr* B/C1) Odhos Samou.
Directions: Across the street from the Park, on the stretch of Odhos Samou between Filadelfias and Leof. Metaxa Sts.

A small, convenient, souvlaki pita snackbar, run by a very friendly chap. A souvlaki and a bottle of beer costs 150drs.

Buses: Trolley-bus No. 1 pulls up to the right of the station. The fare to Syntagma Sq is 30drs.

THE ACCOMMODATION Even early and late in the summer a number of the hardier stretch out on the pavements around and about the stations (and at the nearby *Hotel Oscar's* rates I'm not surprised). Arrivals, even whilst on the train, are bombarded with offers of accommodation, so much so that the touts are a nuisance.

To the right (*Station behind one*) across the concourse and on the corner, is the:
Hotel Lefkos Pirgos (*Tmr* C1) (Class E) 27 Leof. Metaxa/Deligianni   Tel 821 3765
Directions: As above.

Seedy looking establishment. All rooms share the bathrooms. Singles start off at 790drs & double rooms 1580drs. These prices increase, respectively, to 1190drs & 1685drs (1st May-30th June & 16th Sept-31st Dec) and 1360drs & 2180drs (1st July-15th Sept).

Hotel Nana (*Tmr* C1) (Class B), 29 Leof.Metaxa   Tel 884 2211
Directions: Alongside the *Hotel Lefkos Pirgos*.

Smarter, much smarter (well it is B class) with the charges reflecting this pre-eminence. All rooms have an en suite bathroom with a single room charged at 2670drs & a double at 3400drs, rising to 3740drs & 4660drs (16th March-31st Oct).

Directly opposite the main station entrance is the:
Hotel Oscar (*Tmr* C1) (Class B), 25 Samou/Filadelfias   Tel 883 4215
Directions: As above.
  I hardly dare detail the room rates, which for a double room kicks off at 5720drs rising to 6740drs en suite, naturally. Breakfast costs 465drs. I must own up to one staying at the Oscar. But it was at the end of a long stint on the Greek islands, added to which there were a couple of other (good) reasons. Firstly they accept payment by *Amex* which, as I have written before, may be of great assistance in eking out dwindling funds, and secondly, the hotel is conveniently close to the railway and the inter-country coach station. Thus the comforts of this hotel, or similar, can be put to good use in order to build up the bodily reserves, prior to a long distance bus or railway journey! That is not to say that even this luxurious establishment does not escape some of the common faults oft experienced as a 'norm' when staying at lower classified 'cousins'. The en suite bathroom of our room had a loose lavatory seat, the bath plug had no chain attached (there was a chain, but it was not attached) and the small bathroom window was tied up with string. The sliding balcony window would not completely shut – there was no locking mechanism and the air conditioning didn't. Mind you, I must admit to making a reservation without Rosemary, who guarded our backpacks whilst I sorted out the formalities. It may have been the sight of the two, towering, aforementioned packs reversing through the swing doors into the reception that resulted in our being allocated this particular 'downtown' room, at the rear of the hotel, overlooking and overlooked by the backsides of a block of flats.

Hotel Elena (Helena) (*Tmr* B/C1) (Class C) 2 Psiloriti/Samou   Tel 881 3211
Directions: Along Samou St, south from Leof. Metaxa St, and on the right.
  Approximate rates are as follows:- single rooms, sharing the bathroom, cost 1400drs & en suite 1995drs; double rooms sharing are charged at 2000drs & en suite 2550drs.

Hotel Louvre (*Tmr* C2) (Class D) 9 Chiou/Favierou Sts   Tel 522 9891
Directions: Next street back from and parallel to Samou St, towards the south end of Chiou St.
  Greek provincial in outward appearance, despite the grand and evocative name. Single rooms, sharing a bathroom, cost 1400drs; double rooms, sharing, 1995drs & en suite 2550drs.

Joy's Hotel (*Tmr* D1) 38 Feron St   Tel 823 1012
Directions: Proceed along Odhos Filadelfias, almost directly opposite the main station, across Odhos Liossion continuing along Livaniou St as far as Odhos Acharnon. Turn left and then first right on to Feron St.
  Reputedly a good value, busy, Youth Hostel style establishment complete with a bar/cafeteria and offering accommodation ranging from a dormitory to quadruples. Rates as for other hostels. A hot shower costs an extra 100drs.

(B) PELOPONISSOU STATION (*Tmr* B1/2)   Tel 513 1601
The station for trains to the Peloponnese, the ferry connections for some of the Ionian islands and international ferries to Italy from Patras.

Tickets: The concept behind the acquisition of a ticket is similar to that of a lottery. Purchasing a ticket results in the allocation of a compartment seat. In theory this is a splendid scheme but, in practice, the idea breaks down in a welter of bad tempered argument over whom is occupying whose seat. Manners and quaint old-fashioned habits of giving up one's seat to older people and ladies are best avoided. I write this from the bitter experience of offering my seat to elderly Greek ladies, only for their husbands to immediately fill the vacant position. Not what one had in mind! Find your seat and stick to it like glue and if you have made a mistake feign madness, admit to being a foreigner, but do not budge.
  At Peloponissou Station the mechanics of buying a ticket take place in organised bedlam. The ticket office 'traps' open half an hour prior to the train's departure. Scenes reminiscent of a Cup Final crowd develop, with prospective travellers pitching about within the barriers of the ticket hatch, and all this in the space of about 10m by 10m. To add to the difficulty, there are two hatch 'slots' and it is anybody's guess which one to select. It really is best to try and steal a march on the 'extra-curricula' activity, diving for a hatch whenever one opens.
  Travellers booking a return journey train ticket to Europe, and routing via Italy, must ensure the tickets are to and from Patras, not Athens (Yes, Patras). Then the purchase of the separate Patras to Athens (and vice versa) ticket, ensures a seat. A voyager boarding the train with an open ticket will almost surely have to stand for almost the whole of the four hour journey. Most Athens – Patras

116 CANDID GUIDE TO ATHENS

journeys seem to attract an 'Express' surcharge of between 100-150drs, which is exacted by the ticket collector.

Incidentally, the general architecture of the Peloponissou building is delightful, especially the ceiling of the booking office hall, centrally located, under the main clock face. To the left, on entering the building, is a glass-fronted information box with all the train times listed on the window. The staff manning this desk are extremely helpful. They speak sufficient English, so pose no problems in communication – the very opposite of the rushed disinterest shown at the NTOG desk in the National Bank of Greece, on Syntagma Sq.

TRAIN TIMETABLES

Peloponissou Station It is easy to read the Peloponissou timetable and come to the conclusion that a large number of trains are leaving the station at the same time. On seeing the single-line track, a newcomer cannot be blamed for feeling apprehensive that it may prove difficult to select the correct carriages. The mystification arises from the fact that the trains are detailed separately from Athens to say Korinthos, Mikines, Argos, Tripolis, Pirgos and etc, etc. There is no mention that the railway line is a circular layout, with single trains circumscribing the route and that each place name is simply a stop on the journey.

Making changes for branch lines on the Peloponnese can be 'exciting'! Stations are labelled in demotic script and there is no comprehensible announcement from the guard, thus it is easy to fail to make an exit on cue!

A. LARISSIS STATION
Athens to Thessaloniki & on to Alexandroupoli:
Depart   0725, 0830, 1100, 1424, 1930, 2120, 2155, 2310hrs

Thessaloniki
Arrive   1450, 1558, 1757, 2213, 0350, 0538, 0614, 0745hrs
Depart   1536, 1721, 1920, 2302, --   0608, --   0925hrs

Drama (for Kavala)
Arrive   1857, 2109, --   0256, --   1026, --   1331hrs

Alexandroupoli
Arrive   2217, --   --   0651, --   1407, --   1727hrs

One-way fares: Athens to Thessaloniki   :B Class 1520drs: A Class 2280drs.
                Athens to Drama   :   2030drs: 3050drs
                Athens to Alexandroupoli :   2410drs: 3620drs

B. PELOPONISSOU STATION
Athens to Patras:
Depart   0625, 0821, 1013, 1303, 1547, 1827, 2141hrs
Arrive   1055, 1218, 1446, 1708, 2024, 2200, 0159hrs

Return
Depart   0230, 0628, 0809, 1101, 1400, 1647, 1854hrs
Arrive   0640, 1000, 1300, 1500, 1848, 2115, 2254hrs

One-way fare: Athens to Patras:B Class 630drs, A Class 950drs.

Surcharge on Express trains varies from 170-300drs.

PELOPONISSOU STATION

Athens to Patras
Depart   0625, 0821, 1013, 1303, 1547, 1827, 2141hrs.
Arrive   1055, 1218, 1446, 1708, 2024, 2200, 0159hrs.

Patras to Athens
Depart   0203, 0628, 0809, 1101, 1400, 1647, 1845hrs.
Arrive   0640, 1000, 1300, 1500, 1848, 2115, 2254hrs.

LARISSIS STATION

Athens to Thessaloniki & on to Alexandroupoli
Depart   0725, 0830, 1100, 1424, 1930, 2120, 2155, 2310hrs.

Thessaloniki
Arrive   1450, 1558, 1757, 2213, 0350, 0538, 0614, 0745hrs.
Depart   1536, 1721, -   2302, -   0608, -   0925hrs.
Drama (for Kavala)
Arrive   1857, 2109, -   0256, -   1026, -   1331hrs.
Alexandroupoli
Arrive   2217, -   -   0651, -   1407, -   1727hrs.

Alexandroupoli to Athens via Drama & Thessaloniki
Depart   0608, -   -   1208, 1505, -   2256, -
Drama
Depart   0939, -   -   1605, 1858, -   0302, -
Thessaloniki
Arrive   1304, -   -   2026, 2245, -   0708, -
Depart   1340, 1500, 2230, 2130, 0010, 0500, 0800, 1100hrs.
Athens
Arrive   2100, 2230, 0726, 0646, 0800, 1330, 1554, 1750hrs.

Train fares in drachmae

		One-way	
		1st Cl	2nd Cl
Athens to:	or	A	B
Alexandroupolis		3620	2410
Chalkis		410	270
Drama (for Kavala)		3050	2030
Gythion (Killini)		-	-
Kalamata		1470	980
Patras		950	630
Pyrgos (for Killini)		1280	850
Thessaloniki		2280	1520
Volos		1620	1080

TRAVEL AGENTS & TOUR OFFICES There are offices selling tickets for almost anything to almost anywhere, which include:
ABC 58 Stadiou St   Tel 321 1381
American Express 2 Ermou St   Tel 324 4975/9
On the first floor is an excellent retail travel service. Admittedly they are mainly involved in the sale of tours and excursions but the assistants are extremely efficient and helpful. They will, for instance, telephone round to locate all or any hotels, that accept an Amex card, to ascertain if they have a room and the cost.
CHAT 4 Stadiou St   Tel 322 2886
Key Tours 5th Floor, 2 Ermou St   Tel 323 2520
Viking 3 Filellinon St   Tel 322 9383

The agency that was most highly regarded by students for prices and variety, was:
International Student & Youth Travel Service (ISYTS) 11 Nikis St   Tel 323 3767
For FIYTO membership. The second floor office is open Mon-Fri 0900-1900hrs & Sat between 0900-1200hrs.

Two recommended offices offering helpful, inclusive and inexpensive travel options include:-
Magic Bus – International Pullman 20 Filellinon St   Tel (Buses) 323 7471
                                                                                                  (Flights) 322 6810

Filellinon and the parallel street of Odhos Nikis (to the west of Syntagma Sq), all the way south and up as far as Nikodimou St are jam-packed with tourist agencies and student organisations. These include one or two express coach and train fare companies. A sample, going up the rise from Syntagma Square, includes:
(Budget) Student Travel (Tel 322 7993), 1 Filellinon St, on the right, opposite a church
and
Stafford Travel (Tel 322 4225), 20 Filellinon St, on the corner of Filellinon & Kidathineon Sts.

An example of the packaged tours on offer, in this instance from **CHAT Tours** but representative of most, includes:-
One day to Delphi from 4200drs; two days to Epidauras & Mycenae 10900drs; three days to Delphi & Meteora from 27950drs & a one day cruise to Aegina, Poros & Hydra, 4500drs.

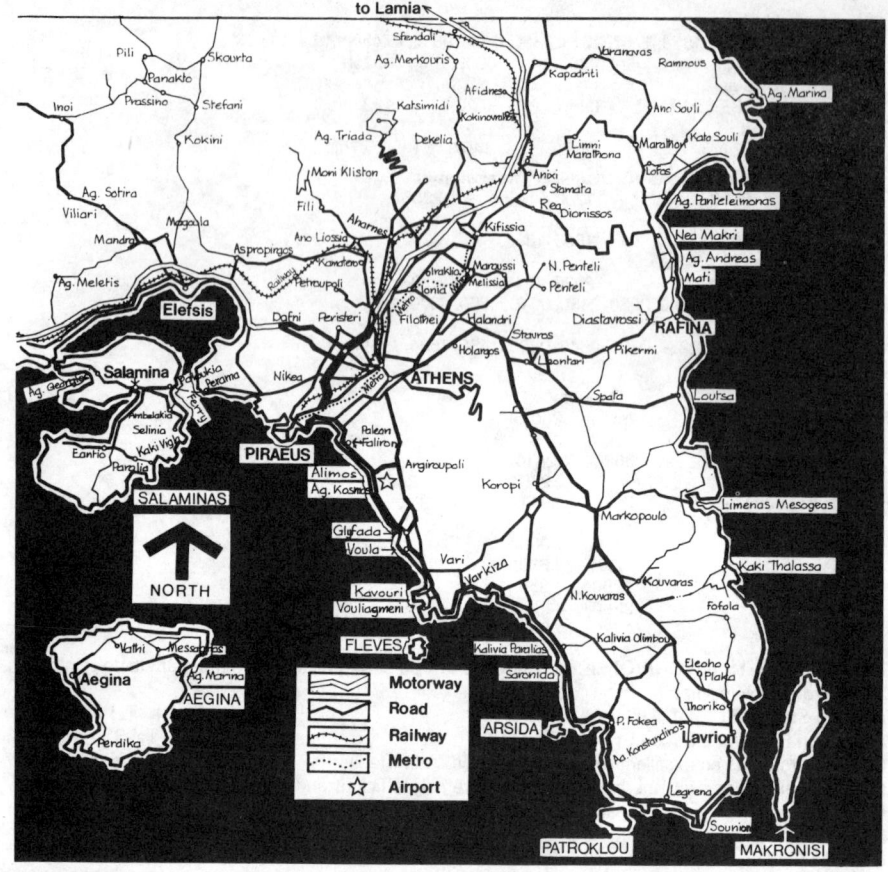

Illustration 8 Athens Environs, Suburbs, Bus & Metro Stations

Callers at the National Bank (*Tmr* 3D/E4/5) usually have to run the gauntlet of 'tour from touts', even if some may only be offering advice ('....I know this white woman'?). They are best brushed aside, otherwise the unwary might well be borne along on an unstoppable tide.

Sample 'charter' air & bus fares available from Athens to various European capitals include (as quoted by **Economy Travel**, 18 Panepistimiou St, Athens Tel 363 4045) the following:
Air to London 25000drs; Paris 24000drs; Rome 17500drs; Munich 20000; Berlin 21000drs; New York 40000drs; Stockholm 29000drs.
Bus to London 13000drs; Paris 12000drs; Venice 9000drs; Munich 11000drs & Istanbul 4500drs.

YOUTH HOSTEL ASSOCIATION *See* **The Accommodation.**

GROC'S Candid Guides to THE GREEK ISLANDS

This highly acclaimed series has been continually refined to ensure that readers, be they armchair voyagers, annual holidaymakers or independent travellers, will be able to plunder a wealth of individualistic information, set out as a travelogue. The text is liberally interspersed with detailed maps and plans. As usual the guides praise the praiseworthy and damn the second rate.

The Cyclades Islands, Athens and Piraeus
2nd Edition
Geoffrey O'Connell
Fully updated including Syros, Mykonos, Paros, Naxos, Ios, Santorini, Amorgos, Astipalaia, Tinos Andros, Sikinos, Folegandros, Milos, Siphnos, Serifos, Kithnos and Kea with excursion details to Delos, Antiparos, Anafi, Donoussa, Koufonissi, Shinoussa, Iraklia, Kimolos and Athens City, Piraeus and the mainland ports of Rafina and Lavrio.
Paperback 392 pages 56 maps and photographs   85253 174 6   £9.95

Crete, Athens and Piraeus
2nd Edition
Geoffrey O'Connell
Crete is not so much an island as a land in its own right. The guide has been divided into a number of regions based on individual cities and towns. The island and town maps are interspersed with pen and ink illustrations. The various routes are described in detail to facilitate holiday-makers' and travellers' exploration of this unique island.
Paperback 226 pages 19 maps and photographs   1 85253 090 1   £7.95

The Greek Mainland Islands
Geoffrey O'Connell
Including the Sporades and Argo-Saronic. Argo-Saronic include - Salaminas, Aegina, Angistri, Poros, Hydra, Spetses and Kithira. Sporades include - Skyros, Alonissos, Skopelos, Skiathos and Evia.
Paperback 280 pages 30 maps and diagrams   1 85253 083 9   £8.95

Rhodes, The Dodecanese, Athens and Piraeus
Geoffrey O'Connell
Including Rhodes, Kos, Karpathos, Kasos, Simi, Tilos, Nisiros, Kalimnos, Leros, Patmos with excursion details to Chalki, Astipalaia, Kastellorizo, Pserimos, Yialos, Angathonisi, Arki and Lipsos.
Paperback 272 pages 31 maps and illustrations   1 85253 066 9   £8.95

Samos and the N.E. Aegean Islands, Athens and Piraeus
Geoffrey O'Connell
Including Samos, Ikaria, Fournoi, Thimena, Chios, Psara, Oinoussai, Lesbos, Limnos, Ag. Estratios, Thassos, and Samothraki as well as Athens City, Piraeus and the mainland ports of Kavala and Alexandroupoli.
Paperback 298 pages 36 maps and photographs   1 85253 898 9   £7.95

Please add 10 % p & p for orders by post

INDEX

A
AA, the, 22-23
A To Z
   Athens City, 104-119
Accommodation
   Athens City, 91-98
   Charges, *See Rates*
   Island, 45-49
   Rates, 49
Acropolis, The, 90
After-sun, *See Lotions*
Agora, The Greek, 90-91
Agora, The Roman, 91
Airline Flights
   Athens, *See Athens*
   Charter, 11-13
   Domestic, 33-34
   International, 11-14, 33-34
   fares, 12,33
Airports
   Athens, *See Athens*
   Crete, 11,33
   Cyclades, 33-34
   Dodecanese, 11,34
   Ionian, 11,34
   Mainland island, 34
   NE Aegean, 34
Air temperatures,
   See Weather
Alarm clock, *See Clocks*
Alcohol, *See Drink*
Allowances, 5,26
Alphabet, Greek, *See Language*
Ancona, 25,27
   (Italy)
Animals, *See Greece*....
Arrival by Air, 85-86
   See Airline flights & Airports
Arrival by Bus, 86
Arrival by Ferry-boat,
   See Ferry-boats
Arrival by Train, *See Trains*
Asteroskopeion(Athens), 90
Athens City, 85-119
   airports, 14-15,33,85-86
Australia, 14

B
Backpacks, 3
Bad buys, 63
Bakers, *See Shopping & Services*
Banks, *See Shopping & Services*
Bank cards, 5,74
Bari. 25
   (Italy)
Bathrooms, 46-47
Beaches, 47,51
Bedroll, 3
Bedrooms, *See Accommodation*
Beer. See Drink
Belgrade, 17,21
   (Yugoslavia)
Best Buys, 71
Beverages, 59-61
Bicycles, 53-54
Bin liners, 4
Books, 5
Bottle-opener, 3
Brandy, *See Drinks*
Bread shops, *See Shopping*
Brindisi, 17-19,27
   (Italy)
British summertime, 6
Broadcasts, *See Radio*
Buses
   Athens City, 85-86,104-107
   domestic, 34,52-53
   international, 21-22
Butchers, *See Shopping*

C
Cafe-bars, *See Drinking places*
Calamine lotion, *See Lotions*
Cameras, *See Photography*
Camping, 47
   Athens, 98-99
Canada, 14
Car
   hire, 53-54
   travel by, 22-26
Cards, playing, 5
Charter flights, *See Airline flights*
Chemists, 4
Cigarettes, *See Smokers*
Cigars, *See Smokers*
Climate, *See Weather*
Clocks alarm, 5
Clothes pegs, 3
Clothing, 3
Coaches, *See Buses*
Coffee, *See Beverages*
Compass, 5
Condiments, 3
Containers, 3
Conversion tables, 6
Cooking equipment, 3
Creams, *See Lotions*
Credit cards, 5,71
   Access (Mastercard), 5
   American Express (Amex), 5
   Diners, 5
Creperies, *See Eating Places*
Cruise ships, 38
Currency, 5,74

D
Denmark, *See Scandanavia*
Department of Health,
   See National Health Cover &
   Insurance matters & policies
Dialling codes, See OTE
Dictionary, *See Language, Greek*
Disinfectant, 4
Donkeys, 52
Drink (& Food), 57-64,71
   Alcoholic 26,60-61
   Non alcoholic, 59-60
Drinking,
   Places, 61
   Water, 60
Drivers & driving
   requirements, 25-26
Duty free, *See Allowances*

E
Eating Out,
   Athens, 99-104
Eating Places, 62
Electricity supply, 3,6
Ercefurly forte, *See Medical matters*
   & medicines
Eurocheques & card, *See Credit cards*
Eurorail pass, 20
Exchange rates, 1

F
Fast Food Joints, *See Eating Places*
Ferry-boats(& Flying Dolphins/Hydrofoils),
   Brindisi, *See Brindisi*
   domestic, 34-36
   international, 26-29
Film, camera, *See Photography*
Filopapou(Athens), 90
Finland, 21

INDEX

Fish, See Food
Flats & houses, 49
Flying Dolphins, See Ferry-boats
Fokionos Negri, 91
  (Athens)
Food (& drink), 57-64
  See Menus
Foot, On, 52
Footwear, 3
France, 16,21,22,23-25
Frozen foods, 59

G

Galaktopoleio, See Eating places
  & Shopping
Galaktozacharoplasteion, See
  Eating places
Gasoline, See Petrol
Germany, 23
Greenwich Mean Time, 6
Good buys, See Best Buys
Greece/Greek
  animals, 82
  Climate, See Weather
  currency, See Currency
  driving requirements, 26
  history, 79-80
  holidays, 82
  language, See Language
  mythology, 79
  people, 81-82
  religion, 80
Guides & maps, See Maps

H

Hair
  curlers, 3
  shampoo, 4
Hill of Areopagos(Athens), 90
Hill of Muses(Athens), 90
Hill of Nymphs(Athens), 90
Hire
  bicycle, car, moped, scooter, 53-54
  insurance, 54
  rates, 54
History, See Greece
Hitching, 52
Holidays, Greek, See Greece
Holiday Insurance, See Insurance
Hostels, 98
  (Athens)
Hotels, 48-49,64
Hotline, Greek island, 1
Hydrofoils, See Ferry-boats

I

Insect cream See Lotions
Insurance & medical matters, 1,4,54
  including Holiday insurance
Interail pass, 20
International Driving Licence,
  See Driving Requirements
Introduction, 1
Ireland, 14
Island
  accommodation,
    See Accommodation, island
  place names, 38
  Maps, See Maps
Italy, 16-19,21-22,24-25

J

Jellyfish, 51

K

Kafeneions, See Drinking Places
Kaningos Sq, 87
  (Athens)
Kaolin (& morphine), See Medical matters &
medicines
Keramikos, 80
  (Athens)
Kiosks, See Street Kiosks
Klafthmonos Sq, 91
  (Athens)
Kolonaki Sq, 88
  (Athens)
Kotzia Sq, 91
  (Athens)

L

Language
  Greek, 6-9,38-44,49-50,55,69,74-76
Liquid containers, 3
Lotions, 4
Luggage, 3
Lycabettus, Mt, 88-90
  (Athens)

M

Magazines, See Newspapers
Maps, 52,72
Map names, 38
Markets, See Shopping
Measures, See Conversion tables
Medical matters & medicines, 4,64
Medications, See Medical matters
  & medicines
Menus, 57
  sample, 64-69
Metric system, See Conversion tables
Metro
  Athens, 109
Milk-shake Bars, See Eating Places
Mini-markets, See Shopping
Monastiraki Sq, 87-88
  (Athens)
Money, See Allowances,
  Currency & Services
Mopeds, 53-54
Morphine, See Medical matters
  & medicines
Mosquito,
  coils, 3-4
Motorists, requirements, 25-26
Museums, 74
Mythology, See Greece

N

Names & addresses, See Useful....
National Gardens, 90
  (Athens)
National Health Cover, 4
National Holidays, See Greece....
Newspapers & Magazines, 72
New Zealand, 14
Norway, See Scandinavia
Nudism, 51

O

Official guides, See Maps
Olympic Airways, See Airline flights
Omonia Sq, 87
  (Athens)
Opening hours, See Shopping
OTE, 75
Otranto(Italy), 22
Ouzeries, See Drinking Places
Overseas phone calls, See OTE

P

Package holiday companies, 12-13
Package tours, 11-13
Packing, 3-4
Paris, 16,21
  (France)
Passports, 5,74
Pavement cafes, *See Drinking*
  & Eating Places
Pensions, 48
Periptero, *See Street kiosks*
Personal possessions, 51
Petrol, 54
Pharmaceuticals, *See Medical matters*
  & medicines
Pharmacies, *See Medical matters*
  & medicines
Photography, 5,72
Phrase books, *See Language, Greek*
Pizzerieas, *See Eating places*
Place names, 38
Plaka,(Athens), 88
Plasters, *See Medical matters & medicines*
Playing cards, *See Cards*
Plumbing, *See Bathrooms*
Police, 45,48,54
Post Office, 74-75
Postage, *See Post Office*
Public Services, *See Services*
Pynx(Athens), 90

Q

R

Radio, 72
Railway Stations, *See Trains*
Rainfall, *See Weather*
Razors, 3
Reading matter, *See Books*
Religion, *See Greece*
Religious holidays & festivals, 82
Restaurants, *See Eating places*
Retsina, *See Wine*
Roads
    international, 22-26
    island, 52
    signs, 55
Roll-bags, 3
Roman Forum, 91
  (Athens)
Rooms, *See Accommodation*
Rotisserie, *See Restaurants*
Rural Centres, *See Restaurants*

S

Saint, *See Ag*
Scandinavia, 14,21
Scheduled flights, *See Airline Flights*
Scooters, 53-54
Sea temperature, *See Weather*
Sea urchins, 51
Services, 73-75
Shampoo, *See Hair*
Shoes, *See Footwear*
Shopping, 71-73
Shops, *See Shopping*
Siesta, *See Opening hours*
Sink plugs, 5
Sleeping bags, 3
Smokers, 5,26,63
Snackbars, *See Eating places*
Soap powder, 3
Solar energy, 46-47
South Africa, 14
Souvlatzidika, *See Eating Places*
Speciality shops, See Shopping
Spirits, *See Drink*
St, *See Ag*
Stomach upsets, *See Medical matters*
  & medicines
Street kiosks (& periptéros),
  See Shopping
Students, 13,19-20
Summertime, 6

Sunburn & sunstroke, 51
Sunglasses, 3
Sunshine, *See Weather*
Sun-tan oil *See Lotions*
Supermarkets, *See Shopping*
Sweden, *See Scandinavia*
Switzerland, 24,25-26
Syntagma Sq, 86
  (Athens)

T

Tavernas, *See Accommodation,*
  Eating places
Taxis, 53
  Athens, 112
Tea, *See Beverages*
Telegrams, *See OTE*
Telephones & office, *See OTE*
Temperatures, *See Weather*
Ticket purchase, *See individual services*
Time, *See Greewich Mean Time*
Timetables, *See individual services*
Tin opener, 3
Tobacco, *See Smokers*
Toilets, *See Bathrooms*
Toilet rolls, 3
Torch, 5
Tourist guides & maps, *See Maps*
Tourist police, *See Police*
Trains
    Athens, 112-117
    international, 15-21
    metro, *See Metro*
    timetables, 20
Travel
    Around an island, 51-54
    Athens to the Islands, 33-38
    Insurance, *See Insurance &*
      Medical Matters
    To the islands, 11-38
Travellers cheques, 5,74
  See Banks & Post Office
Trolley-buses(Athens), *See Buses*
Tummy trouble, *See Medical matters*
  & medicines
Tweezers, 4
Tyropitadika, *See Eating Places*

U

USA, 13
Useful Greek, *See Language*
Useful names & addresses, 30-31,49,83
Utensils, *See Cooking Equipment*

V

Vehicle hire, 53-54
Venice, 16-17
  (Italy)

W

Walking, *See Foot, On*
Washing
  line, 3
  powder, 3
Water, drinking, *See Drinking*
WC(toilet), *See Bathrooms*
Weather, 5
Wind, *See Weather*
Wine, *See Drink*
  measures, 6
Wire hangers, 3
Women, 51

X

Xenias, 49

Y

YMCA, YWCA & Youth
  hostels, 47
  Athens, 82,88
Yugoslavia, 17,21,24-25,26

Z

Zacharoplasteion, *See Eating places*
Zappeion Exhibition Halls, 90